Copywriting

Successful writing for design, advertising, and marketing

Second Edition

Mark Shaw

Copywriting
Successful writing for design,
advertising, and marketing

Second Edition

Laurence King Publishing

For Leilah, Sam, and Fin

Published in 2012 by
Laurence King Publishing Ltd
361–373 City Road
London EC1V 1LR
United Kingdom
Tel: +44 20 7841 6900
Fax: +44 20 7841 6910
E-mail: enquiries@laurenceking.com
www.laurenceking.com

Reprinted 2014, 2015

A catalog record for this book is available from the
British Library.

ISBN: 978-1-78067-000-3

Printed in China

Designed by Studio Ten and a Half

Research by Tim Shaw

LAURENCE KING

Contents

Preface

What's the big deal about copywriting? There's so much writing out there in every shape and form on every topic and field, and everyone is writing and publishing copy all the time these days. Why don't we just let people get on with it? Well, the enormous volume of self-published, unedited writing is the very reason why the skills and techniques of copywriting are more essential than ever before. A friend of mine recently described the situation as "we've all got high-school Math but we wouldn't do the company accounts, so just because we've got high-school English why do we think we can write great copy?"

Since publishing the first edition of this textbook I have spent a few years presenting the key points, lecturing to students, and running seminars for businesses. I've had feedback from around the world, and this is typical of the fantastically random feedback I receive:

A few weeks ago I found Your book "Copywriting. Successful writing for design, advertising and marketing" in Lithuanian book store. I think it's very interesting and really practical to use in different cases. Would like to thank You for this treasure and ensure it will accompany me in the way I am struggling with the words.

I am a student of Vilnius University, Kaunas Faculty of Humanities, Lithuania. Studying marketing and commerce management for master degree. Your book is a good guide for preparing various tasks and helpful source of original ideas. I believe it would be a perfect tool for students of design, advertising, marketing, public relations and even philology. In my opinion it would be worth to translate it to my native language and let Lithuanians improve their skills in writing, editing, and creating presentations. (sic)

We've not translated into Lithuanian just yet, but we launched the Chinese edition earlier this year, and it's very exciting to feel that the skills and techniques I've developed over the course of my career are valued internationally. This is not because of vanity but because the world of branding and messaging is becoming unified, and is increasingly seen as a mature and essential element in normal business practice.

I run a brand and design agency called Liquid Agency Europe and we spend most of our time responding to challenges related to brand management and messaging. Graphic design will always be at the core of branding, but it is increasingly about staying within the brand guidelines. Where in the recent past impact and differentiation could be achieved through pure design thinking, these days it is the way an organization creates and manages its content that is the real unique proposition in the marketplace.

At the heart of everything in this book, and also in the way Liquid Agency practices brand management for global clients, are the values that are behind the brand. A brand is described in various ways as "anyone's experience of you," "someone's gut instinct about your organization," or "what people say about you when you leave the room." One thing is for sure, your brand is not simply your logo. Your brand is the promise that your business makes to its target audiences, and that promise has to be delivered accurately if you are to build long-term relationships with your customers, suppliers, and employees. Increasingly, businesses are being designed from the point of view of the customer experience, with every point of contact being shaped to suit their requirements.

Understanding your own brand takes a bit of thought, and as a copywriter you will do well to follow these processes to identify the qualities within your business that make you who you are, and which you will be promising to your audiences. These qualities are formed from the values within the business. Values are the bedrock of any organization, and are made up of attitudes and beliefs. When you take a copy brief, you will be picking up all sorts of insights into the attitudes and beliefs within an organization. Keep a clear note of these, and build a picture of the values that you are drawing out. Present these back to your client to double-check them, as these will form the foundation of your messaging.

Messaging is the phrase that is being used increasingly to describe the way a business writes. The tools within messaging are typically a slogan or tagline, a word bank of commonly used phrases, a list of core messages that you wish to reinforce consistently, and a tone-of-voice guide, which gives examples of the style of writing that reflects the values in the organization. If you're writing for business, you should start to familiarize yourself with these tools, as they are where the future of branding lies.

Branding is part of every business, no matter how big or how small, and you can play a crucial role in the success of an enterprise by helping it to use effective communication to build bridges and develop profitable relationships with its audiences. Digital messaging is all about creating bite-sized pieces of information that engage and direct the reader. Formats are increasingly diverse, with many new digital channels now in the mix. Customers pick up marketing messages on TV, in the press, and from billboards as much as they ever did, and these are supplemented by websites, social media sites, Twitter accounts, cell-phone messaging, media screens in public places, and just about every place we go. These messages need to be managed well to ensure that the same benefits and calls to action are communicated clearly and consistently throughout all of these touchpoints.

We need copywriters to do the best job of this communication. Too often these projects are left to managers who may know the product inside out but rarely know how to prioritize a message, shape it for a target audience, and instill the values of the organization into the text. Copywriting is content design, and requires all of the design thinking that goes into any other creative aspect of a business. I am hoping that readers of this new edition will feed back their thoughts and experiences to me, and that we can build a network of new writers who can take on this challenge and show the world that great writing is the route to great business!

Mark Shaw
mark@markshaw.co.uk

A brand is a person's gut feeling about a product, service, or organization

Introduction
Copywriters learning from bakers and swimmers

There was a baker in my hometown, and he had a Gold Medal Bakery that ranked with the best in the UK. His bread was truly something else. After I'd left home I always used to take one of his loaves with me, and when each one ran out I could never find any as good, anywhere.

He protected his recipe fiercely, and refused to tell anyone its secrets— not even his sons who worked in the business, not until he was ready. But then, unexpectedly, he fell off his perch. And with him went his recipe, forever.

The Gold Medal Bakery is now a memory, as are the loaves that we all loved, and the moral of this tale is that knowledge, no matter how precious, needs to be shared. If it isn't, it dies. If it is, it will live, and evolve.

One of the most common ways that knowledge can be passed on is in the form of a carefully prepared textbook. Theoretically, it should be possible for a complete non-swimmer to study an authoritative textbook on swimming, which explains and demonstrates all of the disciplines and approaches, then jump in the deep end and swim with style and grace.

How difficult can it be? He can see how easily swimmers cut through the water, and he can read and absorb all of the relevant principles and techniques. If he breathes, moves, and applies himself properly it should be simple.

Except we know that this won't work. In reality, we learn to swim gradually, adapting to the watery environment and building our confidence over time, through trial and error.

So what about creative business writing? Can a well-prepared textbook teach you to be an accomplished copywriter, even if you've never written copy before?

Not if you've never written a word in your life before, but luckily for you, you're not a complete novice. You have been writing since you were a child, and you are already fully immersed in the world of words.

This textbook shares the knowledge about creative writing so that it can live and evolve, but it is not a guide to sales and marketing, and it is not a manual on grammar and punctuation. It aims to explain the processes that you can follow when writing copy, and reveal the secrets about how the best copywriters do it.

Writing copy is not as hard as it looks. It's the creative thinking that goes on behind the writing that is the challenge, and the focus of this textbook is firmly on these fascinating aspects of the rewarding field of copywriting.

You can dip in and out, or read it cover to cover and complete the exercises; either way I hope you will gain some valuable insights. The bottom line is that if you can understand who you're writing for, what you are really saying to them, what it takes to make this interesting, and how to shape your messages to suit their preferences, you will be writing professional copy.

You know you can already swim, and now you have every opportunity to take on the best of them.

Getting to grips with copywriting

Fresh and original writing oils the wheels of every aspect of commercial activity, and language is a key element of many forms of modern design. Copywriting is not about copying—it's about communicating in an original way. You can put a sentence together, and your imagination is alive and well, so you have everything it takes to be a creative writer. All you need are some guidelines to help you figure out when your writing is good, and a little inspiration from some practitioners in the field.

Why do I need to know about copy?

Creative writing for business is challenging and rewarding in equal measure, and when it all comes together with great design to create innovative communications it can feel like the best job in the world. Copywriting is an essential part of the design communications mix, and those of us who do it for a living will tell you that crafting messages and telling stories is a rewarding mental process, even in the business context. You'll find that being able to generate a response from your audience is a valuable and highly sought-after skill.

Copy (or text, or words) used in design is a very particular type of creative writing that requires the inspiration of an artist and the control of a craftsman or craftswoman. In comparison to the rails on which the copywriter runs, the novelist or poet has no limitations. Poetry and storytelling are flights of the imagination, with no client or news editor to bear in mind. Whether the personality of the writer shines through directly or indirectly, this is the purest creative writing—it can take off in any direction, be as fictional as it wants to be, and go wherever it pleases. Writing copy, however, is all about sticking to a brief, while paying homage to the creativity and style of the poet and storyteller.

Journalists and copywriters are commercial writers, but the essence of their roles is completely different. In most cases journalists have to create the story from scratch, usually by following leads. They will have to research the facts to get to the heart of the matter, discover the different viewpoints and opinions, and bring this material together accurately and coherently. Articles are often written to a tightly defined structure, while features can allow more room for individual expression and the interweaving of the writer's viewpoint. The message has to be factually correct, balanced, and fair, but the writer is allowed to take a stance, which could reflect that of the newspaper or, in the case of a regular column, the writer's own opinion.

"If you are a writer of novels, or plays, or poetry, you can write and take your own time, generally speaking. But in advertising, you've got deadlines, you've got to have the idea, and it's got to be a great one, and you've got to have it Tuesday morning."
David Ogilvy

Copywriting borrows from all other fields of writing in its quest for creative expression, but there is no room for your personality in the copy that you write; you are simply a scribe, a hired mouthpiece for your client, and it is the **brand**'s voice that must come through, loudly and clearly. The starting point, whether you're working on a one-off project or are writing copy every day, is to set aside your ego, forget all ideas about expressing your own thoughts, and put on the company coveralls. You'll be surprised how well they fit and how good you look in them.

Good writing makes things happen

In Mesopotamia, the earliest cuneiform writing was developed to record ownership of animals and goods. Writing was at the heart of trading, and its invention was the catalyst for the dawning of modern civilization. It is now one of our greatest forms of expression, and, whatever the brief, is a powerful tool for all types of business. The techniques of creative copywriting are really about finding the most natural way to communicate well with others.

Business has one aim: to deliver a profit. Everyone in every sort of commercial enterprise is trying to sell a product or service for more than it costs them to produce it, and make an honest profit to live off. Selling—which is what you're doing when you're writing copy—used to be a case of steering customer demand by pointing people in the direction of the leading brands.

Before the competitive nature of the global marketplace really hotted up, all you needed to do to have a viable business was to identify and satisfy a customer need. Our abundant times have created a huge amount of choice, and with choice comes competition: it is no longer enough to hold up your hand and tell your customers where you are; you now have to tell them why you are better, why they should bother to knock on your door, and why they should keep coming back to you.

There has been an enormous increase in the different media that can be used to reach customers, from blogs and microsites to talking retail displays and e-mail campaigns. Customers now have even greater control over which of these messages they will give the time of day to, which means the results we can achieve through traditional advertising and marketing are increasingly less predictable. The reality is that we as customers consciously select and deselect the promotional and advertising messages that we wish to listen to.

Innovative graphic design is a powerful way to catch and hold the attention, but we're becoming a bit blasé about stunning visuals, amazing concepts, and slick photography, and they no longer have the power to make us sit up and think as they used to. The messages they carry and the way those messages are expressed are the essence of effective communication.

It is not enough to splash out on expensive media campaigns and expect high-profile visibility alone to deliver results. If the customer isn't watching, or doesn't like the message, you won't attract a response. The starting point has to be to select the best way to reach people, whether this means sticking posters at the top of ski lifts or sending specific text messages to shoppers as they pass your store. Then you must make sure the overall message you're communicating is targeted, relevant, and inspiring. For this you need great copy.

The attitudes and principles that apply to copywriting for external customers apply equally to any written or verbal communication. The clearer and more accurate your communication, the more successful you will be.

"I'm sure that everything a man does is grist for his copy mill. I'm sure of that —what you've done and what you've experienced— if you can put more thinking and more interesting things into your copy, you're that much more provocative."
Bill Bernbach

What's stopping you writing great copy?

Your essential objective as a copywriter is to create clear, easily understood messages that target a defined audience and encourage them to do something for your client. If you get to know the basic processes and avoid the common pitfalls, you'll find that this is not as difficult to achieve as you might think.

Being a natural creative writer will give you a head start, but it is not enough in itself, and you do not need to be a natural writer to be a good copywriter. Some agency writers have got by on their natural talent for decades, and actually have little idea about process or technique.

One of the latest executions from a long-running and consistently award-winning campaign, this uses a few simple words to speak volumes to an intelligent target audience.

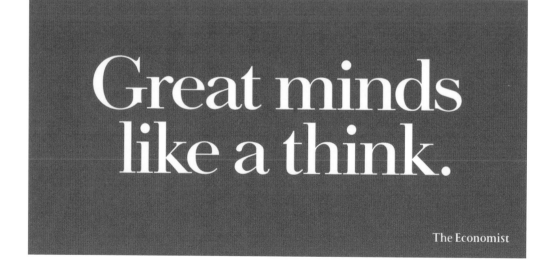

Great minds like a think.

The Economist

"A writer should be joyous, an optimist ... Anything that implies rejection of life is wrong for a writer, and cynicism is rejection of life. I would say participate, participate, participate."
George Gribbin

The best way to write copy is to focus completely on the true nature of the target audience so that your messages are crafted with them in mind. This will produce compelling copy and your reader will feel at home with your writing. Using a clever play on words, a pun, or a quick witticism is becoming less important than being able to craft a well-constructed, stimulating message.

Understand the heart beating at the core of your message, consider the makeup of your quirky audience and their particular habits, such as their buying patterns, and make sure your copy plays to these at all times. Most of the copy that you will be working with will require clear, uncomplicated writing about what you are selling that clearly presents the benefits, not just the features. A creative or conceptual idea should always underpin your approach—you can establish this by giving careful consideration to your overriding message or **call to action** and explaining how the audience can respond.

Too much analysis can hamper creativity. There's no right or wrong way to go about writing copy, yet there are several patterns that you can follow. Every writer will do this slightly differently—you should find the best way of developing your own unique approach that blends proven techniques with your own preferred way of tackling a brief.

Take aim, you're targeting your audience

Whatever the brief, you will have a message to communicate to a specific audience. Build up a profile of this audience, develop an understanding of what they're like and what their situation is, and decide on a style of language that they will relate to. A good word for this process is **profiling**, and anyone can do it.

The most comprehensive briefs can give you an in-depth picture of your audience based on economic profile, geographical location, and even the type of street they live on, the papers they read, and cars they drive. If you haven't been given this sort of information, you can compile it yourself without having to leave your desk or search Google, simply by using your common sense and experience to determine the characteristics of the people in your audience.

You'll be surprised how much you already know about your profiled audience. For example, if you're writing toiletries product copy for women aged between 25 and 40 you may be given the insight that they're professionals, with a reasonable disposable income, and are regular shoppers with the client. An image—a stereotype—will come to mind immediately.

What can your profiling add to this? Well, think it through. It's likely that our 25- to 40-year-old women are busy looking after a family, or juggling home responsibilities with work, or pursuing a career that takes up all of their time. Being this busy will mean that they are living with stress. At the point when they read your copy they are likely to be tired and not have much time. When they stand in the store with your product in their hand, they have their kids with them, or have sore feet, or are being jostled by other customers. How do you cut through all of this?

Now you're building up a picture of a real human being and are writing for someone who is bright, and enjoying life, but who's being distracted and has a lot on her mind. You need to make sure that your messages focus on helping to reduce her stress (and don't expect her to study the text for very long). You need to catch her eye with a strong product name and description, the **tone of voice** you use should be friendly and on her level, and you'd better have something good to say—a clear benefit or an inspiring proposition—otherwise you're wasting her time.

By contrast, if you're writing advertising for the business customers of a computer supplier your profiling will again tell you how to develop this tone of

Taking an ugly subject and turning
it into an imaginative concept,
this poster works very hard by
keeping the message short, sweet
and benefit-led.

voice. Your readers are IT-procurement managers of large corporations, who will be sourcing computers for 50 to 200 people at a time. They control company expenditure, and as well as getting good value for money they require excellent service and support and unbeatable quality. They are also career professionals looking for their next big promotion. The tone of voice you adopt must be confident, reassuring, and extremely credible. Deliver clear benefits without overpromising or trivializing the purchase with quirky headlines. You still need to present the whole message with a powerful idea and a clear call to action, but this needs to be backed up with evidence—in the form of facts and figures to justify any claims you are making—because these people want hard facts.

Sell the benefits, not the features

When you are selling something you don't tell your customers what it does, you tell them how or why it will improve their lives. This takes the "so-what?" factor into account: assume your customers say "so what?" to every claim that you make, and then give them the answer before they've even thought about the question.

The point of this is simple. Your readers are not all paying full attention—some of them are just browsing, others have the radio on in the background, some are about to go out, others are lazy. They don't all have the time or inclination to work out that the features you're listing will provide them with really good **benefits**. You're the copywriter, so do the hard work for them. If you work out the benefits and present them appealingly, far more of your audience will respond.

Every feature has an associated benefit, it's just that some are easier to spot or more compelling than others. The core benefits often lead into peripheral benefits, and you'll need to decide which one to focus on. There are the classics—for example, when people buy a new home security system, they are not buying an alarm, they are buying peace of mind. Working out the benefits is a logical process, as long as you always focus on your audience. It is also important to remember that the benefits of a product or service for one audience will not necessarily be the same as the benefits for another.

Take any product, for example a vacuum cleaner. There are two main types of benefit: those associated with the product as a type (an immaculately clean, dust-free house), and those that distinguish your product or service from the competition (how your vacuum cleaner outperforms others). Be sure to focus on the benefits that set you apart from the pack. If you're not careful, you could do a great job of selling the idea of a vacuum cleaner without leaving your reader with the impression that your brand is the best choice.

It's your role to determine which benefits are the most compelling and which benefits and features are not essential to the brief. Less is often more, and by highlighting one clear benefit you will capture the readers' attention and persuade them to look into what you are offering, so don't be afraid to describe only one benefit in your overall statement.

How to improve the odds in the numbers game

No matter how good a writer you are, you can't achieve the impossible, so focus on what you can achieve. You won't get every member of your target audience to respond in the desired way—some just won't allow you in. Conversely, there will be some people who will buy into your message even if it is unclear and badly written. Both of these sections of your target readership have already made up their minds: they will definitely buy—or not—and there is little you can do to make any difference.

Concentrate instead on your "floating voters"—those members of the audience who may be tempted to buy but need a little nudge, an extra reason, before they commit. This is where you can work some magic. Target those who are predisposed to buying, who have some interest in your product, and you will be reaching the most receptive people in your audience.

Hold their attention by promising, delivering, and reminding

Your finished copy should follow a consistent thread from start to finish so that your readers will stay with you to the end. Fire their interest by explaining what they are about to discover, and why this will be interesting. Giving your copy a hidden structure will ensure that you don't just ramble on, listing facts and features. It also gives you a means of keeping the message fresh and stimulating.

The readers expect you to deliver, and if you don't let them down (either by overpromising or under-delivering) you'll have established the start of a good relationship with them. Don't make these promises too overt. You're not standing there with a bullhorn trying to force people to come into your store; you're welcoming your guests on to your premises and letting them know that they will have an enjoyable time. Your tone should be inviting and warm, and your promises should be subtle and measured.

Intrigue keeps interest alive

It is much better for people to want to buy from you than for you to have to sell to them. Being sold to is an invasion of privacy and it's annoying, yet we all like to shop for our favorite things. Warm up your audience to want to buy from you and you won't have to sell at them. Hard-selling is much more difficult and generates less response.

Make use of intrigue. It's hard to resist finding out about something that we think we really want to know about, especially when it's right there in front of us. Adding intrigue is as simple as asking people if they'd like to find out a bit more about the product.

There's an old chestnut about how to sell a kitten. You don't talk about the joy of owning a pet, the companionship and fun, or how cute and playful the kitten is. You say nothing, put it in the customer's hands, and stand back. It sells itself. There are times when a few choice words achieve more than paragraphs of text. Don't oversell when your customers already want to buy. Invite them in, intrigue them to make sure they remain interested, and let them make up their own minds. Just make it as easy as possible for them to respond.

Get the tone of voice right

As well as creating the right structure for holding your reader's interest, you must select the correct tone of voice, making sure that it is both appropriate for the client's brand and is totally relevant to your audience.

In many cases a clear, informed, and interested tone of voice is the best approach, and you will be able to draw on this same voice for a number of different clients. This should be your baseline, and any copy that you write must achieve this standard at least. Ask yourself: Am I involving the reader? Is the message interesting? Have I included a clear call to action?

If you really want to touch someone, send them a letter.

Part of every day.

AUSTRALIA POST

The copy literally bursts out of the page and hugs you—well, almost. The perfect way to show the warmth and intimacy of a handwritten letter to a loved one. This is a great concept, making the most of digital applications to achieve things that were previously impossible.

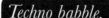

Techno babble.

We looked at our language—and at the other lot down the road. We decided that 3's competitors in the mobile world are a funny bunch. They all sound a bit similar. And some of them have a tendency to philosophize while also lapsing into impenetrable techno-babble.

Verbs.

So, focusing on verbs, ask these questions of your language for 3:
1. Can you turn a noun into a verb?
2. Can you make the verb form active without a trace of the passive?
3. Can you choose verbs that give out energy rather than simply exist?

The tone-of-voice guide for the mobile media company 3 explains how to write for the brand, recommending that the writer clear away adjectives to leave real simplicity and use immediate emotion and a simple energy without making it dumbed-down.

The tone is created by increasing the number of verbs and reducing the number of nouns (these make it more difficult to gain a full understanding in a quick reading). An example of this would be changing "our quality control is good" to "we check everything."

Checklist: Hidden structure

HEADLINE
A STRONG CREATIVE HOOK TO GRAB ATTENTION AND PROVOKE INTEREST.

First paragraph: Creative copy giving clarification to the headline, rewarding the reader for looking into it, and promising lots of interesting discoveries in the following copy.

Body copy: Deliver the promises, clearly linking these revelations to the promises.

Further temptations: Offer new promises later in the text, delivering them before the end of the article.

Final paragraph: Remind the readers about the promises, how they will be fulfilled, how they will benefit them, and what they need to do, if anything.

Achieve a consistent tone of voice
These tools can help you and your team to maintain consistency,
especially where a campaign has a number of different elements,
or if a marketing program continues over many months.

Word bank

This is a collection of evocative words that create the feeling that you wish to maintain in your copy.
It could be pages long, split into different categories, or it might simply be a short list of appropriate
words. Start or begin? Purchase or buy? Complete or finish? Frequently or often?

Brand dictionary

The dictionary builds up a collection of your brand's particular words and phrases.
There are two types:

1. Generic terms and the correct way to use them for this client (for example, "staff must always
be referred to as 'our people,' not 'employees' or 'staff,'" or "our retail outlets are always referred
to as 'our stores,' not 'our shops' or 'our outlets'").

2. The common jargon from your marketplace or industry that needs to be explained. Don't use
industry-standard abbreviations—the RDC is a Regional Distribution Center to your readers—and
be careful when using phrases such as "cascade communication." You might know what it means
but do the readers know that this is where you communicate the message to senior managers, who
will then communicate to their teams? Some brands or sectors have a lot more jargon than others,
but it must always be rephrased in plain English—ambiguity must not be tolerated.

Examples of tone of voice

Your guide can be loose and unstructured—it is simply a collection of phrases and words, short
sentences, and expressions that characterize your brand. The Smart car tone of voice will tell
the writer that the Smart car can "shoot over. zoom up. nip through. whiz by. scoot down. swing
in. pop out. drop round." This is for writers only, and perhaps some "brand police," and will not
be seen by the customer. This is what gives other writers the direction they'll need to write in the
upbeat and positive voice you've worked so hard to create for your client.

Revisit your audience profile and ask yourself if the tone of your copy is the right one for them. Be clear about your role. If you're explaining the benefits of a back-to-work scheme for 16-year-olds who've left school with no qualifications, you're not expected to use hip-hop street language. What you must do is show that you understand the teenage audience, using phrases such as "sometimes it can feel like you haven't got a chance of getting a decent job, and you haven't even started yet" or "you may have felt that school was simply a waste of time, but now you can really make the start you've always wanted." Stick to a simple vocabulary (they may not read well), treat them with respect (they will be very cynical), and be real (they'll see through any waffle).

Keep it simple

If only we'd paid more attention at school. If only we knew what the past participle was and which pronouns to use, whether our tenses are consistent, if we are splitting our infinitives or have a tendency to overuse gerunds and subordinate clauses. It's a minefield out there, and there is no way we can walk through it without stepping on something serious. Yes, grammar, punctuation, spelling, and correct sentence structure are all major considerations, but don't be fazed. Take a closer look and you'll discover that there is a clear route through that you can follow.

That route is simplicity. Your copy should be as clear and digestible as possible, so make life easy for yourself and keep everything simple. This is not about dumbing down, it's about clarity of expression. You do not have to possess an enormous vocabulary or a detailed knowledge of the subtleties of grammar (although this does build up with time), because your role is to express ideas, concepts, and messages in a succinct and compelling way.

Avoid long words (use your thesaurus if you're struggling for a simpler alternative) and steer clear of complex sentences. Be consistent with your style, and make sure your spelling is perfect. There's never an excuse for a typographical error (typo)—use your spell-checker and dictionary. Get to grips with punctuation, particularly apostrophes, and establish a consistent style for the use of initial capitals, dashes, and so on.

"It's as difficult to become a good copywriter as a good brain surgeon."
Rosser Reeves

For the purists who police our language and raise merry hell when a sentence starts with "but" or "and," remind them that Shakespeare himself spelled his name many different ways during his life, and that English is an endlessly changing and developing language, with new words coming in to and old words slipping out of use all the time.

Typography is the icing on your cake

Living in your own bubble as a copywriter is not acceptable. You may feel as if you are a creative island and that you need solitude and privacy to write your best copy, but you are not working in isolation, you are part of a team that includes designers.

Design and copy really come together in **typography**, a true craft with generations of tradition and one of the most stylish and powerful expressions of graphic ideas. Whether the idea comes from the designer or the writer, a phrase or word set in a skilled way can have enormous impact.

The designer will be working to the same brief as you, but is coming at it from the visual perspective. Some designers pay a lot of attention to the copy, reading it and absorbing the content; some get into the words from the typographical point of view, without knowing the subject matter at all. Others regard copy as the black lines that have to go on the page somewhere, getting in the way of the design integrity. In some cases the designer sits in the same room as you and you can discuss the project as it progresses, yet in others you may never meet. The real magic can take place only when the writer and designer are "in sync," when they have a common understanding and complement each other's work.

Discuss the profile of your audience with the designer. Compare notes on who they are, what makes them tick, and the approach you should take to communicating to them. What are they like? Why will they be interested? How will the design grab their attention and set the scene? What will be your core message? Is there a visual concept that will encapsulate this? What overall effect are we trying to create?

Let your ideas flow, accept that most of them will be half-baked, and fish around in them to see if a strong picture starts to emerge. Always refer back to your audience profile, core message, and the overriding benefit that you're focusing on. Your designer will be concentrating on creating impact, being different, and remaining on-brand. Your job is to process your raw material, organize the messages, and draft your copy, in the right tone of voice and in line with the creative concepts being developed by the designer.

Exercise: getting to grips with a tone of voice

Select a brand that you know something about, perhaps one of your favorites, or a very well-known one. Look at a few examples of their communications, whether it's booklets from a branch, press advertising, or their website. Prepare a word bank, brand dictionary, and tone-of-voice guide, on three separate sheets of paper.

For your *word bank*, look at content and vocabulary and list all of the words that you can find in the text that seem to characterize the tone of voice and are particular to that brand. A word bank for a suncare brand might include words such as "adventure," "aglow," "awash," "nutrients," "soothing," and "sunkissed." You could add other words of your own that capture the spirit of the brand.

For your *brand dictionary*, pay attention to the style of language. Is it relaxed or formal, high-brow or aimed at the lowest common denominator? Make a list of specific words and phrases that seem to define the style. For example, do you say "telephone us" or "call us," "pop in to our branch" or "come in to our store," "we will" or "we'll," and are your people called "staff" or "employees"?

For your *tone-of-voice guide*, look for specific sentences or phrases that evoke the essence of the brand's style of writing. Take three or four examples of copy that is clearly "on-brand," and then write a couple of similar but off-brand versions for each one, showing where the copy would not be in line with the brand voice. For example, if you are writing lipstick copy for a cosmetics brand, you could say "perfectly plump, deliciously dewy" and be on-brand, but "it's the only one to plump for" or "plumping lipstick for a dewy finish" would both be off-brand.

Round-up

There is no room for your personality in your copy.

Your customers consciously select the promotional and advertising messages that they wish to listen to.

Using puns and witticisms is becoming less important than crafting a well-constructed and stimulating message.

There is always the need for a creative or conceptual idea to underlie your approach.

Build up a profile of the audience, developing an understanding of what they are like.

Don't tell your customers what something does; tell them how or why it will improve their lives.

Target those who are predisposed to buying, who have some interest in your product, and who will give you the time of day.

It is much better for people to want to buy from you than for you to have to sell to them.

It's hard to resist finding out more about something that we think we really want to know about.

Your copy should be as clear and digestible as possible, so make life easy for yourself and keep everything simple.

The art of writing
great copy

Great copy that gets good results can sometimes be so simple and clear that it looks as if it's written itself. It attracts the attention of the audience, compels them to take an interest, and guides them as they decide to involve themselves. Writing copy like this is a delicate process, which is not set in stone, so the best approach is to find out what makes the most sense to you by seeing how the professionals do it.

Make sure you take a great brief

Great copy comes from a great **brief**, and receiving a brief is an active process, not a passive one. While the client or employer may feel that he or she is giving you everything that you require in the brief, it is up to you as the copywriter to take a great brief. It is common to find that the brief you're working to does not contain all of the information you need. Certain jobs require you to conduct original research, so consider bolstering your content with additional insights, facts, and figures where relevant. Google is the source of many great research adventures.

A copy brief is the one aspect of the communications process that should not involve a long chain of command. It is vital that wherever possible the writer takes his or her own brief from the person commissioning the work, and builds on this by interviewing other key people associated with the project. The golden rule in every aspect of copywriting, design, and communication is to assume nothing, and this is never more appropriate than when taking a brief. So what do you need to know before you start writing, how do you assess the quality of a brief, and how do you get to the source of your information?

Every brief has three essential elements: a profile of your target audience; clarification of the **core message** that is to be communicated; and a good reason why the target audience should be interested—what benefit does it give them? There is a lot more that can be included in a brief, but without these three key elements you cannot hope to hit the nail on the head.

The client, or employer, or whoever is giving you the brief, will not necessarily be able to provide all of the information that you will require. This brief could be one of many projects he or she is looking after and it may not be easy for him or her to stand back and see your brief as clearly as you do. The best writers will not accept a half-baked brief; they will make sure they have everything they need before they begin to write. The best way to do this is to ask "stupid" questions. It is all too easy to have a friendly meeting, discuss the brief in general, shake hands, and disappear to draft your copy. When you're halfway through your project you're likely to realize there's not enough to say, or very little substantial material to use.

When you take the brief you must challenge the briefer to provide detail, but be diplomatic. Take a collaborative approach, and put the client at ease with a phrase such as "it's a good brief, but I need to ask you a few stupid questions." You can then go through the brief and ask for clarification and expansion of the content without treading on anyone's ego. Ask for definitions of terms that seem obvious, and you may dig up all sorts of new insights.

When you've taken a full brief you can conduct further research or interviews to gather more content and help you make the decisions you need to in order to shape your copy in line with the brief, the target audience, and the overall objectives. A lot can be achieved on the Internet, and Google is as good a place to start as anywhere. Your client should be able to put you in touch with key people whom you can interview face to face, over the phone, or using e-mail.

Find the best environment for creativity

"You must be as simple, and as swift, and as penetrating as possible. And it must stem from knowledge. And you must relate that knowledge to the consumer's needs."
Bill Bernbach

Having taken your brief and gathered your raw material it is time to lock yourself away and get your creative juices flowing. It doesn't matter where or how you work, as long as you feel comfortable and can concentrate. Some writers like to be in the middle of a busy studio or office, while others prefer total solitude. Some like to use the latest IT while others prefer a pen and paper. Some are highly efficient and get off to a flying start, while others prevaricate for ever and end up burning the midnight oil in order to hit the deadline. Ultimately, creative writing involves wrestling with your mind, and, however you manage this process, your rules are simple: never miss your deadline and never compromise the quality and integrity of your work.

Copywriting is a highly disciplined type of creative writing and many new writers are worried that they are simply not sufficiently imaginative or concept-driven to undertake this type of work. Copywriting is challenging because it exposes the writer to direct criticism and there is no hiding from the words and creative ideas you put on the page. Although the degree of creativity required does vary from brief to brief, in general 70 percent of your copywriting will be concerned with organization and decision-making, while perhaps only 30 percent of the process will require you to focus purely on the most creative aspects of your writing, so you are dealing mainly with hard facts and you are not as exposed to criticism for your conceptual thinking as you may feel.

You've put a lot of time and effort into taking a thorough brief, so make full use of it. If you have ten working hours available for writing your copy, spend seven of them relentlessly preparing and developing your raw material, processing your notes, and playing with different thoughts and ideas. The remaining three hours will be sufficient to draft your copy. The more thoroughly you process, order, and prepare your copy, the easier it will be to write. Immerse yourself fully in the project. Take on the mindset of your target audience, understand their likes and dislikes, attitudes and beliefs, and create the right viewpoint for writing to them in a clear voice that they will relate to.

There are many types of creative brief

It's your job to create the best copywriting brief possible for every copywriting project you work on, and you can't rely on your client, or your colleagues, to do this for you—although giving them a blank copywriting briefing template is a great way to get most of the work prepared in the way you need it to be before you even start.

Smaller clients will rarely have a written brief for you to follow, often because they aren't clear about what they require, just what they want to achieve—or to put it another way, they know the results they are looking for but they don't know how to create them. In this case you will need to interrogate them to find out the information you need to create great copy. This could be in the form of a one-to-one meeting across a desk or, if you've got the confidence, could be an interactive workshop with a group of people. Once you've gathered your information (following the checklist on the opposite page) write this up and give it back to the client to check, amend, and approve.

There are usually three main types of written brief involved with your copywriting process: the client's creative brief; the studio's creative brief (this could be an internal, in-house team or an external creative agency); and your copywriting brief. The client's creative brief is likely to be fairly generalized, more a set of instructions, but it will have deadlines and should identify the key **milestones**, **sign-offs**, and **stakeholders**. The studio brief will be prepared by an account manager (if agency) or marketing manager (if client) for the creatives, with specific direction on design, media, production, budget controls, and all sorts of other stuff that you don't need to know about—as well as the messaging and copywriting (hopefully). You'll be responsible for preparing your copy brief, which should be shared with the team and client early on so they can contribute or make comments that could save you a lot of hassle later on. As the best carpenters say, "measure twice, cut once."

Checklist: Taking a copy brief
Start with the big picture and drill down into the fine detail.

Basic details

Client's name, address, and contact details.
When was the brief taken and when is the copy needed for?
Does this relate to any previous jobs?
Will it be part of larger communications or is it stand-alone?

Overview

What is the requirement of the brief, what is the client expecting from the project and, specifically, from you?
What is the background and context for the communication (what was the previous marketing or advertising activity, and what are the reasons for doing this new brief)?
What is the timeline and when do you need to respond by?

Background and raw material

What material has the client produced before and how did it perform?
How does this campaign fit in with other communications from the client?
What is being provided as content to develop?
Are there further sources of content (by researching or interviewing)?

Target audience

Who are we trying to reach, and what route are we using?
What is their profile, and what type of people are they?
What do they think about the client?
What's going on in this marketplace—how crowded is it?

The core message

What is the single, compelling message that must be communicated?
What supporting evidence is there to back up any claims being made?

The Unique Selling Point (USP)

What benefit does the core message provide to the audience?
What makes this different and compelling in the marketplace?
Why should the reader bother to read all of the copy and respond?

Creative direction

How should the finished work look and feel?
Is there a brand style that must be adhered to?
Are there examples of similar work that can be used as a guide?
What's the most appropriate tone of voice?

Anything else?

Make sure that any directions that don't fit into the categories listed above are noted at the end of the brief. Examples would be overall word count, or the number of pages in a brochure, or how much room there is for headlines, intro paragraphs, subheadings, and a summary in an article.

The challenge of creating your first draft

Before you begin creating your first draft, you must process and prepare the material provided in your brief, even though you may prefer to simply start writing your copy. The more work you do on it, the smoother and more polished your first draft will be. Read the brief, then reread it slowly a couple of times, taking it all in and pondering the implications of each piece of information.

Identify all of the raw material where the content overlaps and can be seamlessly linked. Lift phrases and points from the brief and note them carefully on a sheet of paper, grouping them under suitable categories such as "target audience," "key message," "supporting details," and "tone of voice." This process will extract core content from the rest of the brief and help you to identify patterns.

For example, if you're working on a brief for a press advertisement for an antiaging beauty product launch you'll be limited in the amount of copy you can work with, and will need to condense the raw material into very succinct points. You may be told the product's **USP** is that it reduces the appearance of fine lines around the eyes. Elsewhere in the brief you discover the cream is very easily absorbed and allows makeup to be applied over it. In your notes you would bring these points together, using a shorthand such as: "reduces appearance of fine lines," "easily absorbed," "allows makeup application."

In another category you will link together points such as availability, **price point**, and promotional offers. Your notes may say: "In supermarkets nationwide from June," "very competitive price," and "buy one get one free in first week."

It is essential that you process every point from the brief, because you will be using these refined notes as the sole reference point for drafting your copy. As you progress you will reshape the content into its core elements, reducing these to a few distinct messages. These notes will give you accurate and highly condensed raw material and a focal point for your innovative creative thinking.

You can now start to make the decisions that will shape your finished copy. The decision-making responsibility that rests on a copywriter's shoulders can be immense, and is largely overlooked. Many people may have contributed to your brief, there may be sensitivities concerning the project, and the individual stakeholders (those who will be signing off the copy or who own the overall department or product group) will have their own priorities and needs. As the writer, you may decide to lead on a single message and leave out the other points that don't support this. This requires confidence and clear reasoning.

Consider the format you are working to and be clear on the parameters, as established in the brief, such as limited space, that will restrict you.

"I try to get a picture in my mind of the kind of people they are—how they use this product, and what it is—they don't often tell you in so many words—but what it is that actually motivates them to buy something or interests them in something."
Leo Burnett

"Know your prospect and know your product—and know both in considerable depth."
George Gribbin

BECOME AWARE OF NO

Idea generation is a different exercise than idea selection. So when new ideas come up, don't judge them just yet. Let them be, no matter how retarded you think they are. But if you simply cannot stop yourself, if the urge to reject them outright is stronger than the potential of an untested idea, you'd better contribute another one to take its place.

EXPAND YOUR TOOLBOX

The more you depend on a tool, the less it does for you. So let go of the mouse and pick up a pencil. And when the pencil loses its point, stop drawing and make a collage. Or even better, abandon your toolbox completely, and invent a new tool. Because sometimes a new tool is what it takes to do the job right.

Words of wisdom from the forward-thinking copywriters at the Language in Common blog, getting to the heart of the matter and showing that good copy can work just as well on a blog as it does in client marketing.

The evocative copy in these advertisements for recreational vehicles (RVs) captures the spirit of adventure and fun that goes with RVing. The camper van is the feature, the great outdoors is the benefit.

Spot a spotted owl. Whistle while you walk. Nestle in at night. Do just about anything, and go just about anywhere with an RV. Go to GoRVing.com for a free video and visit an RV dealer. What will you discover? *Go RVing.*

Marvel over the Milky Way. Hop aboard Saturn's rings. Count your lucky stars that you can do just about anything, just about anywhere with an RV. Go to GoRVing.com for a free video and visit an RV dealer. What will you discover? *Go RVing.*

You're four times
It's hard to
more likely to
concentrate on
have a crash
two things
when you're on
at the same time.
a mobile phone.

It's illegal to use a hand-held mobile phone when driving.
From February 27th 2007 you will receive a £60 fine and
three penalty points on your licence.

www.thinkroadsafety.gov.uk

Published by the Department for Transport. ©Crown copyright 2003. Reprinted in the UK Dec 06 on paper containing at least 75% recycled fibre. Product Code TINF886P

This copy walks the walk: not only
does it explain how dangerous it
is to use your phone when you're
driving, it demonstrates how
confusing it is to try and do two
things at the same time—it's a
double-hit for the reader.

Creating the concept behind your solution

The 30 percent of your time that you'll spend on the creative thinking side of your writing (having spent the other 70 percent on preparing and organizing your raw material) is where you can have the most fun as a writer, but flights of fantasy are very risky. Make sure you have a technique for keeping your train of thought on brief and for checking that your ideas are on track too, once you've finalized them. Focus on building a profile of your audience by establishing what type of people they are. Depending on the target your client gives you, this may be a very defined description or a wide spectrum—either way you must create in your mind a sense of who they are and what "makes them tick."

Conceptualizing is all about lateral thinking—following thought patterns that lead you into new territories where you can create messages that ring true for the reader and which deliver the content so effectively that they get a great response (positive reactions from the audience, leading to practical actions to the benefit of the client). Where do you get your ideas from? They're right there in your notes.

First of all, look for word plays, phrases, or suggestions in the key words in your briefing notes and note them all down without worrying what you're going to do with them. Sometimes a good phrase or message will jump out straight away and can form the center of a headline and approach to your **body copy**, but the ideas that come to you most readily are likely to be clichés or, if not, will have been used already in similar situations. You usually have to work past your first and second rounds of ideas, even though they are good or great, and push yourself into your third or fourth round of ideas before you are in truly original territory.

Next, identify the features and follow your train of thought on the associated benefits, and really take this to the limit. Everything useful has a benefit to someone, so start by identifying this, and then push yourself to think of even more detailed benefits. Try thinking in obscure corners, set your imagination free to roam into strange places, consider the cause and effect of each feature and benefit in surreal ways. You don't need to come up with a brilliantly creative headline or theme because sometimes a simple message is the best solution, but at the same time there should be no limits to your thinking at this stage. Anything goes, and often what seem to be the craziest ideas can be shaped into the most compelling messages.

"If you have all the research, all the ground rules, all the directives, all the data— it doesn't mean the ad is written. Then you've got to close the door and write something—that is the moment of truth which we all try to postpone as long as possible."
David Ogilvy

There are many ways of conceptualizing or "brainstorming" and all are valid. A lot of writers can come up with good ideas and proposals, but the trick is to know which idea is the one your client should invest his multi-million-dollar budget in. After conceptualizing, take a break and return to your notes with a more rational (and less lateral) mind. This is where you go back to the process side of your copywriting, by returning to the brief and the notes you've prepared and checking how accurately your concepts fit the intended direction. You could categorize by type, so that the client can see the structure—for example, headline ideas might follow certain themes that can be grouped together. Be strict with yourself and cut out anything but the really good, or really weird, suggestions, making sure that each is on-brief, or if not on-brief then so striking and different that it still delivers the requirements of the brief.

Editing—your secret weapon in the struggle for clarity

No copywriter drafts finished copy at the first sitting. The secret to great writing is the way you edit your original draft, regardless of whether your text is two short paragraphs or 2000 words in length. The process of reviewing and

The Rolls-Royce Silver Cloud—$13,550.

"At 60 miles an hour the loudest noise in this new Rolls-Royce comes from the electric clock"

What makes Rolls-Royce the best car in the world? "There is really no magic about it— it is merely patient attention to detail," says an eminent Rolls-Royce engineer.

1. "At 60 miles an hour the loudest noise comes from the electric clock," reports the Technical Editor of THE MOTOR. The silence of the engine is uncanny. Three mufflers tune out sound frequencies—acoustically.

2. Every Rolls-Royce engine is run for seven hours at full throttle before installation, and each car is test-driven for hundreds of miles over varying road surfaces.

3. The Rolls-Royce is designed as an *owner-driven* car. It is eighteen inches shorter than the largest domestic cars.

4. The car has power steering, power brakes and automatic gear-shift. It is very easy to drive and to park. No chauffeur required.

5. There is no metal-to-metal contact between the body of the car and the chassis frame—except for the speedometer drive. The entire body is insulated and under-sealed.

6. The finished car spends a week in the final test-shop, being fine-tuned. Here it is subjected to ninety-eight separate ordeals. For example, the engineers use a *stethoscope* to listen for axle-whine.

7. The Rolls-Royce is guaranteed for *three years.* With a new network of dealers and parts-depots from

Coast to Coast, service is no longer any problem.

8. The famous Rolls-Royce radiator has never been changed, except that when Sir Henry Royce died in 1933 the monogram RR was changed from red to black.

9. The coachwork is given five coats of primer paint, and hand rubbed between each coat, before *fourteen* coats of finishing paint go on.

10. By moving a switch on the steering column, you can adjust the shock-absorbers to suit road conditions. (The lack of fatigue in driving this car is remarkable.)

11. Another switch defrosts the rear window, by heating a network of 1360 invisible wires in the glass. There are two separate ventilating systems, so that you can ride in comfort with all the windows closed. Air conditioning is optional.

12. The seats are upholstered with eight hides of English leather—enough to make 128 pairs of soft shoes.

13. A picnic table, veneered in French walnut, slides out from under the dash. Two more swing out behind the front seats.

14. You can get such optional extras as an Espresso coffee-making machine, a dictating machine, a bed, hot and cold water for washing, an electric razor.

15. You can lubricate the entire chassis by simply pushing a pedal from the driver's seat. A gauge on the dash shows the level of oil in the crankcase.

16. Gasoline consumption is remarkably low and there is no need to use premium gas; a happy economy.

17. There are two separate systems of power brakes, hydraulic and mechanical. The Rolls-Royce is a very safe car—and also a very lively car. It cruises serenely at eighty-five. Top speed is in excess of 100 m.p.h.

18. Rolls-Royce engineers make periodic visits to inspect owners' motor cars and advise on service.

ROLLS-ROYCE AND BENTLEY

19. The Bentley is made by Rolls-Royce. Except for the radiators, they are identical motor cars, manufactured by the same engineers in the same works. The Bentley costs $300 less, because its radiator is simpler to make. People who feel diffident about driving a Rolls-Royce can buy a Bentley.

PRICE. The car illustrated in this advertisement—f.o.b. principal port of entry—costs $13,550.
If you would like the rewarding experience of driving a Rolls-Royce or Bentley, get in touch with our dealer. His name is on the bottom of this page. Rolls-Royce Inc., 10 Rockefeller Plaza, New York, N.Y.

JET ENGINES AND THE FUTURE

Certain airlines have chosen Rolls-Royce turbo-jets for their Boeing 707's and Douglas DC8's. Rolls-Royce prop-jets are in the Vickers Viscount, the Fairchild F.27 and the Grumman Gulfstream.
Rolls-Royce engines power more than half the turbo-jet and prop-jet airliners supplied to or on order for world airlines.
Rolls-Royce engines now employ 42,000 people and the company's engineering experience does not stop at motor cars and jet engines. There are Rolls-Royce diesel and gasoline engines for many other applications.
The huge research and development resources of the company are now at work on many projects for the future, including nuclear and rocket propulsion.

Special showing of the Rolls-Royce and Bentley at Salter Automotive Imports, Inc., 9009 Carnegie Ave., tomorrow through April 26.

In this classic long-copy ad from the 1950s, the benefit-led approach came directly from the raw material provided in the brief. David Ogilvy wrote 26 different headlines for this advertisement, and then asked half a dozen writers from his agency to go over them and pick out the best one. He then wrote about 3500 words of copy and had three or four other writers go over it to cut out the dull and obscure parts and reduce the overall word count.

revising your copy can transform it from well-written, logical text into a highly compelling proposition.

There are a few rules to editing. It is usually the case that shorter is better. This is not to say that short, punchy copy is always more effective than long, carefully constructed arguments; however, whatever length you're writing to, you should be concise and to the point, and avoid repetition or unnecessary text.

Be merciless, like Ming. If you've included statements that make similar points, parallel arguments, or lengthy descriptions, they have to go. Your remaining copy will be tighter, easier to read, and more effective. Less is usually more, and you should follow the mantra "if it can go it should go," without being precious about your beautifully crafted paragraphs. Your reader will not tolerate waffle, lack of structure, unfocused messages, or ambiguity, and even concise copy can lose a bit more if you are truly merciless.

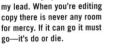

Look into my eyes and follow my lead. When you're editing copy there is never any room for mercy. If it can go it must go—it's do or die.

Never repeat words—there are always alternatives. If you can't find a single word to replace one you've already used, use a description instead, or rephrase the sentence. Replace long, obscure words with shorter ones that are in general usage, cut down wordy sentences, and avoid anything that clutters your core message. Be ruthless with yourself when assessing whether your copy is truly on-brief, targeted, and benefit-led. If you're not this hard on yourself, others will be before the text is approved.

What to do with your early drafts

It's likely that there will be a number of interested parties who will wish to comment on, revise, edit, and amend your original text. Always remember that although you are creating the copy you do not own it and will have to accept direction, even if you think that it compromises your work. You can always argue your point, but only by referring back to the brief and your tone-of-voice guide for justification. Remember that the views of these critics are valid and must be incorporated, or at least considered.

So don't keep your copy hidden away until it is finely tuned and highly polished. Identify the stakeholders in the project and consider the value of involving them at an early stage. Your stakeholders will be in the client team, and are usually the people who brief you. Work with them as closely as you can. Their senior managers are sometimes referred to as project "sponsors." They may have the ultimate sign-off, so try to ensure that they are kept up to speed during the development stages.

"Some of our best successes have been in industries that I knew nothing about."
Leo Burnett

Share the overall brief (and your copy brief, if there is a separate one) with your stakeholders and ask them to approve it. Any comments or directions that they have can then be incorporated from the very start, and you can explain how you will be approaching the copy in order to deliver the correct solution. When working on larger projects you should check in with these key people as you progress. Show them your rough concepts and test their reactions, discuss your approaches with them to see which one they prefer, and incorporate their thoughts into your final draft as you see fit.

There is no room for anyone on the team to have personal opinions, only professional opinions. It is not acceptable for a 50-year-old marketing director to tell you that he or she "doesn't like" a headline that is targeted at 18- to 25-year-old men. "Not liking" is not a valid criticism. If he or she tells you that the headline is poor because, in his or her opinion, "men aged 18 to 25 won't buy into it because it doesn't relate to their lifestyle," there may be a case and you can discuss this. This is a sensitive area and you may need to be subtle in your approach—try saying that he or she is not in the core target audience and personal opinions are not necessarily valid, and see how far this gets you.

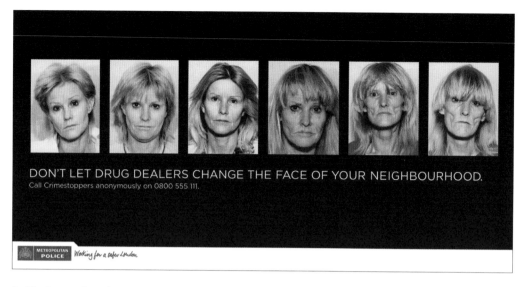

DON'T LET DRUG DEALERS CHANGE THE FACE OF YOUR NEIGHBOURHOOD.
Call Crimestoppers anonymously on 0800 555 111.

METROPOLITAN POLICE   Working for a safer London

A subtle play on words creates a very powerful and accessible headline, but here the copy plays second fiddle to the very moving imagery.

Getting that all-important sign-off

It is important to understand the psychology of approving creative work, and to use techniques to achieve sign-off that don't involve watching your work being pulled apart.

Consider the attitude of those signing off your copy. In the words of the great Edward de Bono, we all live in a critical society, we are trained from birth to criticize, and it is very rare to find constructive feedback in any field. Most of us find it easy to knock things. We always know what we don't like, and we tend to highlight problems and issues rather than build on the elements that we do like. Unfortunately, we rarely have a natural capacity to build constructively on concepts and are rarely clear about what we do like—being precise makes it too easy to be criticized by others! It is unrealistic to expect to show a senior figure some creative work, ask for an opinion, and emerge unscathed. Negative criticism is human nature.

Once your senior players are looking at your finished copy, observe their behavior. If they pick up a pen when they start to read your copy, you can politely remind them that they may not need to red-pen the text, that the copy has been carefully crafted and that their role is to check for factual accuracy (content) and not for style. They will have opinions on style and tone, and these can be discussed, but make it clear that you're not actually inviting them to write copy themselves by amending your text.

Present yourself in the best light

Sometimes you will be presenting your copy to a colleague (possibly a fellow designer, or a creative director or account manager) and at other times you may be presenting your work to a client during the project's development or as part of a competitive pitch against other designers and writers. One technique that may assist you in this involves breaking a lot of the rules already laid down here.

The golden rule is to ensure that your work is on-brief. However, when you line up a collection of different creatives in a pitch situation, and they all adhere rigidly to the brief, the resulting solutions are likely to have similarities of tone, look, and feel, especially where the brief has been conservative. One technique for winning a pitch in this scenario is to go off-brief and present highly creative, forward-thinking, and impressive solutions that show some wider possibilities.

Think of this as your runway approach. Karl Lagerfeld sends his Chanel models down the runway in amazing and stunning creations that the core Chanel customer couldn't seriously contemplate wearing. Yet the customer is inspired by the designs, which appear in all of the magazines because they are so newsworthy, and will visit Chanel to buy her twinsets and handbags. If Lagerfeld were to send his models out wearing these twinsets and handbags the fashion press would say he was losing his touch.

For your runway approach you need to show your client what you can do if you are unrestricted by a brief, and what they might consider if they felt like taking a lead in the marketplace. To avoid the risk of missing the mark entirely, present at least two fully worked-up concepts, one that is completely on-brief, hitting all of the requirements squarely on the head, and another that is your runway showpiece. Do this well and you will stand out from the competition for your confidence, your skill, and your creativity. Don't show too many options.

Manage your copy through to sign-off

There is an art to presenting your copy, whether informally to a colleague or formally to a major client. It is often the case that the best copy solutions, using clear messages to communicate simple concepts, can be underappreciated or undervalued by the client, especially if you're presenting the copy as word-processed documents in isolation from the design concept. The best way to present copy in this format is to include some basic typesetting. Make the headline larger and center it, lay out the page in landscape, give some prominence to the lead paragraph, and ensure your typography is clear and well laid out.

"A lot of copywriters think they're good judges of their own work. I know I'm not."
David Ogilvy

You must be confident but not arrogant. Set the work in context by quickly summarizing the brief and your approach to it and saying what you have done:

Checklist: Assessing copy

☐ Does it answer the written brief?

☐ Is it interesting or compelling?

☐ Can you reduce the word count?

☐ Does it run in the right order?

☐ Do you believe the message?

☐ Does it tie in with the design concept?

☐ Does it include a clear call to action?

☐ Is it using the reader's language?

☐ Is there a better way of doing it?

☐ Maybe it's time to stop now?

"I've got three concepts, two of which I feel are on-brief, and another that explores the other options open to us."

Always finish on a high note, which means saving the work that you consider to be your best until the end. If you show your most stunning and creative work at the start, everything else you reveal will seem like a comedown. Begin with the most solid and reliable concepts, and sell them confidently, with a great deal of enthusiasm—as if you feel this is your ultimate solution. Show how it answers everything in the brief and point out the structure and techniques that you have incorporated. The client will feel confident that you know what you are doing, and should be pleased with the proposal, because it answers the brief.

As you reveal each concept, continue with your enthusiastic and positive approach, taking care not to show off or appear overconfident. Ask for reactions and opinions and build rapport during the meeting. By the time you reach your runway showpiece the client will have had plenty of stimulating material to consider. The brief has been answered but even more solutions are being presented. Whether this final piece is liked or not is irrelevant; its role is to show unrestrained creativity, make you stand out from the competition, and prevent them from outshining you. Explain that although you are totally confident in the recommended solutions, this is conceptual work, and the real solution will incorporate the client's direction and thinking.

Once your initial presentations are completed, you will probably have a number of work-in-progress meetings where the client and others will have opportunities to make changes to your text. This can become very political, and you must take a purely professional approach to this. The client will know the target customer and the products or services in far more detail than you, and you will have to pay close attention to this direction. However, the client will often be too close to the project to be objective, will rarely have enough experience of creative writing and design to genuinely lead its development, and may make suggestions simply to challenge your confidence or test whether you're taking a chance with the product.

The way to handle client comments is to relate everything back to the target audience, core message, and USP that are being highlighted. If the client's suggestion improves these, build it in; if not, prepare a clear explanation of why you wish to override it. If you find yourself in an impasse, go with the client's views. There is no point fighting to the death; it makes a lot more sense to go with the recommendations, make the best job of it that you can, and live to fight another day.

Exercise: familiarizing yourself with a good brief

Type in the criteria listed on "Taking a copy brief" on page 27 to give yourself the main headings for your briefing template.

Choose a piece of advertising or marketing that appeals to you, or look at a selection of communications material from a brand that you like.

Retro-write the brief, filling in all of the elements. You won't know all of the details, so make some up, using your common sense to second guess the client's original directions.

Once you've completed a full brief, follow the processes listed on pages 28, 33, and 35 to prepare and prioritize your raw material, then draft some new creative concepts of your own. Work with a designer if you can, or do some thinking about design yourself.

Work up your best concept as a rough **mock-up**, the same size as the original. If it's an ad, stick it in the magazine over the original. If it's a brochure, keep it next to the original.

Come back the next day and look at your work with a fresh pair of eyes. How did you do? Is your effort as good as the original? Would you show this work to a prospective employer?

Round-up

Great copy comes from a great brief; receiving a brief is an active process, not a passive one.

It doesn't matter where you work or how you work, so long as you feel comfortable and can concentrate.

Never miss your deadline and never compromise the quality and integrity of your work.

The more thoroughly you process, order, and prepare your copy, the easier it is to write.

When searching for creative inspiration, do a mini brainstorm on your own.

The secret of great writing is the way you edit your original draft.

Don't keep your copy hidden away until it is finely tuned and highly polished.

It is important to understand the psychology of approving creative work.

Show your client what you can do if you are unrestricted by a brief.

The client will have a far greater knowledge than you of the target customer and of the products or services being promoted.

Writing for brand
and marketing

We all know the world's best brands, and we all have our favorites. They speak to us, we understand them, we have valid expectations of them, and they rarely let us down. Brand identity shapes perceptions, and if these perceptions prove to be correct, a brand becomes a trusted part of our lives—the objective of all brand marketing strategies. A brand's use of language is its primary form of expression, and by controlling and managing a brand's voice you create the opportunity to build mutually beneficial, long-term relationships with customers.

Language is the brand's personality

Branding has come a long way since it involved burning a mark of identification on the hide of a cow. How language is utilized, how a brand's personality is presented, and the messages it projects are being given increasingly greater importance as markets become more crowded. It is the content, the copy, the unique message the brand delivers that counts today. Graphic design provides the **brand identity** and copywriting provides detail to the brand personality.

Many brands—both product and corporate—have made huge progress over the last decades through their use of graphic design and imagery, but so have consumers, who are now very brand-savvy. In today's saturated landscape everyone has a brand, but it is not always clear what the brand stands for. It is not enough just to have a smart identity. The brand copywriter must understand the brand's essence, its reason for existing, and explain this, with supporting information, using a voice that reflects the brand's characteristics and appeals to the target audience.

"The more you engage with customers the clearer things become and the easier it is to determine what you should be doing."
John Russell, President, Harley-Davidson

Organizations face growing competition all the time and, for many, a strong brand is the way to build **market share**. However, the opportunities to create future brand innovations purely through design expression are diminishing, and the shift toward delivering meaningful content consistently is the new battleground, where good copywriting comes into its own. This emphasis will increase, and as a brand and marketing copywriter you could find yourself playing a key role as the owner and guardian of the tone of voice of a client's brand.

The brand expression has to be ahead of its time

You have to give careful thought to every aspect of a brand's language and its tone of voice, because it mustn't chop and change to suit the mood of the day. This means thinking ahead about the market, the customer, and how things will evolve. You're not just looking at plans for the brand this year or next, but for the next five, ten, or more years.

Consider how the marketplace is likely to adapt and evolve over this time, and the role that your brand is going to play within this. How will its products and services adapt over time? There are no firm answers, but your aim is to allow enough freedom for the voice to evolve without needing to be redefined in the near future.

It's not enough to create a style and tone that suits the current conditions or reflects the company's heritage. This means taking a few chances in the short term in order to be strong in the future—the voice you create may need to move on a lot from where it is has been. The brand has to avoid being fashionable, but it must be forward-thinking. This means you must be prepared to craft messages and use a style that are ahead of their time, so that the brand tone of voice is still current in three or four years.

The challenge of rebranding or creating a new brand

What's in a name? A rose by any other name would smell as sweet. Does it matter what the brand's name is, or is this the most important aspect?

"A brand that captures your mind gains behavior. A brand that captures your heart gains commitment."
Scott Talgo, brand strategist

It is unlikely that you will be given the brief to come up with the new corporate brand name for Nike or Coca-Cola, but you may be asked to create the name for a new range of sneakers or a new drink for these giants. You may also find yourself in the team that is repositioning a tired or unfocused business and everyone is looking at you, the copywriter, for the new name. If it were that simple everyone would be doing it. It's not easy, but there are a few useful techniques that you can learn.

Giving a name to an identity

Brand naming is a tough call. Where a lot of the challenges of copywriting require a number of language crafts and creative skills, creating a single name, a word, is anyone's game. Having the eye to know which will work well, and which won't, is not as easy as it might seem.

You develop your critical eye for assessing a brand name over time, and through experience, but no one can claim to have all the answers when it comes to backing a specific name, and there are always surprise hits and misses. Branding requires vision, and vision requires nerve and commitment. Naming a brand is like naming a new baby. At first the name can seem unfamiliar and possibly unsuitable, but very soon the child "owns" the name and the idea of giving the baby another name is unthinkable.

"It is a pretty recognizable brand name. Originally it was 'Jerry's Guide to the World Wide Web' but we settled on 'Yahoo.'"

Jerry Yang, founder of Yahoo

In most cases the word that is selected as the name for the new brand will seem strange. It doesn't exist on the shelves anywhere, and doesn't have the tangible nature of existing brands. You have to rely on your vision, and picture how the audience will respond, and how it could fit into its marketplace. If the graphics and market positioning have all been thought through and the new identity resonates with the audience, your brand will soon find its feet.

There are several routes to creating a shortlist of brand names. You could experiment with amalgamating industry terms or words to create a new hybrid name that has some relevance to the industry. You could trawl Latin and Greek dictionaries to find interesting words with good connotations. You can brainstorm your rough ideas with other creatives or business brains, pool the ideas, and see if you can come up with a couple of contenders.

Use a pencil to scribble down all of the possible words and relevant short phrases on a large sheet of paper. Try lots of routes, including looking up relevant words in dictionaries and thesauruses, searching on the Internet for other possibilities, and even making up entirely new words that have a good sound or feel to them. While you're doing this research, note any competing brands. Think laterally, play with the words and mix them around, keeping the brief in mind at all times, and establish whether hybrids can be formed. When you've exhausted this process have a break and return later to assess the words.

If you're lucky, one or two of the rough ideas will appeal to you, and you can draw up a very short list of serious contenders, supported by a second list of possibles. (You should keep the rest of your roughs to one side for future reference.) Otherwise, you'll have to repeat the brainstorming, and spread your net wider, looking for inspiration in other areas of life once the well of business language runs dry.

Next, pressure-test the words in the serious contenders list. Do any have double meanings? Could they be misinterpreted? Are they like any existing brands? Can they be spelled differently? What are the alternatives?

You'll then have a shortlist of top potential names, some second-division alternatives, and the "also-rans." It is worth prioritizing these as soon as possible and having two or three hot solutions that stand out confidently above the rest. Giving your client too much choice can be overwhelming and the poor ideas can water down your good ones. Never present ideas that you are not completely happy with, even if this pares down the options to the bone.

At first sight this powerful branding poster for the San Jose Music Festival appears to be simply a strong graphic image. Look again and you'll realize that the use of copy, or typography to be more precise, is just as innovative. It's chopped up and the letters are in different weights, but despite its ambiguity you immediately know it says "Music in the Park." Simple and striking.

Interview: John Simmons, The Writer

Having been head of copy at Interbrand for many years, John Simmons, now at The Writer, has extensive experience of brand communications and tone-of-voice management. As well as training copywriters in the rigors of creative writing, he consults some of the world's largest corporations and a number of smaller outfits on how to utilize language to represent their organization clearly and build strong relationships with their audiences.

I work to a wide variety of briefs and still write a lot of copy myself. I think it's important as a writer not to get carried away with your own ability to use words, and remember that sometimes no copy is better, as words could detract from an image.

When you are aware that someone speaking is choosing words very carefully you will listen more intently, but you will tend to cut off those people who don't. I have recently been working on a brief for a series of 48-sheet billboard posters that convey the skill of the writer, and we don't allow the copy on each poster to be more than six words. Hemingway is credited with writing the shortest story in the world, using only six words: "For sale: baby shoes, never worn."

I have a big problem with management writing, and also with brand strategists who are allowed to put words on paper. They are not writers and usually choose the wrong ones. Brand people have an urge to fill every space, and tend to take a scientific rather than a creative approach, preferring to replicate other big brands than create something new. It's not so easy as that. The copy must define a brand in its essence.

It's important to use that part of the brain that you use yourself, relating to your reader as a human to a human. I put notes in a notebook, the things I want to keep and go back to. I write the first draft by hand and then type it up, editing it as I do so. I read the copy out to the client. I do this when I'm proud of copy and it works. It goes back to childhood. We all like listening to a story, rather than a PowerPoint presentation.

It is also important to maintain a consistent story across all expressions of the brand, globally. Guinness is in 150 countries and had been putting out different brand messages in each one. We rationalized this around the theme that Guinness reflects your inner strength, showing how Guinness helps them in a situation.

A recent copywriting and tone-of-voice project has been the cosmetics range ILA. It features spas, products, and skincare with pure natural materials, which they describe as "beyond organic." The client, Denise, is an ex-nurse. She developed products for a client of hers who was "allergic to water"; this became The Himalayan Goddess Company, which we rebranded as ILA. Pentagram, with John Rushworth as partner, created the identity. There was no grand model, it was simply based around "purity."

They required pack copy for a new range of products. The range was hardcore, drawing on ideas of vibrational energy from Vedic scriptures and involving chanting of mantras when making products. I was slightly skeptical at first. I aimed to get across what we felt was good in the range and broaden the market.

I began by researching ILA's story. As a writer you sense a company. It is vital to visit and get to know a business. How can you work if you've never met or spoken to its people? You'll probably not be true to its absolute essence. The key with ILA was going to the Cotswolds [England] to see where the products are made. Denise gave me a head massage and talked for three hours about her company and products. I just absorbed it all, the words and the atmosphere.

ILA is about essential oils, so their "essence" was even more vital than with other brands. I'm always skeptical about straplines, and instead I suggested we say "Purity, Energy, Balance." This came from John's original brand definition. ILA's tone is different to commercial companies, but shouldn't be too off-puttingly "spiritual."

I found out where the products came from, and the beliefs behind them: a blend of Hindu, Buddhist, and Christian thinking. Three ingredients are used: pink Himalayan salt crystals, argan oil, from the seeds of a tree only found in the Atlas mountains in Morocco, and Rose Damascene from Rajasthan in India.

When it came to the booklet, I started with the stories of the three ingredients (and the barn

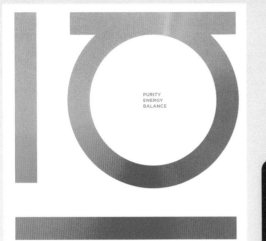

PURITY
ENERGY
BALANCE

In the foothills of the Himalayas you will see slopes covered with Indian Rose Damascene with an exquisite smell. Here we found Pawan and his family, who have been growing and distilling roses for many generations while also supporting local rose farmers.

Pawan knows the soil, he knows the plants, and the way he tests their qualities is as natural as breathing. He smells the roses, knows the precise moment to pick them and use their petals for immediate distillation.

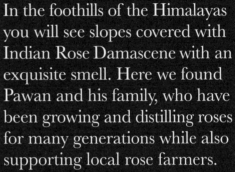

"Keep saying to yourself 'there's always another way to write this.'"

where the company operates). I'd enjoyed listening to them, and thought, "well, if I like them others will too." They worked well beside beautiful photographs of the ingredients being harvested and prepared at source. I was limited for space, and the designer wanted captions, but I said no as they wouldn't have added anything. The introductory copy fires the imagination and the images, without any copy, let it go.

The ultimate role of the booklet is to sell, but we approach this in a subtle way, building brand values and letting customers discover benefits. The right tone of voice is about light touches. It's more believable to say "known for centuries" instead of "will remove …." ILA products are tested in high-tech laboratories but we don't lead on this. We expect readers to take time to discover the qualities and benefits of the products because we know that the people we cater for will do this; the audience is women in their late 20s onward who shop in upmarket stores and on the Internet. They are attracted first by the emotion, the sensuousness of the approach; rationality confirms what emotions have decided.

I remembered the John Donne poem "At the round earth's imagined corners," using this as inspiration. We made the booklet square, with four "pegs" to the corners, Rajasthan, Kashmir, Morocco, and the Cotswolds. The theme was the love and care that goes into the products, the sense of discovery that accompanies them, and Phil Sayer's beautiful photographs.

You have to find out about a company to inform your brief. I've recently been developing tone-of-voice and Internet copy for an accountancy firm that offers professional services to large businesses. Their brief to me is about defining their brand, and I was lucky enough to share the project with designer Angus Hyland of Pentagram.

When I met the senior client team they gave a PowerPoint presentation about how their brand was defined, but it was not to the essence, lacking

clear vision. They said "our people are different, and are encouraged to speak out on issues affecting the professional and the business world in general."

Previously the copy on their website was dry, drudgy, with long sentences, no personality, and a bureaucratic, formal feel, which they knew didn't represent them. I took on the roles of writer and brand consultant, writing some copy with the right feel, then breaking it down to determine what the values were, and checking to see if the new tone-of-voice definitions reflected these values.

The three values were "bold, clear, and positive" and I developed a three-part narrative structure: always start with something bold, develop the message with something clear, and work toward a positive conclusion. The next stage was to evolve a distinctive feel to the copy to set them apart from their competitors.

I presented this to a committee. You have to have principles behind your writing, and before presenting draft copy to the client I showed the tone-of-voice definitions, using only a few pages. It's important to get full agreement and consensus from the start, because it makes it hard for them to disagree among themselves later. There is a large element of politics in this process. It was approved, and we also used the tone-of-voice and style guide to train their own people how to write and talk publicly on behalf of the company.

I always try to help provide the client with the eye and the ear to appreciate the copy. I let them read it and read it to them as well. The ear is the most important thing for a writer— the reader is listening to the words in their head.

My advice is to continually return to the brief you've been given, or the one you've formed, and be as objective as possible. Go with your instinct, use this as your guide to creating a natural feel, and hone the copy. Keep saying to yourself "there's always another way to write this"—it's part of the editing process. I do lots of alternatives for myself, but I don't show them all.

Interview: Steve Manning, Igor International

Steve Manning is one of the US's leading brand-naming copywriters. After running a highly popular blog about brand naming, he launched Igor International where he is busy naming and shaping the identities of some of the most high-profile brands across every type of business.

I find the whole idea of work obnoxious, and I'm not qualified to do anything. I don't like work. I worked for many years as a film editor and cameraman for a travel channel in New York, but it had been a random choice, like everything else in my life. I decided I'd had a great time traveling the world, but I was going to make a complete change.

I sold everything and flew to San Francisco. I told the cab driver to "take me somewhere nice" and he took me to Sausalito, where I booked into the best hotel. After about 100 days the money ran out; I found work as a cab driver, which I did for three years. It was a truly horrible existence. It was a small town, but a guy from a big New York agency got in my cab regularly and we got to know each other. We talked, and he'd seen my press over the last five years. He told me that he owned an agency, and he asked me if I wanted to be an assistant in a new naming company.

The two of us started an agency that we called ahundredmonkeys.com—it was during the dotcom boom and we were getting a lot of work in. My boss was charging $15,000 for a naming job. I was looking to earn more for myself, and I proposed to him that if I could sell the work in for $20,000 I wanted 10 percent of the fee, for $35,000 I wanted 15 percent, and so on, up to $75,000 where the scale went up and I wanted 35 percent of the fee. He didn't believe that I had a chance, but he let me have a go.

The next time we quoted, the client accepted the price of $75,000, and I got my bonus plus the lease on an Audi A8. It's a numbers game, and by sticking to it we know it will work. We don't mind if we miss out on work because of quoting a high fee. We lost a lot of clients, and many would ask if we could do it for cheaper and I'd say "no." A couple of hours later they'd invariably call back to hire us. They can't tell how to assess the fee—it's all about confidence.

Next, I started my own agency, called Igor, with my partner, Jay, who I'd met at art school. We don't have degrees, and we didn't have any money. We thought that if we kept adjusting our website, taking notes of our observations on how these changes affected our listing on Google, maybe we could crack the Google search-criteria code. Thousands of pages later we cracked it! There are books by professors on how to figure it out, and we've done it! It's given us a huge profile.

Our name needed to do so many things, and one word needed to capture so many ideas. The best names are the ones that are demonstrative of the qualities rather than being purely explanatory. Everyone said "Igor" won't work, no one will hire you. But a few years down the line we're working on the MTV downloading service, naming top hotels, and working for the Navy and Department of Defense. Igor says "hunchback grave robbers" to most people; a corporation would say this is a negative connotation. But I see us as the ultimate assistant. We chose to use Igor because we had to demonstrate we believed in turning around a negative connotation associated with a name.

The brand name Igor eliminates the need for advertising, PR, and sales calls. We get a ridiculous amount of press, because when journalists search our field they see lots of bland names and then spot Igor and think "this looks interesting." Also, we know that our clients are risk-tolerant if they have the nerve to recruit a company called Igor.

Our blog was critical of the war and of the Bush administration, and we had a surprise call from the Department of Defense. Two days later they came round and grilled us. We realized that they clearly wanted to hire us, but they were very creepy. I quoted them a month's time for their brief, fairly randomly, sending them a high price ($55,000) to send them away, then we worked on projects to name the next generation of their command and control systems.

Finally, something truly sexy from Australia.

Australia is up for it.

Eyes wide open.

Life's a blur.

INTRODUCING AUSTRALIA'S LATEST ESCAPE

THE PRIMORDIAL SPIRIT

vodka australis

Dive in.

THINGS ARE A LITTLE DIFFERENT IN AUSTRALIA

Pure pleasure.

WICKED. GOOD.

CATCH A PIECE OF AUSTRALIA

EYES WIDE OPEN

SEDUCED BY THE DEVIL DOWN UNDER

Sliver PREMIUM VODKA   **SLIVER** VODKA AUSTRALIS

SLIVER
Premium Vodka from Australia. Pure pleasure.

Australia is up for it.

SLIVER Premium Vodka from Australia. Are you up for it?

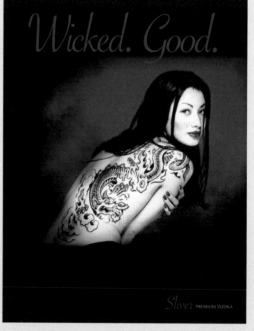

Wicked. Good.

Sliver PREMIUM VODKA

"I never attempt to write anything over 100 words, because I specialize in brand naming."

I never attempt to write anything over 100 words, because I specialize in brand naming. When we quote a price we provide a week-by-week breakdown of it, but this is all hoo-hah really. I named a hotel in Dubai for $40,000, which took two weeks of naming, and I have just turned down a brief from a major corporation because they only wanted to pay $35,000 and they said that we couldn't use the name we create for them in our portfolio. We e-mailed them back and said we were not interested.

A large organization that we didn't like too much approached us for a quotation for creating the name for a significant new brand. I didn't want the work, so I quoted $150,000, and said I wouldn't look at it until they deposited $75,000 in our account upfront. They said "no way," but a few days later they called back. After they put the money in my account I took six weeks before I started the project, but they came back with new briefs a further six times.

If you're a company and you are launching a multi-billion initiative, you have to figure out which naming company to hire, so you approach three of the leading agencies. Two say they can do it for $15,000, or $10,000 if you'd want them to, and another says it's $150,000 and we won't even think about it unless you deposit half in our account upfront. You're launching a multi-million dollar brand, so which naming agency are you going to choose?

When we sell it in we do several funks to help get the client dialled in, excited, and confident, and get them on board with the whole concept. A lot of people want to get their two cents in, but they are always critical and they don't know how to achieve their objective. I tell them to forget the name we're naming now and dissect existing brands. I take them through the top ten US brands—for example, looking at airlines. We agree that the name should say "experience, dependability, confidence, and professionalism."

Something like "Transatlantic Air" would cause no problems. Then I reveal the Virgin Atlantic brand, and show that "virgin" says "never done this before, inexperienced, young, and naïve," and how it is likely to offend Catholics. My client starts to understand they would never have created the names of the top ten US brands.

We critique them all, and then they collectively go "these are all good brand names, but we've got the wrong attitude—we would never choose these names." We then present the leading five to seven proposed names and some basic visuals that we have created, that we call "contorted support," which usually consists of about 15 print advertising treatments [see left].

Some think the availability of the dotcom name should lead the brand-naming process, and if it's not available not to use the name. Having the name.com is seen to carry cachet—it's the prize. Clients say they'd rather have the dotcom, but I don't see it as a priority; we didn't have the dot.com for Igor but that didn't stop us choosing it as our brand name. We show up in the top three when you search product naming, and that's what counts.

We show hundreds of options, and make sure that the client feels at the end of the project that they've examined every possibility. Clients keep checking dictionaries when considering the proposed brand names, but they have to realize that people—their audience—don't run to dictionaries every time they see a brand name that they don't understand. We have created the scientific name for new chemicals when we know nothing about it at the start.

A recent project was to brand a new vodka that costs $50 a bottle. It had to be all natural, really sexy, with worldwide trademark availability (for any beverage, not just alcohol). We use online sites to search for trademark availability and always search a name before we show the client. The new brand is named Sliver.

Searching for availability

The rule of thumb is that if you create a brilliant brand name then it is bound to be registered somewhere. You have to be confident that the names you are presenting are unrestricted and at this point you must have the names checked (or check them yourself) for availability in the relevant **trademark** categories. This can initially be done via the Internet, and the searches can be free and quick. Try the following websites—US trademarks: www.uspto.gov; UK trademarks: www.ipo.gov.uk; international trademarks: www.wipo.int; European Union trademarks: www.oami.europa.eu. A full search for trademark availability should be carried out by experienced intellectual property lawyers before the client commits to the concept. This can be expensive, and should be quoted to the client upfront.

"Any damn fool can put on a deal, but it takes genius, faith, and perseverance to create a brand."
David Ogilvy

Clients may use formal or informal **focus groups** to test your proposed brand names, and you will need to be strong-minded and diplomatic to manage these sessions so that they remain objective and focused. Set your proposed brand names in a clear, well-known font such as Helvetica and print them out in a large point size, one per page. Present them one at a time, and don't sell them in. The aim is to get a balanced and considered response to each name, one that you can use to guide your creative thinking. You may find new ideas within the research group, so listen intently—this is your target audience.

It's fine to use research to guide work, but never let the results make the decision. A few years ago the president of Renault ignored customer research rejecting a new car concept, and launched the Scenic, which become one of the bestsellers in Europe. Unfortunately, not every launch is so successful.

There are increasingly fewer words available for brand names and this is forcing creatives to come up with increasingly unusual solutions. This can be dangerous territory—there are rarely strong arguments for rebranding an existing business with a strange new name, as the brand equity that has been built up over many years can be lost overnight. It is much better to retain the existing brand name and refresh its personality in these cases. Entirely new names are more appropriate for start-up businesses or new groups.

Brand language is all about the big picture

Don't confuse your objectives for the overall use of language of a brand with your objectives when writing each specific piece of communication. The role of a brand's language is to communicate its core principles and messages clearly and consistently, so that every time customers have contact with the brand they receive the same impression of what the brand is all about. It's about long-term relationship management.

On the other hand, the writing you create for marketing activity and other creative communications is intended to promote something and generate a response from the audience, which is more about short-term promotion. While marketing campaigns come and go, the brand is ever-present. Both are vitally important and have to live alongside each other in harmony.

Most of the individual communications that you will write will have a short shelf life. A marketing brochure should have a shelf life of two years, but this is still a relatively short time compared to the lifespan of the brand itself. If the leaflet you're writing is being mailed out, or if your advertisement is appearing in the press, it will be an active piece of marketing material for only a matter of weeks. These communications tend to burn brightly but fizzle out quickly. Make sure you use the basic brand tone of voice, but be prepared to flex it to suit specific briefs, bringing more impact to direct marketing, and being more conceptual with advertising and more succinct with point of sale.

5 days until New Year's Eve

12 potential alter egos considered

26 chats with co-conspirators, decision: we'll be ABBA!

4.1m search results for "get the ABBA look"

4 jumpsuits purchased at Flagshipfancydress.co.uk

3 visits to Toptable.com to find seating for 4 dancing queens

7 inch heels on 4 pairs of glitter boots bought on eBay

2 wigs (platinum blonde + brunette bob) bought on Partydelights.co.uk

4 winners-taking-it-all on the high street

9 tabs open

0 crashes

1 browser

Chrome by Google

A fast, new browser. Made for everyone

google.co.uk/chrome

This gives readers a sense of the journey they take when deciding how to entertain themselves, and how Chrome can help them rapidly move from ideas through to making things happen. It takes a bit of reading, and understanding, but your effort is rewarded with a summary of benefits.

Major news publications including the *New York Times* and *Fortune* magazine have run stories featuring several well-known lawyers who led the charge against the tobacco industry. Last June, these same attorneys held their "First Annual Conference on Legal Approaches to the Obesity Epidemic."

No sooner had the proposed settlement been announced than questions arose about who would receive the money.

Mackey, 50, is a unique entrepreneur, as you are about to discover.

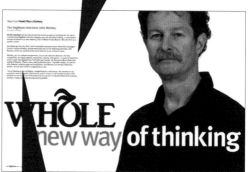

The case is being appealed, millions of dollars are at stake, and the outcome is in doubt. What's the story?

In 2002 he hiked the entire 2,168-mile Appalachian Trail with two friends. Yet *Business Week* titled their profile of Mackey "Peace, Love, and the Bottom Line."

The subject matter presents challenges, which are handled with skill. *VegNews* has to support the vegetarian cause and reflect the views of the reader, yet must retain complete integrity and avoid being perceived as biased. The approach taken is to keep body copy factual and objective, with a few light touches to steer readers and hold their interest.

Writing and managing a consistent voice within a client's overall brand communications require you to stand back and consider the personality being projected by the combined messages of the organization. For better or worse, they always reflect the personality of the organization. Bear in mind the heritage, performance, and vision (past, present, and future) of the brand and develop a tone of voice that will create a strong sense of credibility and build a lasting and positive relationship with the customer. This is not necessarily about fabulous creative writing, it is about the appropriate and controlled use of fresh and inspiring language. The overall look and feel of your brand messages may not dazzle in their intensity, but they will cast a strong light across a wide area.

The elements within the mix of a brand's communications, from the website and company brochures to advertising and promotional messages, target diverse audiences and may well be generated by different teams or individuals. Each of these writers will be taking contrasting approaches to their copy. Controls are needed to manage the way everyone writes within an organization. These usually take the form of a restriction on who can generate high-profile copy, and training these writers to understand what is on-brand and off-brand in terms of tone of voice, use of language, and style of writing.

"Economics is now about emotion and psychology."
Professor Robert Shiller, Yale

There are two key factors to consider: the correct tone of voice or personality that should be communicated across the organization; and the way that this is managed and controlled for maximum consistency without hampering creativity or ignoring the real needs of different target audiences.

Creating a brand tone-of-voice guide

Copywriting for effective brand communications centers on consistency, and there is enormous value in coordinating the messages that a client organization projects to the outside world. Achieve this and every piece of communication supports the others, backing up the core brand messages that lie at the heart of the business. This continual reinforcement—and lack of contradiction—builds credibility and trust, increasing the likelihood of customers buying into the products or services on offer.

Many organizations have a brand design manual that provides templates, color and imagery guidance, and direction on how to make sure every item produced has the definitive brand "stamp." The correct approach to copy is rarely included in these, partly because it is not often clearly defined and also because it is difficult to encapsulate, manage, and control the way copy is written within a large organization.

Your starting point for creating a tone-of-voice guide is to consider its role. Why produce a guide at all? How many different writers will be working on the brand in the next few years? Are they professional copywriters or in-house staff? What type of material will be produced? What are the core values that are being projected? Answer these questions and you will be able to build yourself a brief for the guide itself, knowing what its function is, who the audience is, and how the guide will be utilized.

Your audience will be the writers and managers who are working on the brand communications. They will need clear guidance that is easy to understand and makes sense. A crucial element is explaining when they must stick to the rules without fail and when they might be allowed to break free and use a more creative or unpredictable voice (which is sometimes allowed for creative advertising campaigns, for example). Be very clear about this from the start and you will have a better chance of controlling their approach.

Having determined the role of your tone-of-voice guide you will have an idea of the best approach to take. If it's a formal brand for a large organization and a number of writers will be working on it, a detailed document is most

"Your brand is created out of customer contact and the experience your customers have of you."
Stelios Haji-Ioannou, chairman, easyGroup

appropriate. If it is a younger brand, you may feel it is best to keep your guide short and sweet by focusing on the ideal language and the fun expressions that can be used. Whatever your approach, the tone of the guide should always reflect the tone of the brand. Most companies will have a written **mission statement** supported by some detail on attitude, values, and purpose. If these have not been defined you should try drafting some of your own so you have firm guidelines to follow and refer to. Studying these statements gives you the direction you need to create an effective and relevant tone-of-voice guide.

If the guide is too long and ponderous no one will refer to it; if it is too short and punchy it will be open to many different interpretations. You should aim for something that is between five and ten pages long, makes perfect sense, and gives the approved writers lots of support and guidance without taking away their freedom to create strong concepts and ideas.

Marketing communications are all about the audience

With the brand defined and the tone of voice being guided, you can now focus on delivering the marketing communications for your client. Your objective with any marketing communications activity is to reach your audience, attract their interest, and elicit a positive response. It's worth remembering a few of the basics. Short, clear words and simple sentences (depending to a certain extent on the audience and the nature of the marketing) are far more effective than complexity.

Clarity usually means simplicity, and while this is relatively straightforward to achieve by controlling the voice and style, you also have to have worthwhile things to say. You can't cover poor messages or lack of content with good technique, so be sure to understand the core of your message before you start. This means thinking through and researching your ideas and concepts, arguments, and logic.

If your material is weak it is up to you to strengthen it. Conducting original research to boost your raw material is a good way to discover a suitable creative angle. A compelling fact, revealing piece of information, or unusual insight can form the whole concept and help your finished communication to stand out.

Another important technique is to question your client. Simply tell the person from whom you're gathering the raw material that you need to ask a few "stupid" questions and then ask for clarification of the points that everyone assumes are understood. "What is your business really about?," "Why would the audience find this interesting?," "How is this better than the current products on the market?," and so on. This approach allows you to dig deeply into the brief in search of great selling messages.

Be clear about the role of each piece of marketing

The function of a brochure or leaflet dictates the approach you should take to writing it. Most marketing falls into two distinct categories: education (in healthcare, for example) and selling.

Brochures that are intended to educate the reader will require you to process all of the information without any ambiguity or error, and to structure the copy in the most logical way. Your titles and subtitles must guide the reader through the content and ensure that the information makes perfect sense.

By contrast, a brochure that is designed to sell a concept, service, or product needs to work a lot harder. Your copy has to be compelling, which means the reader can't help but read it because it is presenting information to them in a way they can't resist.

**Elements of a brand
tone-of-voice guide**

Brand essence

Define the brand, its values and purpose, and the company's mission statement. Why does this brand exist and what makes it unique? Don't try too hard; simple statements of fact will do just fine.

Word bank

Create a collection of suitable words to be used in brand expression. Categorize them by sections within the business if necessary. Focus on the type of words that are preferred, for example "our people" rather than "employees," and "our branches" rather than "our stores." For a product brand it might include evocative words such as "sumptuous," "delicious," and "extravagant."

Company dictionary

It is likely that the client organization has all sorts of words, phrases, and abbreviations that are unique to itself. There is no room for jargon in good copy, so set up a company dictionary that explains it all (not everyone will admit to not knowing all the jargon!) and gives the best alternative in plain English.

Brand hierarchy

There may be sub-brands—smaller brands within the business or different versions of the brand for different marketplaces. Show how they relate to each other, how the core values have to be the same, and how each can have some unique personality.

Sample copy

Having explained the best approaches, it is important to give clear examples, showing good copy and versions that are not acceptable. This has to be done for each defined part of the brand, including sub-brands. Cover enough ground to give examples of each type of copy, but only provide enough to make the point.

Strong copy sells strong coffee. Ritual Coffee focus their brand around the message "revolutionize your daily routine" and play with all sorts of provocative lines that stimulate some kind of a response—even first thing in the morning. A great tone of voice, bursting with humor and attitude, drives this distinctive brand in a crowded market.

"A brand is a living entity—and it is enriched or undermined cumulatively over time, the product of a thousand small gestures."
Michael Eisner, CEO, Disney

The distribution method is also a key consideration—the way in which it is being picked up or received by the audience will affect the way you write your headlines. Is it being sent to their homes? Are they supposed to pick it up instore, or is it a leave-behind brochure to help with sales calls? A powerful, benefit-led headline is essential if the brochure is to be picked up in passing, but a gentler, more intriguing approach is more suitable for a brochure that is being given personally to the reader.

Not all of your readers will pore over every word, so cater for the skimmers too. If the only words that are read are the cover title, subtitles, and picture captions, the core messages must still come across effectively and completely. Test this by reading your headlines and picture captions, and consider adding a few highlighted quotes from the body copy to bring out other vital points. Link your copy to the imagery where you can so that the completed item is fully coherent and integrated, not the merging of two separate directions.

Staring into space—or getting on with it?

Creative writing for business is like any other form of creative writing—it can be slow, hard work and you may struggle to find inspiration. A copywriter hard at work may look like a normal person sitting at a desk staring out of the window. Exploring your head for ideas and chasing lines of thought does work, but this can be an interminable process, and one thing you won't have much of with a commercial brief is time.

Fear not the blank page, for writer's block is a myth, it does not exist. Writers get blocks only when they rely on inspiration springing into their minds out of thin air. You are not searching for a wonderful new concept for a novel, you're not grasping for the perfect emotional poetic resonance, and you're not a Hemingway or Burroughs living the life of a tortured writer. Not yet, anyway.

There is an efficient process for preparing and drafting copy that will help you focus on the ideal solution by breaking down a job into small, manageable tasks. Every copywriter will use different techniques; there is no definitively right or wrong way to approach the challenge. Your deadline is the most effective taskmaster. Don't leave things so late that you can't do a thorough job; do all of your preparation as early as possible and you'll give yourself every opportunity to deliver well-crafted copy on time. It always takes longer to write copy than you think, so start early and get the groundwork out of the way.

Brochures that cover many pages need proper planning in order to maintain balance throughout. Sketch a thumbnail page plan for yourself and allocate content accordingly. Consider the word count, and the spread and flow of information. You can keep it very short or opt for long copy—decide this before you start.

Bad brand names spell disaster

There are always new foreign brands (usually for products rather than companies) being highlighted online where the use of English just doesn't work, and these are a lot of fun. These include a Chinese chocolate bar called "Swine," a Japanese mineral water called "Kolic," and a Greek lemon-lime drink called "Zit." These will keep cropping up, but you can learn from this by making sure you are being careful to understand the foreign interpretations of any new name you create, particularly if there is an international dimension involved. With instant translations online there is no excuse not to know the implications in the markets that your client will be operating in.

Of far more importance is the risk of renaming a corporate brand. How Powergen's choice of name for their new Italian operation—Powergenitalia— was approved is anyone's guess. It's worth looking at what a brand is before looking at what a brand name should be aiming to achieve. A brand is not a logo, it is a promise—that has to be delivered. I always describe brand as an experience and that a company's brand is anyone's experience of that organization, including how it looks and feels, how it presents itself in the media, and how it interacts with its employees and customers. My good friend, colleague at Liquid Agency, and international branding guru Marty Neumeier describes brand simply as "what people say about you after you've left the room."

Your brand is so much more than a name, just as you as a person are so much more than your name. But your name has a big role to play in the experience of your brand—not so much for the name itself, but for what people associate with it. In 1996 no one survived the crash of ValuJet Airlines Flight 592, a disaster that stopped the airline operating for months and created a negative brand impression. The name itself did not build confidence, it suggested a company that might be willing to cut costs and possibly cut corners to achieve this, and the crash gave everyone a sense of nervousness about flying with them. They solved this problem in a single move by buying a smaller competitor and adopting its name—AirTran Airways. By the end of that year customers were flying ValuJet again, under the new brand identity.

Opinions vary, but it is generally felt that Datsun was a powerful leading car brand in the US but that Nissan is seen to be an also-ran, and that Kentucky Fried Chicken lost a lot of their strong brand identity when they renamed themselves KFC. These days, the power is with the customer not the organization, as shown when GAP changed the design of their logo and their customers boycotted the store until the old logo was restored.

Trying too hard is a route to disaster. Advertising can be eye-catching and fashionable because it never lasts for long, but a brand lives on, and on, and has to be rock solid. A famously bad rebranding exercise in the UK happened in 2003 when the Post Office decided it should be known as Consignia. The branding agency presented the name on the basis that: "It's got consign in it. It's got a link with insignia, so there is this kind of royalty thing in the back of one's mind. And there's this lovely dictionary definition of consign which is 'to entrust to the care of.' That goes right back to sustaining trust, which is very, very important." They also used three bread-roll shapes bearing words such as "ambition" and "scope," and claimed to bring together "the hard and soft aspects of the brand's desired positioning." From day one the media and public united in their disgust at this decision. It was boycotted by unions and reviled by customers. Even the new chairman, Allan Leighton, abhorred the brand name and pledged its demise, setting an instant deadline of 2004 for the brand's replacement—with Royal Mail.

Hammering home the brand tagline "ready, steady, yo!," these marketing posters for the express service at YO! Sushi follow the theme of a "quickie," tempting the reader to be indulgent and spontaneous and have a fling at lunchtime, with a box of sushi. All good healthy fun.

Great copy makes the reader feel good
Here are a few tips on how to find the right
voice for your copy:

2

Don't chat to them—95 percent
of the body copy should
be clear, well-structured
information that highlights
the benefits to the reader.

1

Don't focus on your client,
focus on the relevance of your
messages to the reader. Instead
of "We have been leading the
field and are the biggest … "
use "As market leaders, we
know how to give you … "

3

Use short, clear words
and sentence structures. Keep
to the point—don't editorialize
or pontificate by adding your
own thoughts or reflecting on
the implications of the points
you are making.

4

Keep the creative concept
to the headlines and your
opening and closing
paragraphs (top and tail).

5

Work with the designer to
share the creative concept.
Be prepared to let the design
imagery dominate the
message, or to lead with
your copy concept.

6

Write for one person. The
print run may be seven million
but only one person reads your
copy at a time. Stay relaxed
and friendly, and maintain a
consistent tone of voice.

7

Instead of sitting thinking about
the best approach just get on
with it. You'll cut out your early
attempts and fine tune the whole
thing, so give yourself some
material to work with.

Techniques for preparing and processing copy

1. Gather as much raw material as you can, conduct some research of your own, and then gather it all together.

2. Read the brief again, and then reread your raw material, looking for patterns, common themes, or connections.

3. Build your working notes. Lift off the key facts, figures, details, and arguments from the raw material and make very concise but full notes for yourself. This should be no more than a few sheets of paper, depending on the job.

4. Put away all of the raw material and reread your notes a few times. Immerse yourself in the content and go as far as you can to "take on" the mindset of the target audience.

5. Decide on the most logical structure for your body copy. Sketch a page plan for a brochure or leaflet. Group facts together so that your paragraphs are packed with good information. Decide what will stay and what will go.

6. Decide on the overall, compelling message, but don't try to crack the main creative line yet. Scribble down ideas and options, even poor ones. Then set up a new document on your computer.

7. Now sit down and put together a full first draft of your copy. Don't worry about the creative concepts, just turn your notes into coherent, logical, structured body copy.

8. Having immersed yourself so deeply in the job, it's now time to decide on the creative concept. Look back at your scribbles in the light of the structure of your text. Do they hold any water? You don't have to set the world on fire, you just need to create strong conceptual lines.

Exercise: creating a brand name

Choose a product that you like, something that you use fairly often. Create a basic brief based on this product, but without including its name or brand, by considering who the product was created for, why they would like it, and what makes it special or different from others. Your brief should be split into "target audience," "core message," and "point of difference."

Your brief is to create a new brand name for a product entering the market to compete with the one you have chosen for this exercise. Study the information you've collated, and brainstorm possible names, searching in dictionaries and on the Internet, in books, and in the recesses of your mind. Scribble down all of your ideas.

Review your names, and shortlist the best ones and the possibles. Discard anything you don't like. See if you can improve the shortlisted names, and select the one that you think will answer the brief in the best way.

Now take another look at the competition for the product you are branding, and see how well your new brand would compete in the marketplace.

Exercise: create a tone-of-voice guide

Select a prominent product or corporate brand and take a good look at the communications they produce. How does the copy work on their packs, or on their annual report? What does the website copy say about their brand? What impression of the brand is created by the communications they publish?

Your brief is to create a five-page tone-of-voice guide for the copywriters who work on the brand. Begin with a page plan along the following lines: summary of the brand, definition of the brand essence, company missions and goals, a summary of the principles behind the tone of voice, a basic word dictionary showing how language is used, a basic word bank showing suitable types of words, examples of good and bad copy, and any other information.

Analyze the tone of voice you are studying and determine the principles behind it. It might be "upbeat, informative, and fresh." It's up to you to define it. Under each of the headings listed above, draft a few sentences explaining the tone of voice.

Return to it later and imagine you are a copywriter about to use the tone-of-voice guide. If you knew nothing about the brand previously, would you be able to write on-brand by following the tone-of-voice guide?

Round-up

Graphic design provides the brand identity and copywriting provides detail for the brand personality.

The brand copywriter must understand the brand's essence, its reason for existing, and explain this.

It's not enough to create a style and tone that suits the current conditions or reflects the company's heritage.

Branding requires vision, and vision requires nerve and commitment.

Never present options that you are not completely happy with, even if this pares the selection down to the bone.

If you create a brilliant brand name then it is bound to be registered somewhere, so search for trademarks.

It's fine to use research to guide your work, but never let the results make the decision.

The role of a brand's language is to communicate its core principles and messages clearly and consistently.

Your objective with any marketing communications activity is to reach your audience, attract their interest, and elicit a positive response from them.

If your raw material is weak, it is up to you to strengthen it.

The function of a brochure or leaflet dictates the approach you should take to writing it.

A copywriter hard at work may look like a normal person sitting at a desk staring out of the window.

Fear not the blank page, for writer's block is a myth, it does not exist.

Every copywriter will use different techniques and there is no absolutely right or wrong way to approach the challenge.

Your deadline is your most effective taskmaster.

Bad brand names spell disaster.

Case Study: Serious Waste Management

Roger Horberry has 20 years of experience writing all types of brand, marketing, and advertising copy, both as an in-house and freelance copywriter. The rebranding brief for a local waste-management firm didn't set him on fire initially, but he soon found his copy solutions were leading the development of a powerful and highly successful new brand.

The Objective:
create competitive advantage through branding

The owner and managing director of Envirotech Waste Services, David Birkett, met with Jonathan Sands, managing director of Elmwood, a design and branding agency that I worked for as a copywriter. The brief was to rebrand a sewerage processing plant. The client specialized in small- to medium-sized organic sewerage processing units for those not connected to the main sewers, and was trading across the UK's North Midlands.

David explained his business to Jonathan along the lines of "it's important that MDs of all businesses take care of their waste processing. If not, they can be personally liable for up to £20,000—this is serious shit." Jonathan briefed me that his idea was to call them "Serious" and that I should develop "serious"' as the angle. I worked alongside a project manager and designer to build the brand.

The copy brief was to play around with the idea of "shit" and how to bring this to life and make it interesting, and not to be afraid of adding a bit of humor, of the saucy seaside postcards type, aiming to be "naughty but nice" but avoiding causing any offense. The team next to me in the studio had just been given a really glamorous brief for fashion retailer Marks & Spencer's lingerie, and all I could think was "why do you mock me oh Lord?"

The Approach:
*straight-talking and tons of bulls**t*

My motto is "make it interesting" because people remember what interests them. In *Information Anxiety*, Richard Saul Wurman says that people don't "forget" things, they just never remember them in the first place because they are too boring.

Everyone always wants to get involved, and great original ideas can become mixed in with other ideas. We have to find them and tell them apart from the bad ones, and this is an instinctive process that requires a lot of experience—it is all about spotting the interest.

Once I have formulated an idea I stress-test it, and optimize it. I get it down on paper in the optimum form of words. Once it has been through this process, the mechanical side of writing the copy is the easy bit. Once you get the thinking right, the words will come.

I love creating copy systems, where we can crank the handle and the solutions can just run and run. However, it requires care because if we fiddle with it, the house of cards can come tumbling down.

We only did one concept for Serious and there was no need to revise it, create alternatives, or develop second ideas. There was no conflict or drama.

The brand was not something to hide behind the scenes. The brand tagline ("It's serious **it") is basically a play on "it's shit," using asterisks to avoid offense. To fully express the brand, we painted the company's tankers brown and dressed the staff in brown uniforms. Unfortunately, some staff left, but others joined because they liked the brand image.

Once we got the theme right we could run with it. We did wordplays around the words "shit" and "it" and created a list of words and phrases that we could use. Our team loved the list, and we set them in the brand style and presented them to the client. He is a very conservative North Midlands businessman, but went with our ideas from the start. He had the courage to implement a radical idea.

The Result:
where there's muck there's brass

Serious is the clearest example I've ever seen of a brand, and its copy, paying off. The client's business made a lot more money after the rebrand and business is booming. There was no other marketing activity or additional spend on advertising, and turnover and profit has increased. The communications consisted of the brand, and the tankers—great big, shit-colored tankers driving around Macclesfield!

The brand did not so much come from an initial vision of the end result, it was built up in stages. Jonathan led with the "serious" theme, I developed the taglines and advertising lines, the designer brought it to life visually, and the project manager ensured the brand was implemented in the right places. It was very easy really.

Clients will often say "my manager might not like it" but in the case of Serious, David is in charge and has no shareholder opinions to worry about. Having one decision-maker in the process is the key to the successful use of language in brand communications. Trying to maintain creative ideas when the approval has to go through a board, committee, or middle-managers can be soul-destroying, and the writer usually has little influence or power in the process. Wherever possible I want to deal directly with the guy or girl who makes the final decision.

The quality I love the most in a client is the balls to go with an idea and not stamp out its originality. Some clients actively strip out language and ideas on the basis that it will offend someone, but I believe that if you don't risk offending, you will never interest anyone.

Case Study: Olive Media Products

Liquid Agency, San Jose, is a "branding farm" delivering brand strategy and execution. Founder Alfredo Muccino has 25 years experience in the field, mainly with technology companies in Silicon Valley, including Apple and Intel. He worked with a long-term client on the development of Olive, which offers the versatility of digital music management and the quality of high-definition files, doing a lot of the copywriting himself.

The Objective:
creating and launching a new product and company brand

A brand is the relationship you create with the consumer: how they feel about it, how it reflects on them. Technical companies tend to have a problem with communication. Engineers speak to engineers, but customers don't want to know how something works, they want to know what it will do for them.

The iPod gives you 1000 songs in your pocket—convenience and portability. It's an accepted way to digest music, but people are giving up on sound quality. Olive's founder is a technologist and audiophile. He combined his interests to develop a new system to store and play large, uncompressed files, retaining the original quality. It replaces hundreds of CDs, yet is a return to the idea of quality of experience. There is a truly remarkable difference in the sound it delivers.

We worked out the brief together. In Silicon Valley it can be informal: meetings were usually over lunch or dinner, sketching out the marketplace and the audience. At Liquid we have a formalized briefing process that includes discussion with the client to define the objective, in-depth evaluation of market landscapes, and audience profiling. We develop an idea of where we can take a brand and how we can differentiate it. The target audience here are "early adopters" who will pay a premium for the latest and greatest technology. We focused on audiophiles (competing with $10,000 systems).

The Approach:
ensuring a strong, clear identity

The quickest way to create disappointment on these projects is not to clarify communication at the start, both for the agency and the client. Creatives are not always disciplined and we need to strike a balance between logic and magic.

The idea we developed is "save the sound," a call to arms protecting the quality musicians create. Naming can be complicated, as lots of names and URLs are registered. In the bar having martinis we came up with "Olive." The client's name is Oliver, so this was one connection. He had always admired Apple; this is a similar quirky approach, where the brand comes across seamlessly in each expression. We looked at lots of alternatives before settling on Olive, adding "Live Better" to highlight the quality of the experience and reference "live" with "Olive."

There was a lot of trust on both sides, enabling us to develop every aspect of the brand. On our small scale we were able to get every expression right. Industrial design in this sector of music equipment is not sophisticated and we upped the level of design. The surface of the product is etched with jazz and opera symbols, subtly suggesting the range of music. It connects with people, and has a depth of design that the customer can discover.

The copy we use is crucial, and it's the little things that make the difference. When you buy an Olive system, you send your CDs to Olive and they load them up, so on the box we say "hear, hear, your music is here." The copy forms conversations with the customer—on a one-to-one. The brand is friendly and approachable. A brand's relationship with a customer has certain expectations, including consistency. If it goes from informal to formal it can become confusing. Design uses a consistent color and typeface, and in the same way copy has to maintain a consistent tone and voice.

We needed names for Olive products. Starting with a long list, we settled on "Opus" for the key product. It has the "O" of Olive, is short, stands for a work of art, and has classical-music references. This represents both the product and the music the product enables. Other names we use for products include "Melody" and "Sinatra"—both have a music link and are obvious at some level. If Olive is the main trademark, we can then use names such as Melody—Olive Melody. Olive is all about music, and everything we do is connected to that ideal.

The Result:
a strong brand generating widespread interest

The brand connects on an intellectual and an emotional level and the press we've had has led to substantial sales. The first product was launched in September and by November sold over 1000 units. We did some clever marketing: American Express offered discounts to members, generating sales of 750 units in three days. We were watching the figures and getting excited as we sold one, then 10, then 50, then 80. We couldn't believe it reached 750!

Olive is only a couple of years old, yet enjoys more coverage than many larger companies. *Rolling Stone*, *Playboy*, *Business Week*, and the *New York Times* all requested information when Olive launched. As a firm it is incredibly small. It's super-efficient, with four to five people achieving these great results, showing the power of a strong brand. It is a good product with a good story. Music companies that create content are looking at Olive as a distribution channel; Time Warner is talking to us about creating high-definition music files. I'm very proud of it: I was trusted to build the brand and it's a major success.

Writing for advertising and direct marketing

When writing for advertising or direct marketing you must assume that your target audience are tough. They automatically select the sort of media and information they choose to let into their lives, they don't like being intruded upon, and they're not predisposed to believe your messages—at least not to start with, anyway. Your audience want only what they think they are looking for, they don't have much time to spare, and they are cynical. But give them what they want and they'll love you for it. So, as the writer, all you have to do is figure out exactly what it is they're looking for.

There's nowhere to hide when you write advertising copy

Such fun—baring your soul and pouring out fresh new conceptual ideas into a hard-nosed world of executives and bean counters. You'd have to be either stupid or mad to want to do this, or perhaps it's the only thing that's ever made sense to you. There is nothing to stop you joining those single-minded, creative wordsmiths who live and breathe advertising copywriting.

Most ad writers work in a specialist agency alongside art directors and designers, and often with account managers looking after the client relationship. Increasing numbers of copywriters are based in-house within a business, sometimes teamed with a designer or, more usually, a creative artworker helping to produce finished results, with advertising included in their mix of other briefs. This may offer less variety, but often allows you to have a lot more control over the copy. The other ad writers are freelance, working alone or in collectives. Some find themselves freelancing after redundancy, others to get their fledgling career moving, and some simply because they are in great demand for their consistently excellent work.

In every case the writer will be commissioned with a brief that will have originated with the client company. It may have passed through a few hands, and it is your responsibility as a writer to take the best possible copy brief, gather as much relevant raw material (background information and sources to follow up) as possible, and to make sure that you are completely clear about the objectives and expectations of the person briefing you. Any errors at this stage can escalate into big problems down the line.

How advertising developed

Advertising is constantly changing. The way in which messages are crafted and communicated is becoming increasingly sophisticated and your writing has to keep up and stay ahead. George Orwell described advertising as "the rattling of a stick inside a swill bucket" and he was right, at the time. Early advertising was little more than an attractive sound and a directional sign, pointing people towards what they already knew they needed or wanted. It began as simple flag-waving. By the 1950s and 1960s advertising was trying a lot harder, telling us that the qualities of the new Cadillac included a more powerful engine and better top speed, or that a soap powder "washes whiter." The audience were now being told what to think and, in general, they went along with it.

As western economies grew, increasing competition in the marketplace and the growing awareness and sophistication of the consumer forced innovation in the way consumer products were presented, positioned, and sold. If the new Cadillac has a superb, faster engine, what this really means is not that the owners of the new car could arrive at places sooner, it means that they can look (and sound) cooler, have more fun, and feel more special while driving to their destination. So let's tell them. They'll imagine that the car will genuinely improve their lives, not just get them around. They may even pay a premium for this. Advertising messages had now started to focus on the customer's lifestyle and self-esteem, fueling increasing demand by promising the fulfillment of dreams. Recent Porsche advertising exemplifies the state of the art in the automotive industry. The line "A devil on both shoulders" beautifully complements the stunning image of the new Cayman, and tips the wink to the target audience by giving the car an aura of dangerous glamour.

The birth of **conceptual advertising** was open season for creative writers. It was exciting and fun, and the 1970s were full of strange ideas such as pregnant men advertising birth control, space aliens telling us about instant mashed potato, and a man in a suit telling us he liked a razor so much he bought the

"Among the best copywriters there's a flair for expression, of putting known and believable things into new relationships. We try to be more straightforward without being flat-footed. We try to be warm without being mawkish."
Leo Burnett

A devil on both shoulders.

The new Cayman. Starting at $49,400.

A devil on both shoulders.

The new Cayman. Starting at $49,400.

With blissfully dark intentions, the new Cayman just begs to be driven. Beneath sculpted curves sits a 2.7-liter, 245-hp mid-mount engine yearning to run. Its rigid body ready to respond instantly to your will. Never has bad felt so good. Porsche. There is no substitute.

Naughty but nice. Car advertising can't encourage fast driving, but combine a beautiful image of the new Porsche with a subtly provocative headline and you can sit back and let the testosterone do the rest.

entire company. Messages, and the ideas behind them, were starting to evolve, and the consumer was ready to handle them. These are the roots of today's advertising and direct-marketing copywriting.

The main lesson we can learn from looking back at the development of advertising is that it was always adapting, staying fresh, being surprising, and breaking new ground, and this is what we must continue to do today. It's about being one step ahead of your reader. With all forms of advertising and **direct marketing** there are two challenges: reaching your audience and interacting with them.

What's the difference between advertising and direct marketing?

The two are closely related but clearly distinct. Advertising is one-way communication; direct marketing (or direct response) aims to be two-way. Technically speaking, advertising is paid-for communication where the client (the company paying for the ad) controls the message, and is identified as doing so (ensuring that there is no confusion between the paid-for messages and the editorial). It's all about grabbing attention and influencing people's habits. By contrast, direct marketing sends its messages directly to the consumer or business, without using any other media, and its marketing objective is to generate an immediate response.

Advertising aims to raise awareness of the client's message to a specific audience, and it operates in every medium and in many different forms. Very high-profile advertising is created by large corporations selling products or services, who are looking to increase demand. Variations of this include charities and government departments promoting humanitarian or policy messages. Recruitment advertising is also a major industry, as is business-to-business or trade advertising. There are many new forms of advertising, especially with the rise of Internet usage and the development of guerrilla advertising (where the surrounding environment is used—sometimes illegally—to display conceptual messages). In today's competitive commercial world, advertising is one of most dominant forms of communication.

"The first thing that marks a good writer is that he avoids the cliché. He avoids the cliché in his speech, not just in his writing."
George Gribbin

Marketers like direct marketing because its effectiveness can usually be measured accurately, unlike that of most other promotional activities. The level and extent of the response to a mailer is tracked and measured, and the information it provides can be used to shape the next brief you work on for the client. **Direct mail**, where addresses are purchased and mailers are sent out in bulk, is the most common type of direct marketing. Next on the list are **telemarketing** and e-mail marketing, as well as inserts in the press or packaging and Internet **banner ads**. A criticism leveled at direct marketing is that it produces tons of "junk mail" and "spam," and this can work against a brand.

Advertising that includes a response form or request to call a number or visit a website also falls within the category of direct marketing. This type of writing needs to use powerful concepts to communicate compelling messages effectively, in order to generate the maximum response from as many people as possible.

Getting the pitch right

Whether we admit it or not, there are always some ads that we like, or even love. We all like to shop for the things that we consider important in our lives. It may be to do with a favorite hobby or it may be the monthly supermarket run, but each of us enjoys shopping once in a while. If we enjoy shopping, we don't mind being given ideas, updates, and information that will help us to shop. This is the attitude to adopt as you tackle each new advertising brief. If you can pitch it correctly, which is a very delicate process, your audience may just lap it up.

You will be briefed by the client or an account manager from a creative agency, and while the main brief will apply to both you and a designer, you will need to take a separate copy brief or at least interview the briefer about the core messages, supporting information, target audience, and USPs on which you will be focusing.

When writing advertisements ask yourself who you are actually writing for. The answer is simple. The only people you're writing advertising for are the members of your target audience. The better you know and understand them, the better your chance of getting a good response from them. You're not waving a flag or rattling a swill bucket with a stick any more, you're moving into their private space, having a quiet word, and giving them new ideas that they simply cannot resist.

Getting to the heart of the problem

In almost every advertising copy brief you will find a core problem that is being solved for your reader by your client, by providing a product or service that addresses a clear need. This should lie at the heart of your thinking when breaking down and analyzing the content in the brief, and when deciding which message or messages to focus on in the advertisement. After all your preparation, these three essential elements will be the focus of your copy:

1. Who is your target audience and what are they like?
2. What is the core message to be communicated to them?
3. Why is this interesting, and what about it is different or unique?

It is not enough to be a creative thinker with a good vocabulary or a clever grasp of English. You're writing about commercial activity and you must understand the business context fully. Too many writers rely on a good turn of phrase, such as "we all know how hard it can be to …," "if you're like most people, you're looking for …," or "these days, it takes all you've got just to …" Focus on hard information and save the padding for a brief that gives you nothing at all to go on.

The Greenpeace ad featured here shows a clear thought process that can be traced back to the brief. The writer understood something fundamental about the audience: they want someone to risk life and limb to stop whaling, but they don't want to risk their own. It seems pretty obvious, really, when you think about it. Turn this into a succinct headline: "Some people risk their lives in the Antarctic to save the whales. Those people are called not me."—suddenly everyone in the target audience can relate immediately to the concept. Apart from the stunning photography and excellent typography, the power lies in the tagline "You don't have to join us, to join us." This is a strong call to action. The whole concept comes from studying the nature of the target audience, as outlined in the brief.

To understand your client's business as a writer you have to view it through the customer's eyes and ask probing questions. Get to know the business by being a customer if you can, or by touring their factory floor. If possible, interview the key directors or managers, and ask plenty of those "stupid" questions to challenge the hype and see what is really going on. You'll be surprised how many original creative ideas can grow from these conversations. You won't know what you're digging up until you find it, so don't worry too much; just cover all of the ground and process it when you get back to base.

"I find if I drink two or three brandies, or a good bottle of claret, I'm far better able to write. I also find that if I listen to music, this loosens me up. I also find that if I read the Oxford Dictionary of Quotations *for 15 minutes, this may start trains of thought."*
David Ogilvy

It's time to commit

You can't process your material forever. Sooner or later it's commitment time. Set yourself up somewhere and get on with it.

Begin by letting your imagination explore the links and connections between the benefits of your product or service and the lifestyle of the target audience. Day-dreaming—the structured sort—helps, as this sort of lateral thinking will help you to make connections that business thinkers will never see. Your goal is to inspire yourself first, and then inspire your audience.

For example, if you are writing advertisements for Harley-Davidson, build a picture of the audience. The brand is clearly aspirational, giving people the sense that they are rebels, individuals, not part of the rat race. Who aspires to this? Free spirits, free thinkers, strong characters, independent minds. And what are these people like? They do their own thing, they make up their own minds, and they don't take any crap. How are we going to advertise motorcycles to them? Very directly, with no sales speak. We need them to recognize themselves in the ad, and then see that a Harley fits into their lifestyle. It has to be their thought process, not ours, that gets them there.

The early stages of developing your creative ideas will feel a bit strange. With your notes from the brief in front of you, you'll consider the selling points and benefits, and how you can link these to your audience. Some sensible connections will come to mind first, followed by seemingly random ideas and loose concepts. Keep jotting these down and revisit them. At this stage it makes little difference if they are good, bad, or indifferent.

Working on your imaginary brief for Harley, you should be sketching out some character profiles that fit your audience. Get the clichés out of the way—the Hell's Angels, the big scary nasty bikers—and steer toward the

Can you tell who this is targeted at, what the core message is, and why it is interesting? This treatment could hardly have more impact, giving you a number of highly compelling reasons to join the organization.

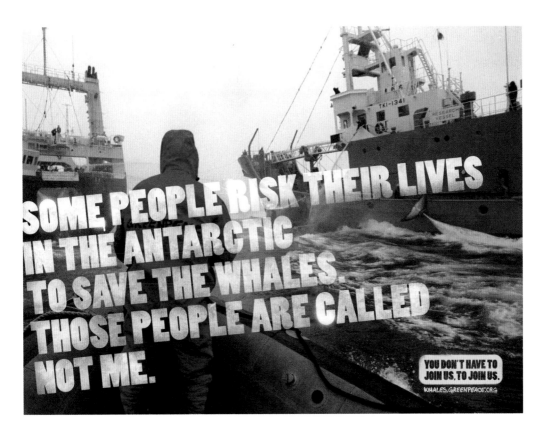

bulk of your audience. We're not dealing with kids here, these are people who have lived their lives, know who they are and what they're looking for. Come up with a few phrases for each of the character profiles you're doodling (using cartoons or words). What sort of things would they say?

At this early stage you're not assessing the quality of your ideas, you're simply getting them (formed and unformed) out of your head and on to the page. Keep pushing yourself and remain confident that you will eventually shape one or more of these roughs into an effective creative solution.

With your Harley ad you've decided, based on your audience profile, that you're not going to try to sell them a bike. You're going to portray their lifestyle, and what better way to do this than putting some of them in the ads, accompanied by typical things they might say. Make sure you get this right, or you'll lose all of your readers and might damage the brand.

Take a break after your one-person brainstorming session. Make a cup of tea or walk around the block, and let go of the brief. When you come back to your desk, review your ideas dispassionately, referring back to your overall objectives. Although some of your ideas will be too poor to be developed, others, though incomplete, will have something good about them. Sometimes the solution lies in the merging of several rough ideas into one new one.

Your portrait-sketches of Harley bikers should be feeling quite real now. It's time to take these and create advertising with them.

Prepare two or three routes that you feel confidently address all of the main elements in the brief: the core message being presented with a clear benefit and a strong point of difference (highlighting the product's or service's USP) in the audience's own language. Consider how your copy lines can be brought to life with imagery and graphics, and be prepared to adjust the copy to facilitate the design treatment. One element must dominate the page, and if this is going to be a visual image your copy may have to be more passive.

If you're showing Harley riders, use the best photograher you can find, and don't use models—only the real deal will work with this approach. Take your best three or four portraits and give each of them the best line you can write. You can let them breathe. Just have a full-bleed shot showing aspects of their lives, let the line speak for itself, and brand it with your logo. No other motorcycle company can claim this territory, so make the most of it.

> *"In most agencies—in all agencies—there's a shortage of copywriters. Good ones. And the good ones are so overworked they almost stagger from one assignment and one meeting to another."*
> **David Ogilvy**

The main types of advertising

High-profile brand awareness

These ads work over the longer term by building visibility without necessarily looking for an immediate response. They must be simple and memorable, and must have enough impact to remain in people's minds for as long as possible. For example, the Alzheimer's advertisements on pages 86–8 don't ask us for our money, they simply build an understanding and awareness of the plight of the sufferers and their families. In time, we will be more inclined to donate to the charity.

Hard-working direct response

These have to persuade the reader to call, write, or go into the nearest store straight away. They work over the short term, and need a sense of urgency, or drama, to wake up the audience and get them to act immediately. They often include a tempting offer. This type of advertising is usually for price-led retail promotions. Instead of appealing to the intellect, they go for the gut, with short deadlines and "amazing" offers. Lines such as "hurry, sale ends Tuesday" or "while stocks last" bring immediacy to the message.

Having settled on the best route or routes to work up into finished design treatments you can now edit your copy into its final shape. You may have a precise word count, or a space on the page to fill, or you may have been given a fairly free rein.

The real Harley ads have beautiful photography, great character portraits, and cracking lines. One has a close-up of a biker's grizzled beard next to the line "May wind be the only product in your hair." Another shows a female crouching to apply makeup, checking her reflection in the chrome of her bike. The line reads "Do this, do that, blah blah blah." No need to water it down or spoil the effect with body copy, you can leave the rest to the reader's imagination.

Take your creative ideas to the extreme

Creativity is not simply about going off on a flight of fancy and painting grand concepts for your audience to decode and interpret. You need a strong nerve and a confident approach to use abstract ideas to make your point, and your concept must be rooted in the core message in your brief. For each format there is a different set of guidelines:

Product-specific
Focus on a single, overriding benefit, keep the whole thing very simple, and let the few elements you use breathe.
For example, Nokia's press advertising for the 6300 model showed an immaculate image of the phone with the lines: "Simply beautiful" and "Beautifully simple," which conveyed everything about the new model.

Service-specific
Outline the problem it solves. Be clear about who provides the service, how it is accessed, and why it is the best value for money.
Clever Wally's direct marketing (pages 84–5) is headed "We make it, you bake it" and "Free delivery," followed by a phone number. Once this has been made clear, the mailer/menu expounds on the fun of cooking a fresh pizza at home.

Business-to-business
Trade customers are primarily interested in making profit. Reassure them about quality, service, and delivery, but focus on professionalism and trust.
The Royal Bank of Scotland once advertised to their business customers using the line "Less talk" to support images of suited men in a meeting spouting the words "bull, bull, bull, bull, bull, bull … " and "bluster, bluster, bluster, bluster …," suggesting the bank was sharp, focused, and on the ball.

Recruitment
Outline the company, the opportunity, the candidate, the package, and the process. It makes a lot of sense to put the bulk of this on a website and lead the readers to the additional content through a press advertisement, which can then focus on attracting their attention.
In the UK's *Creative Review* magazine, a design agency ran an advertisement alongside glossy, half-page advertisements (with 500-word descriptions) that read simply "We would like to meet a passionate designer to work on a wide range of web- and print-based projects," with just an e-mail and web address for following up. The website explained how to apply, and provided all of the necessary background material. This is efficient, cost-effective, and clear, and projects great brand values, suggesting the agency is organized and acute.

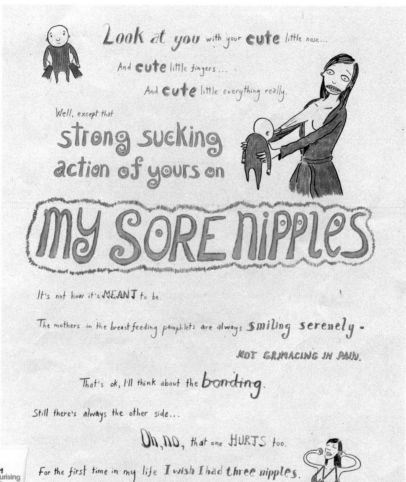

This fun and amusing treatment takes an innovative approach to presenting copy, but it also gets across a serious, benefit-led message. It should appeal to the core audience while building general brand awareness.

To profile your audience you will need to:

1. Build up as accurate a picture as you can, using the following criteria as a rough guide:

Age:

Sex:

Location:

Income levels:

Likes/dislikes:

Current opinions of the client's product or service:

Aspirations:

Lifestyles:

Attitudes:

2. Use this information to understand the characteristics of the audience by:

Imagining the world through their eyes:

Understanding how they might weigh things up:

Estimating how they might react to different messages:

Profiling your audience

Your twin goals are to attract your audience and interact positively with them. You must find out who they are, where they are, and what they are really like, using your own instincts as much as the background information you're supplied with, in the same way that Greenpeace and Harley-Davidson might do in order to create their advertising.

To help develop your ability to get a clear insight into the different characteristics of each audience you'll write for, take a bit of time to think about the people in your life, how they each speak to you, and how you speak to them. What is it that characterizes those people that you most like talking to, and those that turn you off? Could you replicate this on paper? What do their voices look like when written down?

Get you know your audience before you begin

Language is perhaps the most powerful tool in human history, yet it's something that we all take for granted. It's only when we look into the way language operates, and the way it can be used to plant ideas into people's minds, that we start to see the complex structures involved in communicating. Effective use of language builds connections—bridges—between your client and your audience, and those bridges enable relationships to form and develop.

We're all unique individuals but we're social animals, and our society is formed of lots of defined groups, and language is used differently between these different groups. We copy, observe, and imitate our close peers, and share stylistic techniques, vocabulary, and tones. We may all speak English but we are all using phrases and words differently.

I use the phrase "amateur psychology" to describe the processes that copywriters use to profile their target audience. There's no need to go into complex market research analysis or sociodemographic categories in any detail. This is all about drawing on your knowledge of people in your life, or even people in movies, on TV, or online. You want to distill the essential characteristics of the specific types of people so you can find a common ground in terms of their attitudes and beliefs.

The basic questions you can ask yourself are: How old are they? Where do they live? What are their habits? What's their family situation? Think about their interests: What do they read? What type of movies do they watch? What brands do they like? How do they socialize? Where do they work? Where do they go on vacation? Make a note of these "made-up" profiles, and try to be as accurate as you can. This will help give you ideas about tone of voice and messaging later.

The point of this is to try and establish the kind of influences they will take on board. Be realistic not idealistic. Consider the challenges that people who are typical of those in your target audience will be dealing with. What type of income do they have, and how able are they to buy into the messages you're putting out to them? You're looking for ideas about what it takes to "tip the balance" for the target audience from considering the message to acting on the message. The more relevant your writing is to them, the greater the levels of engagement that you can develop with them.

We have to win permission from our target audience to allow our ideas into their minds, and if we want those ideas to stay there and create the desired responses we must make sure they are both engaging and compelling. Are there phrases and words that particularly resonate with your audience? Make up a few phrases or pretend you're writing snippets of a movie script and bring their voices to life, for fun, to warm up.

Establish their tone of voice by writing down some examples, sticking to the content that you've been briefed on but using the voice you're distilling through your amateur research. Think about the rhythm and intonation of their speech: do they speak in short, fast sentences or long, drawn-out phrasing? What about their choice of words, do they use short, stubby Anglo-Saxon words or intellectual Latin-based words? Consider their style of expression: are they loud and brash, oozing confidence and attitude, or are they methodical and considered, particular about the way they construct their point of view? By addressing their preferences, needs, wants, and desires accurately you can show them that you understand the way they think, which goes a long way to winning their trust.

It pays to engage

In discussing how to develop an awareness of target audiences, these days, it is not enough to rely on using traditional advertising and direct-marketing methods, it's also important, as a creative, to understand the phenomenal developments in how audiences interact with each other via **social media**. On platforms such as Facebook, Twitter, and LinkedIn, people are engaging with one another, rather than simply reading content and navigating through pages on a website. Users within these networks can interact with a group of friends, share content with each other, and communicate in a variety of ways.

To write effective social media copy for your client requires you to become a credible part of the conversations people are having with each other within your client's social networks. You should adapt your copy to reflect the specific social network environment that your client belongs to, being acutely aware of the style and tone of voice of the people who are influencing what happens within that environment, and reflecting this without moving away from your client's brand values.

However, it's important to remember that blogs such as Twitter aren't going to be the right media for interacting with certain audiences, since many people simply don't use them.

Most companies integrate social media advertising into their marketing strategy. Copywriters can use the marketing tools now widely available online, which enables them to target an audience by age, location, hobbies, occupation, etc. In addition, it is now even easier to research how your audience is interacting with your copy.

Developing your "bedrock" body copy

For your copywriting bedrock, build up a confident tone of voice that you can draw on in many different situations to convey a message warmly and succinctly. This needs to be inviting, fresh, and very concise and is perfect for all sorts of body copy. Write out your body copy fully and then edit it down as tightly as possible. Use your instincts to develop a feel for the sort of language and approach with which everyone is most comfortable, and use this as the overall tone of voice for your copy in support of the more creative copy for the conceptual elements.

The *Huffington Post* cleverly brings together classic news reporting, blogs, and user-generated content on a range of subjects such as politics, world current affairs, comedy, and technology. It is hugely interactive and uses short, snappy, and active language to make its readers want to interact and add comment.

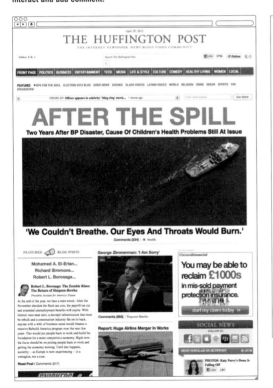

Creative angles for you to consider

There are several tried and tested approaches:

Before and after

Show how greatly life is improved with the product or service you're promoting by comparing life before (miserable) with life after (joyous).

This is the territory of weight-loss clubs and gyms, and also of loan and finance companies. It is all about offering to solve big problems in people's lives, and applies only where the problem is perceived to be serious enough to spoil the reader's quality of life.

FUDing

FUD stands for Fear, Uncertainty, and Doubt, an approach used by professional services such as solicitors or insurance brokers. Ask the audience if they are confident, feel safe, know all the risks, and they're likely to begin to feel unconfident and insecure, and will want you to help protect them.

This is not about creating anxiety, it's about highlighting risks that people can protect themselves from. This approach is often combined with humor, showing people who haven't protected themselves experiencing an exaggerated version of the risk.

Wit (not humor)

Humor is very subjective, but wit is universal. A good play on a word or phrase or a twist in meaning can be very effective, but make sure it works for your audience as well as for you.

When the *Economist* billboard reads "Would you like to sit next to you at dinner?" in huge white letters on a bright red background, you either laugh (to yourself) or you don't. Those who don't get it are not in the target audience, so it's risk-free.

Knock the competitor

This is not something to be done overtly, although references can be made to well-known products and any shortcomings they may have. Comparison advertising is often as simple as showing similar people in identical situations, one having a better time than the other because of the brand being promoted. Innocent Drinks (see pages 110–12) don't knock competition, but their packs say "We promise that we'll never use concentrates, preservatives, stabilizers, or any weird stuff in our drinks. And if we do you can tell our mums." This implies that the competition uses some or all of these substances.

Provocation

You don't always have to be liked to sell a lot. You may even consider trying to tell your audience not to buy the product, because it's too expensive or out of their league. See what happens.

Stella Artois advertising, with its "Reassuringly Expensive" tagline, creates the impression that the beer is so ludicrously expensive that it achieves almost godlike status.

Some radio advertising also provokes the audience by using annoying tunes and lyrics to convey messages and phone numbers that the audience will remember.

Intrigue

A far more positive approach than FUDing, intrigue is a powerful technique for drawing in the audience. Show them something interesting and tell them there's a secret to be told.

Penguin Books use very striking photography in their press advertising, depicting highly dramatic and tense human scenarios, with the line "be here" applied subtly in lower case and their logo in the bottom right corner. It's both intriguing and compelling, especially if you enjoy gripping novels.

Gimmicks

Promotional giveaways and eye-catching tricks such as clever folds in direct mail or an unusually located advertisement in a magazine can work if they are linked closely to the audience.

Running ads along consecutive pages can enable you to develop a sequence of messages that build to a punchline, and including a promotional item with a direct mailer can create lots of opportunities for hard-hitting or witty headlines.

How creative do we have to be?

Let's forget about being creative and get on with the job of writing advertisements. The creativity is inherent in the process, but if you try too hard to make your ad better than anyone else's you'll only skim the surface. Put all of your energy into understanding what presses your reader's buttons, and then think about how to press them, which is the fun bit.

You can brainstorm concepts on your own, but it's more enjoyable and more dynamic to share the process with another creative thinker (usually a writer or graphic designer), especially with the guidance of an experienced creative director. As a beginner you'll experience each brainstorming session as a one-off, bursting with new ideas, but there are patterns to this type of work and an experienced creative director will be able to distinguish between writing that is truly fresh and that which has been done before.

Direct marketing is about generating an immediate response

A great deal of the effort that goes into direct mailers, and other forms of direct marketing, is put into strategic planning and media or **list buying**. Everyone on the team involved in the direct-marketing process is trying to profile the same audience. The strategists should lead the way, explaining to the client exactly who they are targeting and why. The media planners and buyers will then select the mailing lists from the many available from specialist **list brokers**, in order to reach as many members of the target audience as possible within the available budget.

This is all very helpful to you, because it provides lots of information about your audience, as well as how the piece of communication will reach them. If the mailer is inserted into a mainstream music magazine, study the readership profile and work out what it is they like about their magazine, then you can complement or mirror this. If it's going through the mailbox alone it needs as much help as it can get.

You don't have many options with direct-marketing copy, because it has to be so immediate, so it makes sense to follow a pattern in most cases, as outlined below. By following this structure you can put all of your efforts into creating a truly new and appealing approach, and when you have a strong concept in mind simply organize the raw material into the structure provided.

Copy structure for a direct mailer
Each element has to burn brightly for a short time.

1.
A hard-hitting, compelling headline, with the sole purpose of persuading the reader to open up the mailer to find out more.

2.
A qualifying headline that dominates the inside of the mailer, continuing the theme, with the sole purpose of getting the reader to read the body copy.

3.
Highly structured body copy presenting the core argument, facts, and figures as concisely and compellingly as possible.

4.
A very strong call to action, with clear instructions and a range of options, backed by a compelling reason to act immediately.

Copy structure for a direct-mail cover letter
This is your chance to make friends with your reader.

1. **An engaging headline at the top of the letter, clarifying the subject matter and promising a discovery for the reader.**

2. A compelling opening paragraph that summarizes the core argument and entices the reader to continue until the end of the letter.

3. Two or three short paragraphs presenting the details of the argument, highlighting all of the benefits outlined in your brief.

4. A call to action in the final paragraph, inviting the reader to study the accompanying mailer or catalog, visit a website, or respond directly.

— *We make it, you bake it* —
Free delivery 020 8994 8080　85 Chiswick High Road, London W4 2EF

SUMMER MENU

SUMMER 2007

CLEVER WALLY'S
RAW NEWS

Pizza joint triggers "sensory excursions"

WEST LONDONERS OVERWHELMED BY RAW POWER

"I tore open the bag and found myself floating over rolling Cotswold hills. Below me, ripe, golden wheat swayed in the soft breeze," recounted a Hammersmith woman.

A Barnes resident reported "catching the scent of fresh thyme and being transported to my mother's garden in Sussex." She witnessed her retired parents "enjoying a G&T and discussing plans to re-mortgage and blow my inheritance on high-end cruises."

A Chiswick man told us of "standing in the hall handing over a tenner to a delivery man one minute, and the next, perching high in the branches of a Warwickshire tree as happy free range pigs snuffled below."

The cause of the phenomenon has been traced to Clever Wally's Raw Pizza. Wally, raw pizza impresario and freshness fanatic has a ready explanation:

"People are bombarded with the so-called "fresh" everyday, but the store-made dough that we hand shape to order, the free range ham, sausage and chicken, the freshly chopped herbs, are of such high quality, so perfectly fresh and untainted, it can be mind-blowing. What's commonly passed off as 'fresh' is no preparation for an encounter with The Raw."

Wally gives

A percentage of Clever Wally's profits will be donated annually to Médecins sans Frontières. Please give us a call on 020 8994 8080 if you'd like to learn more.

Amazing offers

Wally's Deals on Wheels deliver more love for less dosh. "That's more than cutting the mustard; it's about getting raw for less! Hang on, does that make sense?" said Wally. Judge for yourself on the back page!

Pig "ready for the end"

"I've lived well and ranged free" oinked Porky, 2. "My lawyer has my will and clear instructions to send my best bacon to Clever Wally. Man, they can sure sling one fresh pie."

Wally "all ears"

Clever Wally has been listening to his clever customers and he's changed his menu as a result. Build-your-own pizzas, a new garlic bread, booze... it's all coming together. New menu inside!

Selling uncooked pizzas is not the most obvious new business idea. However, with stimulating branding and a strong direct-mail campaign it seems like one of the best and most mouthwatering ideas in town, and the pizzas are flying off the shelves.

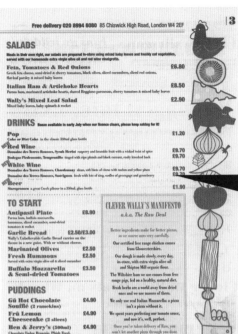

Clever Wally's Manifesto
a.k.a The Raw Deal

Better ingredients make for better pizzas, so we source ours very carefully.

Our certified free range chicken comes from Gloucestershire.

Our dough is made slowly, every day, in-store, with extra virgin olive oil and Shipton Mill organic flour.

The Wiltshire ham we use comes from free range pigs, fed on a healthy, natural diet.

Fresh herbs are a world away from dried ones and we use masses of them.

We only use real Mozzarella: a pizza isn't a pizza without it.

We spent years perfecting our tomato sauce, and now it's, well, perfect.

Once you've taken delivery of Raw, you won't let another pizza through your door.

Leo: A man in a helmet will appear at your door. You will hand him a ten-pound note and he will exchange it for a raw pizza.

jackie's father.

we took his car keys away.

but the car's in the garage. and he knows it.

so he goes and sits in the car.

without the keys.

he sits there and kind of messes around with the buttons and switches.

we have an electric door opener and he opens and closes that.

my mother, she tells him,

"look robert, you cannot drive."

i was sitting on the couch today looking at him when he asked again

and she told him no, again.

he came over and leaned close to me and said,

"you know what? i didn't want to drive anyway."

he was so cute. like a little boy.

my big, strong, control-freak father suddenly looked just like a little boy.

he's acquired a lot of grace.

my personal belief is

that's part of why this has happened to him.

for the people you'll never forget. call 847-933-1000 ALZHEIMER'S ASSOCIATION

Greater Chicagoland Chapter

he came over and leaned close to me and said,
"you know what? i didn't want to drive anyway."
he was so cute. like a little boy.
my big, strong, control-freak father suddenly looked just like a little boy.

Interview: Diane Ruggie, DDB

Diane is a group creative director at DDB in Chicago. She has been at DDB for 23 years, working on international brands such as McDonald's. Find out how she approaches her writing and learn from the techniques of a proven master.

As a child, I realized I loved words. In second or third grade I was inspired by the idea that the 26 letters of the alphabet can be arranged to make people do an endless number of amazing things like laugh, cry, swear, pray, propose marriage. It's infinite. Yes, I always knew that I was interested in the power of words, and always wanted to work with them in some way.

I studied journalism as my main degree, because I thought I wanted to become a reporter. But I discovered that I didn't like prying into other people's private affairs when they had sad stories to tell or were experiencing trouble in their lives. I had a good nose for news and I somewhat enjoyed writing the stories, but I wasn't comfortable with some aspects of the research and interviewing process. Another thing I had to cope with was writing articles that were unbiased and without emotion, despite prying into people's lives to get them.

My professors helped me shift to magazine writing and then other creative writing challenges. I liked how advertising let me use my instincts to understand how a consumer related to a product. Journalistic writing started to feel scientific in nature, following a dry order. It simply didn't have enough empathy in it for me.

So I went into the advertising program, and I bloomed. It was a general curriculum that gave me the whole picture—creative, production, planning, and account management. More than that, it helped me and the other students put together a portfolio, and source a list of agencies to approach for work as a copywriter. I had a few interviews, and got lucky. I netted my first job at a small agency in Chicago.

But I always wanted to work for DDB. I was pretty single-minded about that. So when I finished my first commercial, I took it over to DDB and said "will you hire me now?" Somehow, that did the trick. Now, I try to stay that passionate about coming in every day, because you are all only as good as your last assignment.

Even though I'm a manager of people these days, I still like to write on occasion. I work on branding campaigns and tactical work for large companies including Safeway and LensCrafters. But how does that happen? The planners and account people bring the briefs to the creatives. We take it all in, use the products, and listen to the target audience talk about the product. We will eat the food, walk around the grocery store, shopping mall, or museum and absorb the experience as much as possible so we can let it all cook in our brains. You never know where inspiration will come from.

We challenge the client if we experience something that seems amiss. Then we process the raw material, work up the messages, and come up with ideas until we feel like we've turned over every stone. We often put each idea on individual sheets of paper—words or pictures—and stick them to the wall.

After that, it's best to walk away and let things hibernate. It's like a "cocoon" phase and it lasts for a day or so. This is simply about leaving the thick of it and returning later with fresh eyes. And often when you're not even thinking about the assignment, the answer comes to you.

Normally, when we return to the work after the "cocoon" phase, everything gets assessed with a new sense of clarity. Some of it climbs to a higher plane and some of it drops away. The good stuff starts to have more zing, the excitement builds, and the words and visuals come more easily.

Once the basics of the concepts have been cracked the discipline expands and we can then add more detail and missing media options, such as direct-mail solutions, events, or online treatments. It is rare, but ideas that we threw away at an earlier stage sometimes can be folded into a different concept as things evolve.

We have two or three teams of art directors and writer partners working simultaneously on the same brief. When they come to me saying "we have two ideas," I know that they have had five or six on their shortlist. So I often ask them what else they have just to make sure the territory has been well mined.

The roles of the art director and writer often switch during the early stages of creating the concepts. If a writer simply sits down and types up a television script for example, and then shares it with their partner, it's too one-dimensional. Most media vehicles are visual, after all. Plus if you take the time to get the creative thinking right, the writing becomes straightforward. When I am the writer on an assignment it's only after the concept is nailed down that I lock myself away to put the actual words on paper. It is often already written in the air before that.

I can recommend a little book by James Webb Young called *A Technique for Producing Ideas*. It describes the whole process of conceptualizing, explains a technique using index cards, and the right time to put ideas to one side to let them cook. This process works for any profession you're in, even non-creative ones.

Just out of graduate school I was interviewed for a job that was out of my league, but I was trying to reach for the stars. I had sent my beginner's portfolio out for a position in Paris. I couldn't possibly do it because I didn't speak French well enough, but I felt I had nothing to lose. I have always had a fascination and love for Paris. Soon the creative director in Paris called me. He said he couldn't hire me, but explained that he could tell I had the *feu sacré*— the sacred fire! After that I walked on air, and this compliment never left me. It gave me a huge boost of confidence, and I recommend to any aspiring writer out there to stick your neck out. You may find out you have the *feu sacré*.

Interview: Will Awdry, Ogilvy

Will is a creative partner at Ogilvy, has been writing great advertising for decades, and leads the D&AD Writing for Advertising course. Here we learn how he got started in copywriting, and see how he approaches the challenges of advertising writing. Like many senior copywriters, he mainly oversees creative teams and only manages to write copy himself when he gets the chance in between his busy schedules.

In my current role I spend my time keeping everyone inside the factory gates making sure the people outside the factory gates get the picture. My main job now is writing e-mails, and the art of copywriting has never been so important as in writing e-mails.

I had always felt comfortable with writing, but my first jobs were in account management. During this time I worked in partnership with a designer to create a "book," a portfolio of creative advertising—concepts in this case. We worked on briefs that we were given on D&AD workshops, where we also had exposure to presenting our work to advertising professionals, helping us learn how to show our work in its best light and how to handle criticism.

If you want a job in advertising, remember that they tend to look for teams: two problem-solvers working together who respond with an "idea" for a theme or creative concept. Two heads are better than one, because you can bounce ideas around. One comes up with ideas, the other edits them, and the roles swap from one to the other.

"Begin strongly. Have a theme. Use simple language. Leave a picture in the listener's mind. End dramatically."
Winston Churchill

You have to be able to capture the flavor of what you are trying to achieve. What we really do is turn company stories into a narrative that might be of interest to an audience. The challenge is how to sequence the information so it is of interest. The media, all forms of it, are a series of influences that characterize behavior. Our copy is simply a series of very, very short stories that are looking to rent space in people's brains. It's "mental rental." We're trying to create thoughts that last longer than others.

Copywriting is commercial communication and it won't work unless you engage people. You have to invite yourself memorably into someone's mind. Your approach is to do this in its most compressed form and then leave it for them to act upon. Didactic carpet-bombing doesn't work any more.

In the 1970s, advertising would say "buy this, we're telling you why" and explain that this soap powder gives you the whitest wash. Today, some campaigns give the reader just a fraction of the information, but the best approach is to leave just enough information for the target audience to work out the core message and get the satisfaction of doing this. It is a relationship. Saying "do not smoke, it will kill you" won't work. Saying "Cancer Cures Smoking" is far more effective, and is a perfect example of a slightly cryptic advertising headline. That's what makes it click.

Antonio Damasio writes about the treatment during the Second World War of people who had serious brain damage, and the discovery that even in cases where the majority of the brain was missing—leaving only the emotional receptors at the front—perfectly rational decisions were capable of being made. It is our emotions that steer our decisions. The Institute of Practitioners in Advertising produces a compendium of examples of the most effective advertisements in terms of sales. They publish 10 or 12 case studies each year, focusing on the return on investment. Between 1994 and 2004 they published 230 papers, and of these nearly three-quarters of the approaches used largely emotional ideas. When you are writing your copy you must speak emotionally to your audience; you are not some hack journalist rehashing a spec. Engage their interest by being relevant.

Think of your engaging, emotional point as a dart. Your headline, the compressed summary of the thought (for example "The ultimate driving machine"), is the sharp point. Your body copy, the sustained explanations that support the headline, is the feathers of the dart. If your

"You cannot be a copywriter unless you are a strategist. You attack the problem."

□ wrinkled?
□ wonderful?

Will society ever accept 'old' can be beautiful? Join the beauty debate.

campaignforrealbeauty.co.uk 🕊 | *Dove*

body copy is too brief the dart loses its way; if it's too heavy it won't fly. Achieving the perfect balance is essential.

Humans are now very adept at understanding copy and the most rigorous editors of all are the audience. The advertising community has broadly lost the trust of the audience. It used to be British justice, but now it is French justice. Now you have to prove that your client is not guilty.

Dove and the campaign for real beauty

"I apologize for such a long letter, if I had more time it would be shorter." **Blaise Pascal**

The controlling thought for Dove is "real beauty." The brand originated during the Second World War, when surgeons discovered that most bad gunshot wounds healed better when moisturized. Ten years ago Unilever expanded the brand, which is characterized by having 25 percent moisturizer, across all bodycare products. The seismic change began with the "campaign for

real beauty". This broke down stereotypes, catapulted the brand into mainstream consciousness, and boosted sales.

The trick, however, is not just to gain sales, it is to maintain them, and there is very little loyalty in most marketplaces. Products are given names such as "pro-age," celebrating age, with the line "because beautiful skin has no age limit."

A lightness of touch and a certain freshness takes the messages beyond the hackneyed, and allows you to look at imagery differently. You cannot be a copywriter unless you are a strategist. You attack the problem.

I read the brief, turn it over so that I can't look at it, and then summarize it in one sentence, no matter how clunky or unworkable that sentence is. Then I write it large on a big sheet of paper and stick this on the wall (this is how I get past the blank page). Then I think to myself, "it's easy to do something better than that."

I might then write a short exposition, two or three lines to develop that thought, and sometimes a pithy line may emerge from this that will become a key point. I then go for a walk, and consider how to approach this to bring it to life.

I make sure I get to the end of my first draft before I redraft it. From here it collapses in on itself all the time, and everything "packs down" as I edit and revise the first draft. If I don't do this it looks overwritten and can easily take on the appearance of slick "advertising-ese." Copy needs to be quirky and surprising, and your choice of words should come from outside the mainstream.

"There are just three rules for copywriting, but no one knows what they are." **Somerset Maugham**

A great example of good use of copy is in the UK bookstore chain Waterstones. Tim Waterstone had the idea of letting the staff include their "own choice" recommendations of books, where they write their own reviews by hand on preprinted cards that form a special display in the center of the store. It is very personalized and many retailers are now copying this idea.

Once people understand what you've written down, then you can play. Use imperatives, or questions, or whatever takes your fancy. The average vocabulary of a typical adult in England is 43,000, in Italy it is 27,000 and in France 25,000. This gives us lots of opportunities to play games with words.

Try these exercises if you can't get going. Think of a slightly ludicrous audience, for example, Action Man or G.I. Joe. Write 50 words to him that explain the message you're trying to communicate. If he could write 50 words back to you, what would he say? Do this with understanding and a degree of sensitivity. This will get the arguments flowing. Think about your favorite movie, then write the entire plot in sentences of no more than three words. This will help you get to the nub of what's being said. Your arguments should be ordered, clearly identifiable, and sequential. This lets the audience know that you know what is going on in their lives.

A campaign is a minimum of three expressions of an idea, running consistently throughout. You must have a call to action. If you are not eliciting some form of response it's not working. This takes sensitivity. A bad stand-up comic or circus act will do the act and then stand back and wait for the applause. You have to make the response seem as unlike hard work as possible. If the reader is saying "you're asking us to do the hard work" he or she won't respond.

There are two media types: lean forward and lean back. The first refers to readers who are seeking out information about your client—often online. They want to know, so tell them. The lean-back type is more passive, watching TV, sitting on the train, or listening to the radio in the car. You have to create interest. The bulk of copywriting is targeted at lean forward.

Great copy uses visual words. In mainstream above-the-line copy you are fly-fishing for the audience's heads, and need to be very brief. For example, David Abbott's ad for the *Economist*— "'I don't read the *Economist*,' Management Trainee Aged 42"—gets the whole message across in a few simple words. After 25 years the campaign is still running and still wins awards.

The basics of mailer copy

The less personal, the less interesting
No: "This weedkiller will stop weeds from damaging your driveway"
Yes: "Doesn't it drive you mad when weeds destroy your driveway? Well, you don't have
to put up with this any more … "

Make the message strong, clear, and simple
No: "Do you ever get the feeling that you are paying too much for your gas and electricity bills?"
Yes: "Looking for savings?"

Use intrigue or a promise to attract interest
No: "Reduce the appearance of wrinkles"
Yes: "Discover the secret of younger-looking skin"

Consider using strong sales-offer messages
No: "Sunday Sale—big discounts"
Yes: "Amazing! Two for One on all items this Sunday! Wow!"

Present the benefits clearly, with subheads
No: "These children need your help"
Yes: "You can save the sight of these children"

Include a very straightforward call to action
No: "So why don't you find out more?"
Yes: "Simply call 0800 123 456 now so you don't miss out"

Give a reason to respond now, not later
No: "You simply won't find better"
Yes: "Don't forget, this incredible offer ends this Sunday"

Use high-energy copy to create a buzz
No: "Britain's ancient woodland has been in decline for many decades, for many reasons.
Many new woodlands are planted with fast-growing softwoods that stifle the local
habitat. Your donation will enable us to plant … "
Yes: "It's true that Britain's ancient woodland is dying out, but it's not too late. Together
we can restock many ancient woodlands with indigenous species and provide a
legacy for our grandchildren that we can be truly proud of … "

Be clear about the mailing process—it affects your copy

The way to success with direct marketing is to send carefully crafted messages to a perfectly targeted mailing list. Perfectly targeted and completely current mailing lists are very expensive, but the alternative is to mail enormous quantities and play the numbers game. It's your role to focus on the messages and ensure they are both relevant and interesting.

If a client is looking to increase sales through a direct-marketing campaign, the strategy could be to purchase a premium-quality list of high-net-worth individuals who each have the capacity to make substantial purchases. There may be 300 of these people in the designated catchment area, and the list—guaranteed to be current and accurate—may be extremely expensive. This approach is favored by premium businesses with high-value offers because they are interested in communicating only with the wealthiest individuals. The cost per mailer in these situations can be enormous, but the potential returns mirror the initial investment. Writing for these is a very high-pressure job, made easier by the precise audience profile, which gives you plenty to work with in terms of establishing a relationship with the reader. This low-volume, high-quality list gives you a clearly defined target audience to whom you can speak in their own voice, and use examples directly relevant to their lives.

An alternative could be to purchase a list of 30,000 middle-income households. You might get this list for the same price as the list of 300 high-income prospects, but it will be a different type of audience, and the response rates will be much lower because the list may be slightly out of date or have other inaccuracies. As the writer, you can't make too many assumptions about this broader and more generalized audience, so focus on the product or service instead, and settle for a more "catch-all" benefit statement. This high-volume, low-quality list gives you a broad and diverse audience, to which you'll have to sell harder in order to deliver the right level of response.

Depending on the quality and accuracy of the mailing list, direct marketing works on typical responses of 0.04 percent of the total mailed. Utilities companies commonly use high-volume mailers to offer cheaper deals on gas and electricity, for example. With the high wastage approach (buying cheap lists covering entire catchment areas), the preferred route is to send creatively written and designed postcards as the print and postage costs are far lower.

Direct marketing is a vital tool for relationship marketing

Relationship marketing focuses on retaining existing customers and building stronger relationships with them, and direct marketing—particularly with targeted mailers—is an excellent tool for developing existing customer relationships and increasing customer loyalty.

By definition, your audience for a **loyalty campaign** will be current customers who have given permission for you to contact them. You know what they are like, and you know that they have previously bought into your brand and may want to know more. You simply want them to retain their loyalty to your brand by continuing to purchase. This makes the writing process more straightforward as there is less uncertainty and risk involved. As they are current customers, you could afford to take a more familiar voice than with your main marketing material, and rather than sell to them you can present your information to them clearly and calmly so that they continue to buy from you.

Depending on your client's customer information, you can operate highly targeted direct-mail campaigns. A retail client could mail a specific group of premium customers and invite them in-store for a special evening where they could meet a celebrity, get some tips from experts, see a preview of a new line, or enjoy special discounts. You would write this using a different voice—being more personal and inviting—than if you were mailing the entire customer base with a more basic promotional offer.

Variable data printing allows text in a print run to be changed to suit different readers. This can be as simple as running three or four variations of a text to suit different age or geographical profiles, or it can allow the name and personal details of readers to be printed within the document, as if it had been created solely for the recipient. As the copywriter, make sure that the message is as relevant and credible as possible—it's not enough to use this technique as a gimmick. Your main challenge is to make sure that text reads smoothly with the permutations that may occur in a "mail merge."

Direct marketing is about filtering

"One of the first lessons our copywriters get is this lesson—you must make the product interesting, not just make the ad different. And that's what too many of the copywriters in the US today don't yet understand."

Rosser Reeves

The majority of direct mail never gets read: sending a mailer to someone who has not requested it is about as random as communications can get. The point is that some of the people you mail will read it and respond positively, and as the writer this is all that matters to you.

Your target audience is different at each stage in the writing process. At first, you are communicating to a general audience, many of whom are simply not interested. Some of these people will show an interest by reading your advertisement, and these readers form a different audience profile: they are the part of the audience that may well be prepared to put in a bit of effort to find out more, so write with them specifically in mind. You may need to keep your body copy short and sweet in order to appeal to as many readers as possible. Or you may decide to give them something more substantial in the form of a more detailed proposition. Well-crafted, long copy that presents a case, backs it up, and delivers a carefully constructed argument can win a lot of readers and convert many of these prospects into committed customers.

Once you have completed your copy, leave it overnight, go home, and return to it with a fresh pair of eyes. As the writer you view it from a specific perspective; as the reader this will be very different. How does it work for you as a potential member of the target audience? What would you change? Does it work hard enough? This "next day" test is a vital part of the creative process.

Your clients will always want to make amendments; it's human nature. You have to consider whether proposed amendments improve or detract from the final effect, and argue your point strongly, from the point of view of the brief.

No matter how good it is, edit it down

The tighter your copy the better, so cut out unnecessary words. Previous generations hailed the merits of long copy in advertising and direct marketing, but more recent consensus seems to be to keep it as short and punchy as possible. Both are right, it's simply a question of fitness for purpose. You have a split second to catch the attention of a newspaper reader flicking through its pages, and your creative concept has to hit home quickly. However, once you have the reader's attention, you can work with it and can present your story.

For example, Clever Wally's (pages 84–5) uses the headline "Pizza joint triggers 'sensory excursions'" and subhead "West Londoners overwhelmed by raw power" to tease readers into the body copy: "'I tore open the bag and found myself floating over rolling Cotswold hills. Below me, ripe, golden wheat swayed in the soft breeze,' recounted a Hammersmith woman." Your copy should project personality, and you must be prepared to add human touches wherever relevant, while sticking closely to your original copy brief.

This direct-mail piece is simple yet bold, incorporating a clear message with imagery that gives personality to the obsolete computer. The theme is expanded within the booklet, building to a strong call to action.

I used to work in the financial world.

But was replaced by the younger generation, not that they look any younger.

I retired when I was five.

I used to work in the financial world.

While considering my options, I met with Intechra and they told me that just because I was five didn't mean that I was obsolete.

They said I could get a new start—my hard drive would be triple wiped. I'd have an absolutely clean slate.

Now I could work in the classroom.

Or be transferred to the Ohio branch.

They said I could get a new start—my hard drive would be triple wiped. I'd have an absolutely clean slate.

Even my monitor friend didn't become junk. His raw materials were recaptured and today he is part of an airplane.

They keep track of everything, send detailed reports to their clients and even include indemnification certificates to guarantee against all risk.

My self-esteem got restored too when I heard about the check my old company got for me. I knew I had value.

Don't you just love a happy ending? Yours is standing by.

Even my monitor friend didn't become junk. His raw materials were recaptured and today he is part of an airplane.

My self-esteem got restored too when I heard about the check my old company got for me. I knew I had value.

Exercise: write an advertising campaign

Select a brand that you like or that is well known and collect some of their advertising and marketing material. (Use material from the copywriting exercises in chapters 1 and 2, if possible.)

Decide who the target audience is, what the core message is, and what the USP (Unique Selling Point) should be. Write a summary brief.

Brainstorm some visual and verbal concepts, then sift these down into two or three strong routes.

Select the best route, and work up at least three creative treatments, each following the same style and tone, but each with an individual message. Maintain a clear division between all three.

Draft some body copy and scamp some design treatments, using colored pens or a design program on your Mac or PC. Sit back and assess your work.

Round-up

Direct marketing describes all communications that seek a direct response from the reader.

There are two challenges: reaching your audience and interacting with them.

The way to success with direct marketing is to send carefully crafted messages to a perfectly targeted mailing list.

Direct marketing is an excellent tool for expanding existing customer relationships.

The breakdown of traditional media has created a wealth of new ways of reaching the target audience.

To understand your client's business you have to view it through the customer's eyes.

Creativity is not about simply going off on a flight of fancy and painting grand concepts.

The early stages of developing your creative ideas will feel a bit strange.

Prepare two or three routes that you feel confidently address all of the main elements in the brief.

Consider whether any proposed amendments improve or detract from the finished effect.

Case Study: Amnesty International

Nick Holmes is the creative director and copywriter at graphic design agency Different Kettle in Bristol, UK. The agency is run by creatives and is focused on delivering great creative solutions by getting the brief right from the very start. They have won many awards for their work, and have generated excellent responses through their direct-marketing activity. So how did Nick create this hard-hitting insert for Amnesty?

DICTATORS
TRAFFICKERS
RAPISTS
EXECUTIONERS
TORTURERS
TERRORISTS

DEFY THEM

There's a man in Algeria who tortures people. It's his job and he's good at it. He uses a variety of tools including broken glass and a blow torch.

There's a militia commander in Sudan who wages war on civilians. He commands his men to rape women. As many as possible. It's his way of suppressing the population.

An Iranian official is paid to kill people. Including children. He's been known to hang them in public streets.

A western president authorises an illegal detention centre. Here no rule of law applies. Detainees are subjected to sleep deprivation, hooding, forced nudity and simulated drowning.

A man in eastern Europe runs a profitable business selling women as sex slaves. The UK is one of his biggest markets.

All these people are real. They are all going about their business as you read this leaflet. They all want to carry on undisturbed.

So they all share one hope: that you will not join Amnesty International.

JOIN AMNESTY

Amnesty International is the world's most influential human rights organisation. Simply by joining you are making a stand against human rights abusers.

And they don't like it.

Bertha Oliva de Nativi, a woman whose husband was 'disappeared' by the Honduran military, put it like this: 'Murderers and violators are cowards' she said 'so cowardly that they do it hooded in darkness. They feel under siege when organisations like Amnesty International take action.'

A former torturer in El Salvador was even more succinct: 'If there is lots of pressure, like from Amnesty International, we might pass the inmates onto the judge. But if there's no pressure they're dead.'

We can only apply pressure, because of the members we represent. The more members – the more pressure. It's as simple as that.

That's why we need you to defy the abusers and join Amnesty.

You can become a member by making a regular donation of £3 a month. All you have to do is complete the attached form and put it in a post box.

A lot of people are hoping you won't do it. But many, many more are praying you will.

I'M JOINING AMNESTY

Please complete this form below or visit www.amnesty.org.uk/join

			Title	First Name	
			Surname		

INSTRUCTION TO YOUR BANK/BUILDING SOCIETY TO PAY AMNESTY INTERNATIONAL (UK) BY DIRECT DEBITS

To The Manager of	Bank/Building Society		Postcode	
Address			Email*	
	Postcode		Mobile*	
Name(s) of account holder(s)				

(Signature) | Date

There's a man in Algeria who tortures people. It's his job and he's good at it. He uses a variety of tools including broken glass and a blow torch.

An Iranian official is paid to kill people, including children. He's been known to hang them in public streets.

All these people are real. They are all going about their business as you read this leaflet. They all want to carry on undisturbed.

So they all share one hope: that you will not join Amnesty International.

The Objective:
create a generic fund-raising press insert

We do a lot with Amnesty, and have a long history with them. They decided that they would run a creative pitch for their acquisition inserts, which were to appear mainly in the mainstream quality press. The brief was as simple as "we need a new insert that is not issue-specific and will not date." This was a very open brief—we could write as much or as little copy as we felt we needed to.

The customer profile defined the audience as people who are well read and interested in current affairs. We were up against our previous work, and we decided to do something that was generic and wasn't time-sensitive. We presented four concepts and the client developed two of them. One was a "hefty" read, consisting of an eight-page booklet debating the use of torture and whether it can ever be justified. The other concepts we used were about changing the news by joining Amnesty and making a difference.

People always feel the need to describe the Amnesty tone of voice. The broad essence is about humanity, and about a movement of ordinary people standing up against injustice around the world. We could qualify the tone of voice as: "simplify, humanize, and make it easy to participate." We don't put tone of voice on our briefs, because if the brief is clear the tone of voice will inevitably follow. The tone of voice has to be true to the specific concept or idea.

Corporate guidelines can be inward-looking. As far as I am concerned, I talk differently to different people—to my children, to my colleagues, and to my friends—but I am still a consistent person. The best approach is to aim to avoid corporate speak at all times.

Direct marketing is cruel because there is an immediate measure of success. We shelve this fear and instead of worrying about what the response will be we go back to the original creative idea and see how true we are being to it, looking for ways to enhance it and eliminating anything that detracts from it. We just think about this, not how many people are reading it, or the rules of direct marketing. Like any rules, it's good to know them, but do be prepared to break them. Some rules say that with mail packs you should "always make accompanying letters long," but sometimes we don't have a letter at all.

I think everything should be edited as tightly as possible in every case. It might still be a four-page letter, but it could have started as an eight-page letter. I'm a great one for rewriting and cutting.

The Approach:
developing copy and design in unison

The gold dust is in the raw material. It's critical to have good material to work with, because although you're being creative you are not making anything up. You can't polish a turd. The background research and reading around the subject creates lots of great material. Sometimes if you read a fact there's the creative concept staring you in the face. It'll need crafting and shaping, but you know you've got the essence.

We have an instinctive feel about what will work, but we sometimes disagree amongst ourselves. You can't always predict how well a piece of marketing will perform, but if we're not excited by it ourselves then we usually start again.

We always work as a team, with an art director and writer working in close partnership, and share creative ideas. We develop the core design and copy concept, presenting this to the client before writing body copy. The copy at this stage consists of a main headline and our top-line thinking. In this case, our mock-up was almost exactly the same as the final version, and once they went with it the copywriting was simply about adding flesh to the bones.

It wasn't all plain sailing: the art director had to be talked around to our point of view on designing around the copy's strength before we could present it to the client, as he felt there was not enough creativity in the design. Amnesty's new guidelines included the use of fluorescent colors, which is where the pink lettering came from.

The concept's strength was its simplicity. We know that no one wants to read inserts, so we played on this with the "throw this away" line. But then we very quickly had to tell the reader what this is all about—as soon as they open it up.

The Result:
generating good responses

The insert has done really well. The client seldom expects the inserts to pay for themselves, but on the first outing this insert appears to be bringing in more than the cost of the whole campaign (donors pay by direct debit and it takes a while to properly assess the full response).

It is interesting to consider the criteria for what is "working" and "not working." We did an arms-control pack raising awareness of arms sales. It won lots and lots of awards, but it wasn't one of the client's hardest-working appeals. It is more difficult to raise money in some subjects than others, and it's not always due to the creative treatments.

Case Study: MemoMind Pharma

Steve Wexler runs one of the most successful direct-marketing copywriting firms in the US. He has been writing copy for 20 years, initially for catalogs, and now specializes in writing for direct marketing. He employs 11 copywriters in his creative studio, which also includes two sizable design teams, and believes in the power of closely linking words and imagery. He tells us how his studio improved upon the results of a successful direct mailer.

It is a sophisticated doctor's formula shown to reverse up to 10 years of memory decline in as little as 30 days!

In less than one month, my memory went from terrible to incredible.

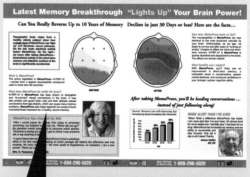

N-PEP-12 in MemoProve has been shown to strengthen and to "re-connect" neural connections in the brain.

The Objective:

generate improved response from a successful mailer

MemoMind Pharma have successfully promoted their neuropeptides memory pill by mailing a 12-page supplement with articles on memory enhancement to their customer base. The control mailer that had been proven to deliver the best responses was an 8½ x 11 in (21.6 x 27.9 cm) "magalog" (a cross between a magazine and a product catalog).

We test lots of formats using alternative headlines and measuring responses. The challenge is always to improve the control; this is hardest of all when it was your own work! We always start by taking a thorough creative brief. After this, I outline the project, write some initial headers and subheaders, and art direct the layout and structure. The writers and designers then fill in the pieces.

The cover, which is prime real estate, was loaded with promises (which every magazine from *Cosmopolitan* to the *Enquirer* uses heavily) about the benefits of memory enhancement, so we looked at the format, and decided to test different sizes, which let us set copy in larger point sizes.

The Approach:

the benefits of different formats

When you're creating direct marketing, leave your ego at the door—our work is not going to be hanging in the Louvre. Remember that the design has to sell the message. Every element of direct-marketing design should push readers to the end sell, so the designer should read the copy fully and understand exactly what it is that they are selling. Some get this and some don't. (If you're a designer and you get this, you get a much larger salary!)

It is important to develop the copy and design solutions together. If direct marketing were a sales representative, graphic design would be his or her suit and style, and copy would be his or her sales messages. It is often underappreciated that design has to create something that sends a message across visually. Graphic design and conceptual images can overshadow a message: it can be more interesting to look at them and ignore the copy.

It is all about presenting a compelling concept. It's important to work with images that will inspire your end prospect. I will sometimes visit a picture library and search for a compelling picture that relates to the message in a brief, and write copy around it. It is very difficult to do this the other way around. You have to tailor the message to the audience, and make it clear what's in it for them.

The memory enhancement supplement is designed to look and feel like a quality magazine. It has newsstand quality and a high perceived value (it included the price tag of US$3.95/CAN$4.50 in the top right-hand corner). It includes a range of different editorial angles, each one leaning toward the proven benefits of the memory pill, for example looking in detail at its ingredients or showcasing a series of testimonials about its effectiveness.

The copy focused on believability, legitimacy, and sales points. Believability came as much from design treatment as copy, which included powerful testimonials from credible people explaining how it worked for them, such as "Wow! What a difference MemoProve has made. I am more alert than I've ever been. It's almost hard for me to realize how 'mentally slow' I had been for so long." The credentials of clinical physicians and findings of medical studies give the messages legitimacy: "Clinical trials on MemoProve stunned researchers when results surfaced in not the usual three to six month time frame, but in 30 days!" Sales points give readers some of the best promises they'll get. As well as offering free samples, the copy promises "to reverse 10 years of age-related memory loss."

We set the mailer in different sizes, the largest being a tabloid. Each had the same copy and design; in the larger formats everything was proportionally bigger. For the tabloid we had to create an extra four pages as it had to be a minimum of 16 pages.

The Result:

the larger copy sizes generate the best response

The tabloid format, with its increased font size and larger images, delivered even better results than the control mailer, making the most expensive format the one that delivered the best return on investment.

We mail-tested with lower numbers than the usual mass mailing; the tabloid won significantly. When it was rolled out to the full list there was a huge increase in response, so it became the control mailer. There aren't usually many quality brochures in the mail because they are expensive, so this is a real point of difference. When mail came, the quality-printed tabloid became the wrap people used to carry the rest of their mail in.

The bigger type made the copy easier to read for our audience, who are in the older age range, and removed anything that might stop them in their tracks when reading the messages. Whatever you do, don't let anything stop your readers in their tracks—let the flow of the messages continue and you'll get the best responses.

Writing for retailing and products

Large-scale retailing is fast-paced and furious. Time is of the essence and new promotions can be required every week, in multiple forms. Clear, positive interaction with the shopper is the key to success, and this requires strict control and careful management of customer messages. The challenge is knowing who you are writing for and what their mindset is—essentially they are looking for something and you are making it easier for them to find it. In this environment people vote with their feet—all you have to do is keep them on your side. Every retailer has a personality, brand characteristics, and product lines, so if your writing reflects these you'll be creating maximum customer interest. Products are the lifeblood of retailing and good product copy is essential—get this right and you'll be boosting the success of the product and the store.

This tone-of-voice guide for Wishes, part of UK Cancer Research, is fresh, appealing, and easy to understand, and best of all it doesn't just say what the copy style is, it demonstrates it in the process.

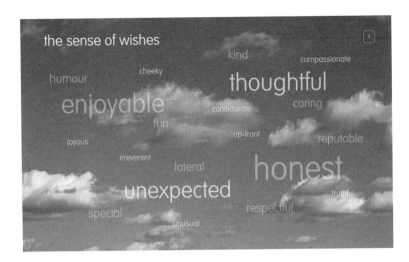

What is retailing about?

Like any other business, retailing is about making profits, in this case by selling products to customers who visit your premises or website. The more you sell, the bigger your profit. Whatever retail format is used, the retailer wants the customer to come back as often as possible. The better the relationship created with the customer, the more products the retailer will sell. Every relationship thrives on good communications, and your objective as copywriter is to present the core messages in a way that fosters strong customer rapport.

Products play an active role in the communications chain by attracting the customer's eye and promoting their benefits in the most appealing way.

The hierarchy of retail communication

Dividing the mass of retail briefs into categories or types is a good way to break down the task of writing and to profile the customer accurately at every step.

The categories are:

1.
External messages
giving customers reasons
to visit the store

2.
Welcoming and directional messages
helping them to locate
their section

3.
Promotional messages
offering alternatives,
additional items, and
discounts

4.
Front-of-pack
messages presenting
the product's benefits
to them

5.
Back-of-pack
messages persuading
them to buy into the
brand more

Turning a passive fascia
into active advertising, this
innovative approach presents
compelling messages to the
external customers as well as
flagging up the brand cues.

Your messages should help create a sense of place

Retailing is a simple process. Stores invite the public onto the premises and serve their needs as well as they possibly can. It's a fundamental relationship. The problem is that the customers are free to go wherever they like. Retailers don't expect 100 percent market share, but they do need regular and repeat custom. While many struggle and fail, the retailer who understands the marketplace in detail and depth, and works hard to give customers exactly what they want, in the way they like it best—whether it's bargain deals or luxury goods—will succeed.

"In the 1960s, if you introduced a new product to America, 90 percent of the people who viewed it for the first time believed in the corporate promise. Then 40 years later if you performed the same exercise less than 10 percent of the public believed it was true. The fracturing of trust is based on the fact that the consumer has been let down."

**Howard Schultz,
founder of Starbucks**

Retail design is highly sophisticated, bursting with graphic displays, marketing promotions, and eye-catching products—all carrying messages as part of the mission to "delight the customer" and "exceed expectations." Most retailers use some form of copy to attract more people into their store, to sell more of certain items, and to encourage them to spend more than they were planning to. Satisfied shoppers will be inclined to return to the places they like and make repeat purchases. If you're writing retail copy your objective is to help create a strong sense of place, of belonging, comfort, and familiarity that the shopper will recognize, enjoy, and feel at home with.

Whether within a local or specialist store run by a friendly shopkeeper or for chains of larger stores, messages that guide or inform the customer and show the retailer's personality greatly enhance the service provided by sales assistants. Shoppers don't always want direct assistance, but will absorb the written messages posted around them as they browse, and will get to know the retailer and the products better. This helps to build a strong relationship with the customers—it's your role to pitch the message to them in the right tone of voice.

It's not just about each message, it's the in-store "clutter" too

Writing individual customer messages, from promotional offers to in-store advertisements, from directional signage to customer service promises, is not too difficult in itself. These could be identifying different parts of the store (men's, children's, outdoor, bargains, etc.), highlighting where to pay, or explaining a price offer next to a product line. These messages usually require short, plain, and simple copy (the sort that you feel anyone could write, but that actually requires a great deal of effort to perfect).

This type of writing is all about the best use of one or two words. For example, is there a better way to say "3 for 2"? Should the message be "Buy two get one free!" or "Three for the price of two!" or "Save 33% when you buy three!" and how do we explain the rule that it's the lowest-priced item that is the free one? Is there a better way of saying "Cheapest item free"? Do customers now know what **BOGOF** (buy one get one free) means, and can we just slap BOGOF next to a product line? Not only are these surprisingly knotty problems to tackle, but a lot of senior people, all with ideas of their own, will have to sign off the copy. This is less about creative writing, and more about the best—and most appropriate—use of language. Your role is to control the language used to ensure that it remains on-brand and is also as succinct and clear as possible. You would probably recommend "3 for 2 (cheapest item is free)," sacrificing your urge to create something wonderful and unique to the cause of impact and maximum take-up.

After all of the sweat and tears that can go into creating and signing off a new promotional line, you can be caught out by the "clutter" of in-store customer messages. Visit a branch of any major retailer and you could find promotions from last month still on display, next to this month's. You could find homemade promotions displayed next to your national campaign (store managers like to do it their way), bits of other promotions mixed in with yours, or bits taken off (store staff can do a lot with the bits of display material they receive from head office). You may also find supplier-funded promotions clashing with all of this, confused even more by the directional signage. In a sea of cardboard, most messages will become soggy and drown.

These issues are all to do with proper and efficient store management, together with central control of the messages being created. The way in which the head office and stores communicate with each other is also a vital component. All of this is out of your hands. As the writer, all you can do is try to be aware of this bigger picture at all times, and to ensure that while the individual promotions may fight for space, they do not clash with or compete against each other.

Many supermarkets and warehouse-style retailers work to a system or hierarchy (in the form of a basic grid or table that categorizes customer messages into three or four types and prescribes how each will be written) that arranges their messages into clear levels and categories, with strict rules that have to be maintained. This is sometimes referred to as a **brand matrix**. This is very restricting, and can be extremely frustrating for you, because your writing will come out looking the same as everyone else's and you will have no room to think laterally. However, it does ensure that the overall effect of the myriad messages will not overpower the customer.

In-store messages can achieve the following:

1.
help to set the scene from
the external viewpoint

2.
welcome the customers
as they come in

3.
promise them
good deals

4.
create and hold
their interest

5.
direct them around
the store

6.
give them rewards in
the form of discounted
prices or offers

7.
encourage them
to return, soon

Typical in-store retail promotions

Vouchers & gift certificates

A good reward mechanism for customers, these bring them back for a repeat visit, and they may tell their friends too. Promote these on the range of choice a voucher offers—"you get exactly what you're looking for"— and encourage the customer to think about the possibilities they present.

Free samples

You can't expect people to take a chance with a new product, so let them try it out. In-store tastings, or free samples to take home, are very effective ways to launch a product. Your writing for these promotions should be evocative and exciting.

Themed campaigns

These usually have a charitable theme, such as raising money for a worthy cause linked to the retailer's marketplace. Don't milk it, just present the facts and benefits under a strong headline.

Store card

Regular customers love their store cards, but only if they know exactly how they work and how to get the best from them. Explain all of this by processing the details and cutting them down into a very short checklist.

In-store events

These usually take place when the store is closed, and can be extremely profitable if the best customers are invited. Celebrities (chefs, hairdressers, etc.) are a big pull, but so is the chance to preview new lines or get extra discounts. Give this the big sell.

BOGOF & discounts

Buy one get one free, two for one, three for two, percentage savings—they all give the customer a reward that will help build loyalty and repeat business. Keep your copy simple, make sure the offer is clear, and don't clash with other deals.

Introduce a friend

This is an effective way of expanding a customer base without changing your customer profile. Make sure the reward for the customer who introduces a friend is appealing and use a peer-to-peer voice; don't talk down to the customer.

Loyalty promotions

You can't get real loyalty—this is only shopping—but you can encourage repeat visits by offering a reward for buying more of a specific item. Keep your copy short and to the point, but present the benefits clearly and strongly.

Supplier-funded

These are jointly branded offers with a key supplier. You'll need to strike a balance between the tone of voice of the retail client and the supplier's brand, so it is best to write in a clear and straightforward tone of voice.

Bargains

Everyone loves a bargain, so make the most of end-of-line promotions or discounted lines by shouting about them. You can go to town on the "last chance to get these prices" or "hurry, when they've gone they've gone" angle, but always stay on-brand.

Advice & insight

Top tips from an expert (in-house or external—possibly you) are very popular with customers. This gives them the ideas and confidence to continue shopping. Lists can be compiled using your own research if necessary.

*"My love of writing came to
me at college by chance."*

Interview: Meredith Mathews, Half Price Books

Meredith is the in-house copywriter at Half Price Books, based in Dallas, Texas, the largest second-hand book dealer in the US. She won the Retail Advertising Conference award in 2007 from the Retail Advertising and Marketing Association for her retail merchandising campaign, which is based around strategically located signs featuring carefully targeted messages relating to the products on their shelves.

I work mainly as a copywriter, but look after some design elements, such as the way messages are set out and the colors we use for signage. The creative side of copywriting drew me to advertising after university. I found so much in it: the business angle, the graphic design element, the need to write in an artful way, but in a different form to pure poetry.

I do write personally; I like to explore core words and their definitions. I always wanted to know where words come from and like the process of copywriting. Some find it painful, but for me it is a free-flowing experience. When I'm looking at a brief I usually find a phrase, word, or idea pops into my head. I prefer typing because I can write faster and keep up with my thoughts more easily. I am constantly editing copy for Half Price Books, and I write a lot of it too. At every reread I edit the copy to make it as concise as possible. The concept might come out quite quickly, but the best lines are crafted in the editing process.

Half Price Books is our retail business, and Texas Bookman is our wholesale business. Writing for Texas Bookman requires a shift in style into business-to-business language. The copy still draws on the same emotions and techniques, but takes a gearshift in terms of the brand personality. We are experimenting with the voice to make it different from Half Price Books.

Our "Love, cherish and let go" campaign was very exciting. Half Price Books buys as well as sells second-hand books, but found the majority of customers weren't selling books back. The brief was to get them to start selling too. During the campaign—featuring lines such as "Already been where no man has gone before? Sell your sci-fi books."—the guys in the stores were overwhelmed. People who had never sold back before were bringing boxes and boxes. The operations end of the business was delighted with the response!

I worked on the campaign with a senior art director, who also works in-house. We spent time . in stores observing our customers' behavior—we observed where they went when they came into the store, which is why messages are right on the shelf next to their books. This research gave us this new information, which led to the creation of the new campaign.

With retail signage, customers do not look above eye-level. All of our messages were positioned at eye-level, and we made each one specific to the genre, with lines such as "Is the suspense killing you? Sell us your thrillers." and "All better now? Sell us your self-help books." The campaign tagline was "Let go."

We ensured that the campaign featured pure copy by setting each on a single-color background without any imagery. It was a tough job to convince the creative director not to include any imagery or photographs—these things usually feature a photoshoot of people with books. We used four colors only, and we found that it was most successful when positioned at eye-level and when the copy just spoke a simple message.

We presented just the one creative idea to the marketing team. There was some resistance because it was a new approach not to use imagery, and was felt to be less of a hard sell, because the message was "sell us your books." We argued that we have to give the customer credit that they'll understand.

Another award-winning campaign was our "Banned Books Awareness" promotion. The lines used were deeper than the boss thought customers could grasp, but everyone liked them. They felt rewarded when they read lines such as "Banned Books Week. Celebrate the freedom to read with one of these hot books." and "Side Effects of Reading Banned Books may include laughing, crying, questioning, anger, gratitude, and learning."

My advice to young writers is to listen to your own voice even when working for a client—it may have been the spark that got you the job in the first place.

Interview: Dan Germain, Innocent Drinks

Dan used to be an English teacher, and always enjoyed writing. He was always a "bit of a show-off" and found writing to be a good way of expressing himself. He joined his friends, the three founders of Innocent Drinks, as their fourth employee and has been looking after the tone of voice and copywriting for this fresh and exciting brand ever since. The messages on their packs have been a key part of their success, so what exactly is Dan up to and how does he do it?

I tend to work a lot with Richard, my creative partner and one of the three founders. We're old friends, so we're good at talking and having ideas. We share the same ideals, ethics, and beliefs, and the copy we write is natural and honest, like a conversation you might have with your friends or your mom. I just write it as I say it or think it. And I try to question the accepted way of doing things. In every bit of our business, from copywriting to how we make the drinks, we've been told "you can't do this" from the voices of experience. And we've usually found that there is another, more innocent way.

Before we settled on "Innocent" the company was called "Fast Tractor." Labels exist to prove this, though they're locked in a cupboard. We liked Fast Tractor because it suggested freshness (to us at least). We also considered "Naked" and "Nude," but at the time they were all just words. We didn't really have a clue about building a brand. But things have changed. These days we use the word "innocent" as an adjective, asking ourselves "is this innocent?" when judging our work, words, behavior—everything really.

I now have a wider role as Head of Creative. We have our own internal agency, which I help to run, though I also work with external agencies when the need arises. When we work with agencies we try to work collaboratively—we have a really clear idea of how we want to look and feel, and I think/hope that agency creatives like working with people who have that clarity. I've learned loads from working with agencies—I've worked with some of the best creatives that there are, and have pinched loads of tips on how to get to the best work.

Policing and editing our copy is an instinctive process. I can give general guidelines and tips but it is really difficult to define. If you held a gun to my head, I would say that the Innocent voice is natural, honest, and engaging. We once spent a whole day analyzing our tone only to come up with nothing much that we couldn't have decided in five minutes.

Our tone of voice is simply the result of us being a group of friends trying to make each other laugh, which is still my aim. I can't write for everyone in our audience, old and young, north and south. So I don't try to. I'd end up with something less than average if I tried to please everyone.

I don't like the word "consumer." It suggests a predictable group of people who will jump if the advert tells them to jump. I like being an individual and my behavior can be unpredictable, and I guess that goes for most other people out there. People see through "clever" attempts to change their behavior, so I would rather present information in a simple, clear way and let people make up their own minds.

Lots of packaging is over-designed in my opinion. Every pack on the shelf shouts at you, especially in our bit of the market, with pictures of fruit and messages telling you to have your five [servings of fruit and vegetables] a day. We try to politely sit there and behave ourselves, and in the beginning being the quiet one got us noticed. Ultimately, we let our drinks do the talking and make sure our labels are calm and polite, and then when you flip the product over you get a nice surprise. But no pack, however well designed, can mask a bad product, and so we know that 95 percent of the success of our business lives and dies by the quality of our ingredients and recipes.

We try to have a conversation with our drinkers. That means it's a two-way thing. People e-mail us or call the banana phone—we get hundreds of calls/e-mails every week, quite often from people who are just up for a chat. The first e-mails that came through, which were from the first few passionate drinkers, helped us to form the voice. These people love the stuff and we made friends, which helped us to find out all about

the perfect smoothie
for summer,
season of
flip flops,
freckles
and
rained
off barbecues

innocent®
pure fruit smoothie

mangoes & passion fruits

innocent™
smoothie for summer

cherries and strawberries

innocent©
probiotic yoghurt thickie

yoghurt, vanilla bean & honey

Innocent Smoothies contain only the purest and freshest fruit. No concentrates, preservatives, or additives of any kind. And they're made and delivered daily. Now that's out of the way I'm using the rest of this space for a personal message: Brian, if you're reading this, do you want to come to the zoo next Thursday? My boss is on a training thing, so it's all cool. They've opened the new penguin bit and apparently one of the pandas is expecting. I've taped this wing mirror to a stick so you don't have to stand on a box or wear those tall shoes or anything. Call me.

Buddha—now there was a nice chap. Never said a bad word about anyone, and always kept his stereo at a respectable volume so as not to disturb the neighbors. Even had his life saved by some yoghurt once—after losing consciousness whilst fasting, a lady brought him back from death by feeding him some. We find that our thickies bring us back to consciousness at around 11am, just when we need a bit of sustenance to help us through till lunchtime, but please don't let us dictate when you should drink them. Choose your own path. Om.

"I just write it as I say it or think it."

Ingredients	Nutritional info	(per 100ml)
2 pressed apples,	Energy	207kJ (49kcal)
17 crushed cherries (21%),	Protein	0.6g
½ mashed banana,	Carbohydrate	12.6g
4 crushed strawberries (16%)	Fat	less than 0.1g
and some freshly squeezed	Vitamin C	43mg
orange juice.		(71% RDA per 100ml)

YOUR RECOMMENDED DAILY INTAKE OF FRUIT
NEVER, EVER, EVER FROM CONCENTRATE

AN INNOCENT SMOOTHIE IS A BLEND OF CRUSHED FRUIT, PURE AND FRESH JUICES AND NOTHING ELSE

OVER 170% RDA OF NATURAL VITAMIN C

Look after your smoothie
Keep refrigerated 0-5°C before and after opening. Once opened consume within 2 days. For use-by date see cap. Gently pasteurised, like milk. Shake it up baby.

5 038862 390101

250ml ℮ 0605 6

the perfect smoothie for summer, season of flip flops, freckles and rained off barbecues

innocent™
smoothie for summer
cherries and strawberries

Spitting is quite rude, but it seems that spitting cherry stones is OK. And Rick 'The Pellet Gun' Krause is the king of stone spitting. Rick is the Pele/John McEnroe/Big Daddy of the cherry stone spitting world, and improved the world record over a period of years until in 1993 he reached 22.12m at the Michigan Cherry Pit Spit. These days, some young interloper has managed to increase the record to 29.19m, no doubt with the help of yoga and a low carb diet. But Pellet Gun is still the man in our eyes.

An innocent promise
We promise that anything innocent will always taste good and do you good. We promise that we'll never use concentrates, preservatives, stabilisers, or any weird stuff in our drinks. And if we do you can tell our mums.

Pop round to Fruit Towers, 3 Goldhawk Estate, London W6 0BA, e-mail hello@innocentdrinks.com, call the banana phone on 020 8600 3993 (UK) or 01 864 4100 (ROI). And join the family at www.innocentdrinks.com/family

This bottle is made from 50% recycled plastic. We're working on the rest.

TM = The Man

the people who drank our drinks, and why they drank them. I used to sit there and e-mail them all day long. Those were the days.

These days it's not just me writing the copy. We have a small group of people writing copy for our packaging—a few people at Innocent plus a motley crew of people I've met along the way who just fancied having a go. We write a brief and then everyone goes off and writes a few labels every few months. It's good to include an external voice or two. Keeps things interesting. We change the copy on our packs four times a year. We generate over two hundred individual messages every year, so we hope that you always get a new one whenever you pick up one of our drinks.

The reality of what we do is so much more important than image. We're creating a reality, and it is easier and more effective to write the way we do because then we don't have to make anything up.

And it's this fact that I often return to. We have a solid, well-run, copper-bottomed business, and that allows us to write what we fancy on the packs, on the Web, or wherever our words appear. If we delivered late, made dodgy recipes, or if they just tasted rubbish, the silly chat on our packaging would become plain annoying.

Support the customer's journey

It's the retailer's job to lay out the store with clear sections, logical product grouping, and attractive displays. As part of the creative team it is your role to attract interest so that the shopper doesn't miss the rewarding offers, promotions, or brand propositions. Your touchstone is brevity and control—every display must be eye-catching and easy to understand. Above all, create a strong sense of atmosphere, interest and ideas by making sure that every message is consistently in the same tone of voice, reinforcing the retailer's core brand values.

As a customer, being bombarded by sales messages when all you want to do is find a product can be enough to make you walk out of a store before you even begin to shop. Every shopper will have similar specific requirements: they want to locate what they're looking for, be presented with a choice of similar brands and products, pay for their choice without any hassle, and leave feeling satisfied. This complete process (from entering to leaving the store) is usually called the **customer journey**, and the messages that guide and support this journey are essential components of good retailing.

Visit any leading supermarket or large-scale retailer and look carefully at their brand icons, **taglines**, and price ticketing—you'll see they are using a **value-pricing system** of one form or another. It will be based on a matrix that separates the core customer messages into a clear hierarchy, organized so that they're not vying for attention with each other and so that the customer picks up distinct directional, brand, product, and promotional messages at the right time on the journey through the store.

Smaller retailers can adopt a similar approach, often more easily, as they don't have to use every element, and they will have greater flexibility and less formality. If you let products sit quietly on the shelf you are relying on the customer to discover them. Use posters or shelf messages to point out key items and their benefits and you're likely to attract impulse purchases. Go for the "wow" factor—try to give the customer a reason to purchase. A good approach is to preprint blank tickets, posters, and signage so that your messages can be overprinted and put up in-store quickly and cheaply, enabling the store to operate short-term promotions and display very topical, specific, and timely messages.

Key elements in a value-pricing system
All retailers take their own approach to communicating quality, value, and service. Many focus on low prices, and most value-pricing systems will incorporate the following elements:

1. Value icon
a logo or graphic device that represents the store's everyday competitive prices.

2. Brand tagline
a memorable sign-off line that encapsulates the store's everyday value for money.

3. Value pricing
a fixed-format price system featuring a graphic device, consistent color and some basic supporting copy.

4. Offer pricing
an alternative version of the value price-point tickets that highlights a short-term offer.

5. Special offer
a further alternative version that shouts out about an exceptional customer offer.

The style and tone of voice you use must represent the client's brand accurately and be concise, clear, and easy to understand. If a retail brand is youthful, wacky, cutting-edge, cool, or funky you have a license to write your copy accordingly, but don't lose sight of the function of your messages. If it's well respected, established, and sophisticated your voice must reflect this. If it takes time for customers to work out the meaning of your message they probably won't bother, so cut your copy down to the bone, use as few words as possible, and be prepared to sacrifice your juicy creative lines for straightforward guidance if necessary. For example, if you're tempted to write "This delicious, aromatic Blue Mountain coffee is supplied to us exclusively and we grind the beans freshly on the premises for you. It's Fairtrade approved and we keep the prices as low as possible. Try a cup for free before you buy your supplies for home!" consider this as an alternative: "Freshly ground, exclusive Blue Mountain Fairtrade coffee. Enjoy a free cup now when you buy 1lb!" This is a reduction from 46 to 16 words!

Understanding the customer journey

"If you do build a great experience, customers tell each other about that. Word of mouth is very powerful."
Jeff Bezos

Your customer's journey in, around, and out of the premises actually begins outside the store, with the enticing advertising and external messages you use to attract attention and draw in passing shoppers. A lot of effort and attention goes into the design of store window displays, but despite this many customers don't pay much attention to the detail they contain. They are either driving or walking past, while others will be heading into the store anyway. Either way, passersby do not have much time to stop and absorb complicated messages. Use short, punchy words, and as few as possible, remembering to reflect the brand's personality at all times.

The key elements in guiding the customer journey

External signage and window displays
giving a reason to come inside

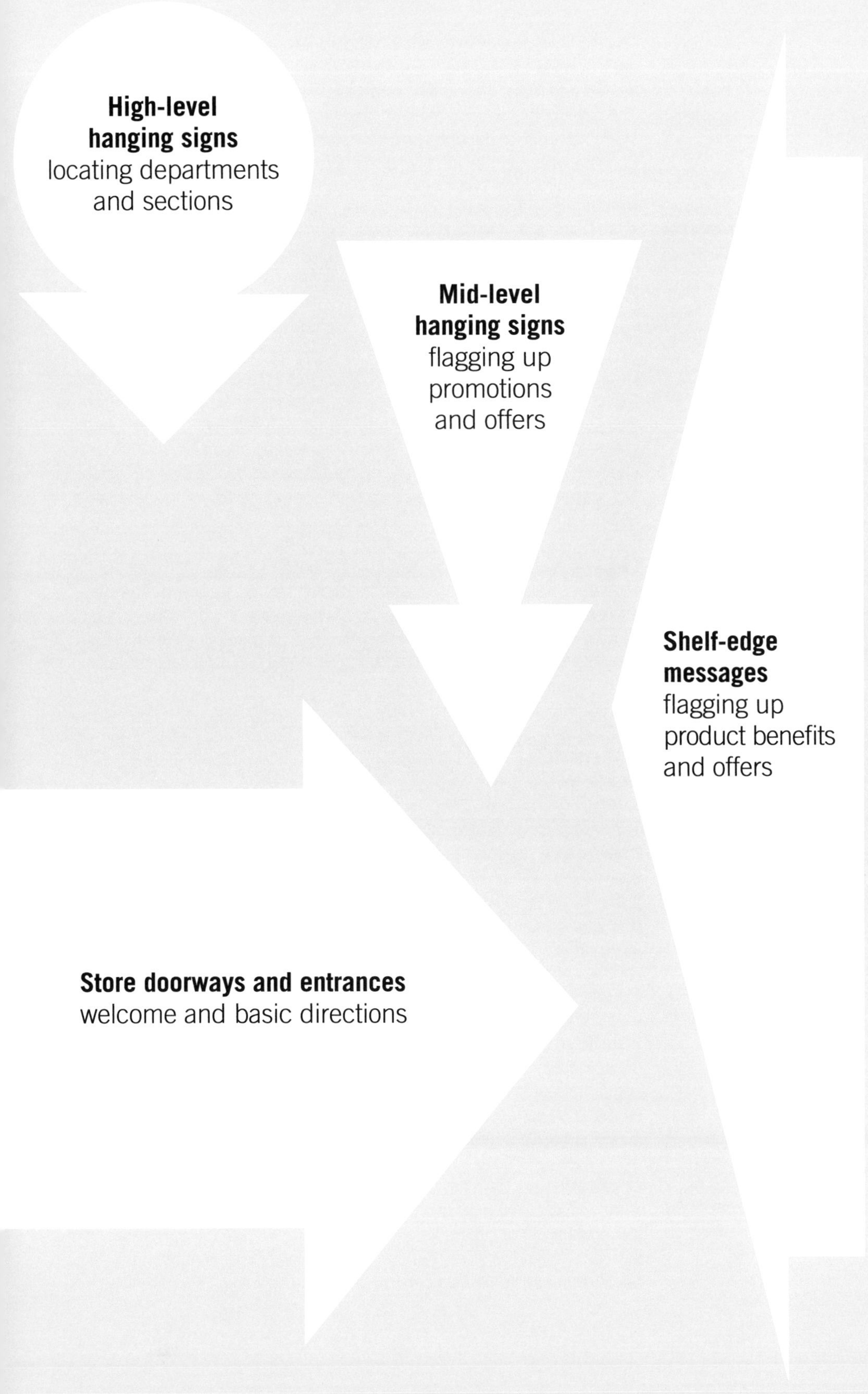

**High-level
hanging signs**
locating departments
and sections

**Mid-level
hanging signs**
flagging up
promotions
and offers

**Shelf-edge
messages**
flagging up
product benefits
and offers

Store doorways and entrances
welcome and basic directions

Customer Journey 1
Window displays

The store window is, in effect, a billboard advertisement and you should approach the copy in the same way as any other external advertisement: keep it short and make it compelling (by flagging up a single, overriding benefit). The sales points you are making must be clear from across the road, at a single glance. Boil the messages down to their ultimate essence—all you need to do is entice people into the store to find out more.

Customer Journey 2
Store entrance

Depending on the layout of the store it makes sense to take the opportunity to display a welcome or brand message at the entrance to the store. This can be a good way to give visitors a sense of the brand that sets the scene for their overall experience in the store. Consider putting up a "goodbye and thanks, see you soon" message here too, facing the customers as they leave—politeness is always well received.

Customer Journey 3
Directional signage

Once people are inside the store they will need direction to product areas. Card signs hanging from the ceiling are an excellent method for flagging up these sections, although they are not particularly efficient ways of running promotions: customers rarely—if ever—look above head height once they know where they are in the store. It's best to focus your efforts on the shelf-edge, eye-level, and end-of-aisle messages—otherwise, you could waste a lot of time on messages that will literally go over everyone's heads.

Customer Journey 4
Hanging signs

Large retailers often operate two levels of hanging cards: high- and mid-level. High-level hanging cards are best for identifying the sections of the store, and it's best to simply flag up a single word, or perhaps two. Mid-level hanging signage is good for messages linked to seasonal promotions (Mother's Day, Valentine's Day, Easter, Thanksgiving, Christmas, skiing season, summer season, and so on) or other promotional marketing messages, as they can be seen from a distance and can lead customers over. The high-level signage requires very basic copy, simply to name the sections, so resist the temptation to use them for creative concepts as this can undermine the clarity of the directional messages.

Customer Journey 5
Eye-level merchandising

The next stage of the customer journey that concerns you as the copywriter is at eye level, and has to clearly identify the products and their prices, and support this with relevant details of any offers or specific product benefits. It makes sense to use a consistent format for layout, colors, and copy, so that your customer can find the relevant information as quickly and easily as possible.

Customer Journey 6
On shelf

Extreme simplicity and clarity are key at the shelf edge. If your client operates a defined value-pricing system this will give you a format for the price tickets that should allow every price to be displayed boldly and clearly. Consider including a few short "bullet points," highlighting the distinguishing features and core benefits offered by each item. This will help to generate interest by enabling comparisons and encouraging customers to try new products and more expensive brands.

Customer Journey 7
Easy purchasing

Once customers have found what they are looking for, and have browsed the store and seen the promotions, they need to pay and leave. It is essential that the location of the cash registers and exits are very clearly signposted from all locations within the store. You don't want to lose the sale at the last minute because the customer has become frustrated.

BRAEBURN
Old-fashioned, aromatic and juicy. Rich and spicy-sweet. Crisp texture stays crisp and juicy when cooked.
One of the best for eating out of hand. Also good for sauce, baking and freezing.

CAMEO
Extra crisp, sweet-tart and juicy. Extra denseness makes it take longer to cook. It holds its juiciness and texture well and resists browning.
A natural choice for salads and fruit trays. Also very good eaten out of hand.

GINGER GOLD
The earliest-ripening apple. Crisp, sweet and mildly tart.
Very slow to brown, making it an outstanding choice for salads, garnish and any other fresh-cut apple use. Cooks well, too.

EMPIRE
Crisp, perfumy and juicy. A cross between McIntosh and Red Delicious. Keeps well.
A wonderful sweet-tart combination that makes it great for everything.

FUJI
Super sweet, super juicy and super crisp. Immensely flavorful. Keeps better than other sweet apples.
Holds its texture well when baked. Great for salads and outstanding eaten out of hand.

GALA
Small, crisp, juicy and mildly sweet with a beautifully striped colorful. Gorgeous set out in a fruit bowl.
Superb in salads and desserts and eaten out of hand. Perfect for kids.

GOLDEN DELICIOUS
Mellow, honey-sweet and juicy. Its sweetness means less added sugar when using for pies.
Resists browning. Good for baking, salads, sauce and eating out of hand. The pie apple of choice of the Culinary Institute of America.

GRANNY SMITH
Very tart, lemony, juicy and extra crunchy. The darker the skin, the more tart the fruit.
Tartness mellows with cooking while texture remains firm. Compliments savory foods well. An excellent all-purpose apple.

HONEY CRISP
Mild honeyed flavor with explosive crispness. Juicy and very sweet. Keeps well.
Good for salads, pies freezing and baking. Exceptional eaten out of hand.

IDA RED
Sweetly tart, highly flavorful and small-cored. Its firmness ensures it holds its shape perfectly when baked.
Cooking with skins on will yield pink applesauce. Highly desirable for cooking and baking. A top choice for traditional baked apples.

MACOUN
Extra-sweet, aromatic and very juicy. Firm textured with an excellent crunch.
Good for sauce and salads. Excellent served with cheese or eaten out of hand.

LADY APPLES
Lovely and petite. Can range in flavor from mouth-puckering to sweet.
Excellent for cooking, caramel or candy apples, even decorating!

McINTOSH
Sweet-tart, tender and highly aromatic. Tender, snow-white flesh cooks down quickly.
Perhaps best eaten out of hand, but ideal for sauce. Also very good in pies and crisps.

MUTSU
Large, juicy, super crisp and spicy. Pleasing balance of sweet and tart. Very refreshing.
Ideal eaten out of hand, but also good for pies, salads, baking, freezing and on sandwiches. Roast and serve with your favorite roast.

PAULA RED
Very tart, juicy and flavorful with firm, crisp texture.
Excellent for eating out of hand and perfect for sauce and cooking.

PINK LADY
Crisp, unique, tangy-tart and sweet. Complex and perfumy, with a firm texture.
Outstanding eaten out of hand. Terrific on a fruit tray, in salads or for fondue. Also good for baking and sauce.

RED DELICIOUS
Mildly sweet, tender and juicy. Maintains its good looks for a long time, making it a good choice for centerpieces.
A nice addition to salads but at its very best eaten out of hand.

ROME
Mildly tart, lightly sweet and firm. Referred to as "the Baker's Buddy" because it retains its shape and tartness beautifully when cooked.
Primarily a cooking apple. It is superb for sauce, baking and sautéing.

JONAGOLD
Uniquely honey-tart, crisp & juicy with spicy fragrance and firm texture.
Excellent for baking and pies. Also good in salads and for sauce. Sauté slices in butter with cinnamon—no sugar needed! One of the best for eating out of hand. Freezes well.

CORTLAND
Crisp and sweet with only a hint of tartness. Tender, fine-grained and snow-white inside.
Resists browning making it the very best salad apple, but also ideal for kebabs and garnishes. A great all-purpose apple that stays firm when baked.

Customers don't always know how to shop a line, or how to differentiate one product from another, and Fairacre Farms have taken a simple and extremely effective approach to explaining theirs. The results are practical, and because of this they are highly compelling too.

It's always great to find someone having fun with their copy, and Loseley know that ice cream is not such a serious business, so why not create some exotic characters and tell some far-fetched stories? It certainly makes them stand out from the competition.

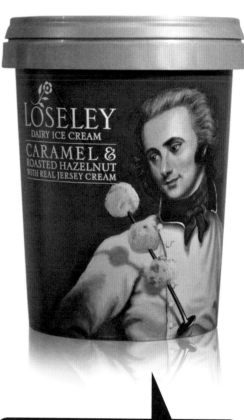

My husband sailed for Madagascar today. Normally I would count the days until his return. For he brings me the most exotic delicacies. Then I discovered Loseley use the finest Madagascan bourbon vanilla in their deliciously creamy ice cream. Strangely, I now miss my husband rather less.

It is true that I am a most accomplished swordsman. But when I truly want to impress, I present Loseley for dessert (though my cook always maintains it is his own creation). The roasted hazelnuts, demerara sugar, and rich caramel sauce never fail to melt the ladies' hearts.

"Next to doing the right thing, the most important thing is to let people know you are doing the right thing."
John D. Rockefeller

You are unlikely to have any control over the number of supplier promotions in the store. These are often written, designed, and produced by the product supplier and are part of the deals made between retailers and manufacturers. Sometimes they come to you in the form of a brief, and you should endeavor to ensure that the same guidelines apply to these as to your client's other customer messages.

In-store posters should be big and bold, and they may require little more than an evocative image and a brand identity. The posters created by Fairacre Farms to promote their apples through educating their customers about the specific benefits of different varieties are perfect examples of clear and powerful communications. They contain a clear, benefit-led message and are warm and enticing (page 117).

End-of-shelf displays—which are highly effective sales points—must have a few basic communications elements and be light on copy. An emotive headline and concise qualifying line will be all that's needed to support the graphics and steer the customer to the products being highlighted.

What are the products saying to your customer?

So much effort has been put into attracting the customer to the products on the shelves, but what about the products themselves? Whether the product line is the retailer's **house brand** or is a stand-alone **proprietary brand**, your pack copy has to clearly show what the brand is, highlight the product name, explain the benefits it offers, and conform to a number of statutory requirements, including lengthy ingredient (sometimes called **INCI**) lists. These elements may seem very straightforward initially, but can be surprisingly complex, as they will have to be applied across many items in the line.

"No matter what your product is, you are ultimately in the education business. Your customers need to be constantly educated about the many advantages of doing business with you, trained to use your products more effectively, and taught how to make never-ending improvement in their lives."
Robert G. Allen

On any product, space for copy is severely limited, and the requirements (generic brand message, product details, benefits, full ingredients list, and legal disclaimers) often take up the lion's share, even before you've had the chance to think about a creative line. It is vital to work with the designers and artworkers to establish the copy area for each specific product, and to calculate the precise word count. This will save you a lot of time and will help you to manage the expectations of your client from the start.

There are distinct differences between the role of copy on the front and back of the pack. The copy on the front of the pack—especially the brand and product names and descriptors—is an advertisement; it has to catch the eye and encourage people to put the product into their baskets. There is rarely time for customers to read your back-of-pack copy in a busy store—it is intended to be read back at home, when they are relaxed and unhurried. Your back-of-pack copy should provide detail and evidence that reassures customers that they have made a good purchase, and create enough motivation or incentive to ensure that they will replace it from the same product line.

Get the tone of voice right

If you are writing the copy for an extensive product line it makes sense to define the tone of voice for yourself, for the people approving the copy (the marketing team, business owner, or senior client), and for any other writers and the rest of the design team. This doesn't need to be sophisticated or cleverly designed. A few carefully prepared pages of paper will be sufficient. The tone-of-voice guide on page 18 is a good example of the approach you can take. As with any copy, keep it as short as possible. A few evocative sentences, set in large type, can be a good way to present the tone of voice.

The core elements of a brand matrix

Parameters such as these present an experienced writer with a clear guide when selecting language, phrases, words, and expressions to evoke the essence of the brand.

What is the brand vision?

For example, "what makes this brand different from any other?"

It could be: "this brand will be a part of women's lives from their 30s onward."

What is the core idea?

For example, "what is the reason that the product or service exists?"

It could be: "this brand makes the latest scientific thinking in skincare available to every woman."

Your tone-of-voice guide has to have some structure, some thinking behind it that makes sense to everyone who will be involved with it. Most follow the direction given by a brand matrix, a chart showing a profile of the brand, which aims to identify and explain its core elements. If a brand structure or matrix has not been provided by the lead creative agency or the client's marketing team, you should consider creating your own to use as a rough guide for your copy.

You need a global awareness when naming a product

"The point to remember about selling things is that, as well as creating atmosphere and excitement around your products, you've got to know what you're selling."
Stuart Wilde

Naming a product is a similar process to naming a brand (a product could also be a brand in itself). The key difference is that a company brand is designed to convey the values in the corporation consistently over many years, and therefore it needs to be solid and reliable and not a victim to fashion trends. However a product brand can take more of an advertising approach, and aim for high impact or standout, and if this is fashionable for a while it can always be updated when trends change.

With such a huge variety of product brand names on the shelves, and new ones coming into the fray all the time, of equal importance to creative brainstorming is the lack of availability of names when it comes to trademarks. You have to search your early ideas thoroughly—and don't present a proposed new product brand name unless you are confident that there's no reason to believe it has been registered already.

What values are associated with this?

For example, "what does this brand stand for?"

It could be: "innovation, performance, credibility."

What is its personality like?

For example, "what characterizes this brand and the way it communicates?"

It could be: "stimulating, friendly, fun."

Why should the customer believe this?

For example, "what makes the brand ring true for the customer?"

It could be: "traditional values coupled with proven scientific evidence."

Work out what your product is associated with and consider the different categories of names that you could select from.

Categories of names:

Arbitrary	(Sun Microsystems)
Classical	(Ajax cleaning products)
Acronym	(DKNY)
Editing	(Travelex)
Description	(Head and Shoulders)
Alliteration	(Automobile Association)
Family	(Ferrari)
Heritage	(Broad Stripe Butchers)

Launching a new product brand requires you to create:

the brand name

range names (for larger brands)

specific product names

the front- and back-of-pack copy

the point-of-sale, merchandising, and advertising text.

Consider the hierarchy of information that you are creating. You may well be dealing with the parent brand name, the product brand itself, product name, and a possible product description. Let one of these dominate.

Product brands are highly competitive and you have to create a name that helps yours stand out among the clutter. The best names are very memorable and sound good as well as look good. It should all add up to a good feeling about the name; if not, you'll have an uphill battle trying to gain awareness of it after it's launched.

GOLD DIGGER *shimmer*

NUMEROLOGY:
128=1+2+8=11=1+1=2
Sensitivity & balance. The diplomat.

 (2)

Pride.

Grab your rewards.
The brazen are due.

COLOR SUITE:
Earthy Low Notes.
The power of earth & connection.

 ▼

Wear it and don't apologize.
You are a legend already.

KISS THE COOK *crème*

NUMEROLOGY:
118=1+1+8=10=1+0=1
Independence & ambition. The hero.

(1)

Move the bed into the kitchen.
You are cooking on all burners.

Contentment.

COLOR SUITE:
Earthy Low Notes.
The power of earth & connection.

 ▼

Some like it hot.

SALT OF THE EARTH *shimmer*

NUMEROLOGY:
133=1+3+3=7
Versatility & adventure. The trail blazer.

 (7)

Truth.

Spend time with those you trust.
You are goodness itself.

COLOR SUITE:
Earthy Low Notes.
The power of earth & connection.

 ▼

Peel away the layers.
Get real. Play unplugged.

CAN YOU DIG IT? *shimmer*

NUMEROLOGY:
127=1+2+7=10=1+0=1
Independence & ambition. The hero.

(1)

Excavation.

Invite the unconvinced.
Get down & dirty. Camp out.

COLOR SUITE:
Earthy Low Notes.
The power of earth & connection.

 ▼

Stay below ground.
Darkness is where it's at.

DEATH BY CHOCOLATE *crème*

NUMEROLOGY:
126=1+2+6=9
Compassion & giving. The humanitarian.

 (9)

Decadence. Definitely order dessert.

Let someone else
pick up the check.

COLOR SUITE:
Earthy Low Notes.
The power of earth & connection.

▼

Stop worrying about
consequences.
You're worth it.

Spa Ritual uses a copy system comprised of a few different elements that appear consistently on all packs, so that the customer becomes familiar with the way the information is communicated, and feels connected with the brand.

Exercise: getting to grips with store communications

The aim of this exercise to is develop your skills in working to a hierarchy of messaging. Choose an existing retailer, or create a profile of an imaginary one, and see if you can break down their brand and messages into the following categories:

Value pricing
1. What will their overall value message be?
2. How will this be expressed as a tagline?
3. What will everyday price tickets say?
4. How will discounts be communicated?

Customer journey
1. Which messages are the most suitable for store windows?
2. What language will you use to guide customers around the store?
3. How will you express core product promotions?
4. What messages would you put on the shelf edges?

Exercise: creating a new product brand

The objective of this exercise is to create a new brand name for a product line, product names for individual items, and copy for both front and back of pack.

Create a short brief for a new product. It could be a lawnmower or a shampoo, a chicken pie or a computer. Include the main benefit, target audience, and point of difference.

1. Brainstorm lists of possible names for the main brand.
2. Shortlist and segregate these by type.
3. Choose an option to develop.
4. Create product names that fit in with the new brand (4 or 5 items).
5. For each item, write engaging and short copy for the front of pack.
6. Write some more detailed copy for the back of pack.

Keep a close eye on your word counts, ensuring they are the same for each item, and that they will fit on the product (easy for lawnmowers, difficult for lipsticks).

Round-up

Present the core messages in a way that fosters strong rapport with the customer.

Create a strong sense of place, of belonging, comfort, and familiarity.

Your role is to attract interest so that the shopper doesn't miss the rewarding offers, promotions, or brand propositions.

The messages that guide and support the customer journey are essential components of good retailing.

Go for the "wow" factor, try to give the customer a reason to purchase.

Be prepared to sacrifice your juicy creative lines for straightforward guidance if necessary.

Work with the designers and artworkers to find out what the copy area is for each specific product, and calculate the precise word count.

There are distinct differences between the role of copy on the front and back of the pack.

If you are writing the copy for an extensive product range, define the tone of voice.

The availability of new brand names is sparse, so you must check your proposals for trademark availability before you show them to the client.

Good design can transform a plain word into a strong brand, but it is best to start with a word that already has impact and resonance on its own.

Be prepared to fight your corner to a certain extent. The best way to do this is to explain all of the parameters and restrictions within which you are working.

Case Study: Method Home Products

Eric Ryan is the founder of Method Home Products, a $100 million turnover home-products business that uses interesting messages and a strong and clear tone of voice to communicate its sometimes radical viewpoints. Method's attitude is communicated powerfully through effective use of copy, and this is one of the core factors behind its outstanding success. Here Eric tells us how the brand was created, and how it uses language to gain competitive advantage.

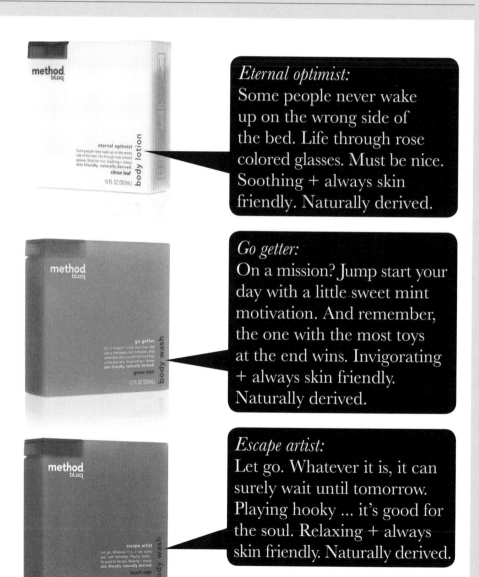

Eternal optimist:
Some people never wake up on the wrong side of the bed. Life through rose colored glasses. Must be nice. Soothing + always skin friendly. Naturally derived.

Go getter:
On a mission? Jump start your day with a little sweet mint motivation. And remember, the one with the most toys at the end wins. Invigorating + always skin friendly. Naturally derived.

Escape artist:
Let go. Whatever it is, it can surely wait until tomorrow. Playing hooky ... it's good for the soul. Relaxing + always skin friendly. Naturally derived.

The Objective:
explaining how our brand is different in every sense

Method had to be a challenging brand, a challenger brand. It had to do things differently to stand out from the competition in a crowded marketplace, and had to make customers think differently about the home products they use. Most consumers are on autopilot when they shop. We used our voice, messages, and language to challenge the status quo.

I'm a strategic planner, not a writer. I'm a terrible writer, but can tell good writing when I see it. I write copy briefs from a strategic point of view, giving as much content as I can. My skill is in creating the big idea that the creatives can develop and bring to life.

Maintaining our tone of voice across our product range is a challenge. We have products in all areas, from candles to detergent. The objective is to achieve consistency with the messages and information on every product, but to be honest we can't get there. We strike a balance between doing the best writing possible for each product, and representing the brand voice accurately and clearly. We know we don't need the copy to look the same, or read the same, on every product, it just has to feel the same.

Merchandising and the way we display and market products in-store is a very important part of our business. We try to utilize every touch point for the customer, giving them clear messages to ensure they understand our environmental credentials. We have a small budget for marketing, and the copy we use has to work very hard for us.

The Approach:
speaking our mind and standing for our beliefs

Our personality, which is about questioning and being rebellious, comes from us and the attitude that formed the business in the first place.

The name Method came from my original brief. I'm from a branding background, and I wanted a "jumping off" word to say we get the job done, with less force. Our inspiration was the word "technique," as by using better techniques we can reduce the need to use strong detergents or chemicals that harm our environment. Adam, in our team, suggested "method" and we all agreed it was a good fit.

The voice of Method was developed by our advertising agency, Crispin Porter, with two aims: it had to be fun (in a category not associated with fun) and had to be both provocative and likable.

Our agencies (Shire and TBWA), together with our freelance writers, look after all copywriting for us;

we now have an in-house writer too. We're trying to find our "Dan" [Dan Germain, Innocent, pages 110–12], someone who can instinctively control our tone of voice and push it forward without losing core values.

Where we can, we like to have fun with product names and be more creative. Creating a combustible cleaning cloth from corn, we called the range Omop to make it sound distinctive. We're following the lead of companies like Apple who make product icons that become part of our culture. Whatever you do, you can't overcomplicate things. It's about keeping it simple to make it stand out and be memorable.

The basic structure to our pack copy is that it must be a single sentence. In Canada rules state we have to include extra information, and have it in French too. It's a real challenge to be simple: there's a constant trade-off between the messages and the necessary detail. We have to keep trying to strike the right balance; we haven't found the solution yet.

We often find at the end of a long brainstorm that many, sometimes most, of the words we want for products are already registered as trademarks, sometimes decades ago. I'm always amazed at how many are gone. Our open and flexible approach to product copy means we can have lots of choices in product names. Checking for availability is a long and expensive part of the process, and we have an in-house legal team who specialize in this for us.

It is easier to get the copy right on every touch point if writers are in-house. It is such a difficult job if you are not based in the business, if you don't understand the categories and context for each one.

The Result:
customers know what we offer them, and they love it

We make sure we're never boring, and we're always experimenting and reinventing how we talk about our products and their benefits. We're always looking for fresh approaches and new ideas. For example, we learned shopping bags were being banned in San Francisco; we created a promotion so customers receive a free reusable shopping bag if they spend $20 with us. The funky bag has "plastic bag rehab" written in big hippy lettering—they've been a hit.

We make statements explaining who we are and what we stand for. They range from "we think perfect is boring, and weirdliness is next to godliness" to "we also believe in making products safe for every surface, especially earth's." We make our attitude felt on the widest possible scale and are not afraid of thinking big. We've recently launched a "Detox Seattle" campaign, and even published a book about our attitude and thinking—it's called *Squeaky Green*.

Case Study: Pret A Manger

Pret A Manger is one of the UK's retail success stories. Selling a wide range of the freshest sandwiches and lunchtime foods, the company prefers to use innovative customer communications rather than slick advertising and PR. Everything in a Pret store carries a message, from the coffee cups to the napkins, from the packaging to the posters on the walls. This creates a strong and unique personality, so what was their original approach, and how do they do it?

We spent months dipping, dunking and tasting until we found the perfect recipe for yoghurty, chocolatey nuts (hard life, eh?).

Almonds, brazils, hazelnuts, macadamias, pecans, pistachios ... we think this little bag rocks!

The goodies in this little bag are packed full of good stuff. Mangos are a fantastic source of vitamin C and they taste amazing.

We buy Fairtrade mango which guarantees fair prices for the farmers. We think this makes them taste even sweeter!

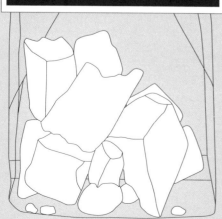

YOGHURT&NUT...
ROCKS!

A little bag full of white chocolate and yoghurt coated nuts.

★ PRET A MANGER ★

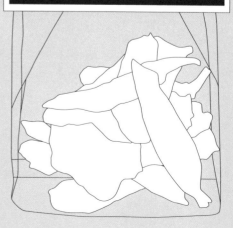

MANGO
SLICES

A little bag full of delicious dried mango slices.

★ PRET A MANGO ★

The Objective:
reflecting the attitude that makes the company so dynamic

The messages mirror the culture that pervades every aspect of Pret's business. It is a relaxed and informal working environment, built on the individual qualities of everyone who works there, and the internal communications are as quirky as the customer messages.

Pret doesn't have a press or PR office and only uses an external creative agency to help manage the huge workload of writing. The stimulating and informative messages that adorn every Pret item are written and managed by three people internally: the company's founder, commercial director, and head of communications, and even they don't follow a rule book.

The Pret tone of voice is based on the personality and ideas of the founder, Julian Metcalfe. It bursts with life, but is never preaching or bragging, and is definitely not "corporate" or "spin." Nothing deviates from the message about Pret's natural food, which is always "just made." Julian himself never uses the word "copy"—to him it's just messages, and every message is designed to make you feel good about Pret.

The Approach:
keeping the copy as fresh as the sandwiches

There is an instinctive approach to creativity and freshness, and an openness that many others could learn from. They have published all of their recipes so that customers can make Pret sandwiches themselves, and they have made public their commitment to not air-freight their ingredients, except in the case of an emergency (or where fresh basil leaves are concerned).

The writers say it is difficult to explain what is on- and off-brand when writing for Pret, but they all know what works and what doesn't—they each have a highly attuned eye for language, both their own and that of the competitors. If a competitor could say it, Pret won't. Yet a style of copy that works for a Pret soup board won't work for a Pret coffee board, simply because they are completely different messages.

The closest they get to an explanation is that their language "has charm, wit, and humility, but is never preaching," and that, while it is fun, "it is a wry smile not a belly laugh." They have also described it as "flippancy, underpinned by serious knowledge." For example, their "Eat with your head" campaign promotes ten very sensible points about healthy eating.

By maintaining such a simple and straightforward process to writing messages, the team at Pret is able to keep a consistent feel with all of the copy. When trying to come up with a phrase to describe chemicals used by competitors, the team settled on "frankenstein food," while one of Pret's coffees has "a velvety foam—gives a jolt in the arm." They also go to great lengths to include their ingredients in plain English, and where they can't avoid jargon they explain what the ingredient is for: "soya lecithin—to stop glooping."

They operate plans and processes—coffee cups are reprinted three times a year, and posters refreshed five times a year—but the rule of thumb is that nothing is sacred. You'll find interesting messages at the bottom of invoices, on training materials, on screen designs, and on the wall at head office (where they keep a swear box for anyone referring to stores outside of London as "out of London"). The way they communicate to their customers and staff is incredibly important to Pret, and every piece of communication comes through the writing team for approval.

It's not as easy as it looks, though. They return many times to each piece of copy, and quality control themselves by reading and critiquing each other's copy. It took six months to write their 16-page brochure, but it is this painstaking attention to detail that makes the Pret A Manger tone of voice so light, tasty, and enjoyable.

The Result:
communications that build relationships with their customers

The copy at Pret builds long-term customer relationships because it is targeted and engaging, but they are clear that the most compelling thing about Pret is the food. Just like the food, the copy has to be turned around quickly so that the messages are always fresh and, where possible, relevant. Critics say the customer is bombarded with emotional overload, but they miss the point. The customer reads what he or she wants and, rather than being overloaded, is given a choice of positive messages to enjoy at will.

This *ugly brown napkin* is made from 100% recycled stock (some white napkins are bleached which can result in environmentally damaging toxic waste). If Pret staff get all serviette-ish and hand you huge bunches of napkins (which you don't need or want) please give them the evil eye. Waste not want not.

Chefs at work

'Just made' with preservative-free, fresh, natural ingredients.

100% recycled

Ian (Head of Crisps) was convinced he could make ours taste even better. (We didn't see him for months.)

He's feeling rather smug now, as we have to agree—they really do taste very, very good.

Pret crisps are good because we chop and change the variety of potato throughout the year. This costs more but results in a better crunch and taste.

CROXTON MANOR
CHEDDAR
& RED ONION

HAND COOKED POTATO CRISPS
* made from 100% natural ingredients *

NEW

Handmade APPLE CAKE

⊰ FLOWERY TINS ⊱

Sorry about the ghastly plastic wrapper. When you bake a cake at home,
you take it out of the oven and cool it on a wire rack. Then you eat a large slice
(as a reward) and keep the rest in a flowery cake tin, like your Grandma used to!

Think of the nasty wrapper as the cake tin.
It's the only way we can keep the cake moist and delicious.
As is often the case, the beauty is on the inside.

PASSION FACT NO.47

When you bake a cake at home, you take it out of the oven and cool it on a rack. Then you eat a large slice (as a reward) and keep the rest in a flowery cake tim, like your Grandma used to!

Think of the nasty wrapper as the cake tin. It's the only way we can keep the cake moist and delicious. As is often the case, the beauty is on the inside.

Writing for company magazines, newsletters, and internal communications

Company magazines and newsletters communicate regularly with customers or employees with the aim of building positive relationships that contribute to the success of the organization. They often follow a fixed design format, and it is the content—the copy, photography, and illustration—that brings the publication to life. This type of copywriting requires a journalistic approach, combining research with original writing, but it also needs you to use your copy skills to engage your reader and represent your client accurately.

News and features are about content as much as style

Newsletters and magazines serve a number of purposes in the commercial world. Some are designed to establish a brand, others to reach a wider market, some to inform and educate employees and others to cross-sell within the existing customer base.

All copywriting thrives on the availability of good content, but where some formats—such as press advertising or direct marketing—rely primarily on the style of communication and the immediate impact this can create with a reader, newsletter and magazine articles (even basic newsletter articles) have to be informative, stimulating, and interesting, and to achieve good content is crucial. Because of the amount of information they have to convey, magazines and newsletters must have a strong seam of raw material to mine, and this mine must never be worked out.

Researching the content for news items, reviews, interviews, and articles will be a key part of your role, and this is where copywriting and journalism have many parallels. The two disciplines require similar skills and abilities, but they are also very different from each other. Journalism is all about reporting the story as objectively as possible, while copywriting requires the writer to tell the story on behalf of the client. This is usually an objective and unbiased stance (any over-promotion within an article will result in loss of credibility), but you are always in the service of the person briefing you and your editorial will therefore be biased toward the marketing objectives of the client.

Magazines and newsletters rely on informative writing

Many, if not most, organizations have identified a need or an opportunity to send out a regular communication to their employees or customers. These differ from one-off communications (an individual leaflet or brochure, for example) in that they aim to communicate regularly with the audience, and build a strong, ongoing relationship with them.

Some magazines are big-budget productions led from the most senior parts of the business, while at the other end of the scale, newsletters often evolve from the ground up, frequently as a collection of memos and updates. Any professional publication will employ the services of a copywriter, or more than one in many cases, either in a core editorial management role or as a regular contributor of content.

Whether editing or writing for a publication, your starting point is to understand the different natures of a magazine and a newsletter. They have many similarities. Both are published regularly, feature a mixture of editorial, carry the client company's message, and aim to inform and motivate the audience to act favorably toward the client. They can use the same types of format and structure, but where a newsletter's function is to keep the audience up to date in a practical way, the role of a company magazine is to communicate the client's brand values and create a sense of lifestyle (even in business-to-business).

"Far more thought and care go into the composition of any prominent ad in a newspaper or magazine than go into the writing of their features and editorials."

Marshall McLuhan, communications theorist

The key is in what they are called. A magazine is a themed collection of interesting material, and a newsletter is an update on what's going on. A magazine is a focal point for stories, comment, updates, and features, and the style in which this is collated and presented is a vital part of its character. Much more time and effort goes into a magazine than into a newsletter. Although it does need to be smart and well presented, it is the content of the information in a newsletter, not its image or the lifestyle it portrays, that counts.

Factual, clear, and informative, the messages in this detailed brochure showcase the great work done by the UK's Meteorological Office without being dry. The copy really brings out the points of interest to make this a stimulating read.

Overall, our focus is on increasing public safety on land, at sea and in the air; which includes helping people and societies cope with climate related and other natural disasters, such as the earthquake-tsunami in south-east Asia.

As the hurricane season progressed, residents in Florida found themselves bombarded by four hurricanes and one tropical storm in quick succession. During this more active than normal season, nine named storms affected the whole of the US ...

"I recommend deep-fried grasshoppers, very tasty, though I am not keen on termites," he says. *"Everywhere I have been in Africa, I have been amazed by the hospitality and generosity of the people. The best reward for me is when you see people realize that they can do it for themselves and they don't have to rely on other people to make things better."*

"Before we had this system we would get a general icing warning and our handling agency would heat up the de-icing rigs. Using the new Met Office system, we're able to give them better information and so cut out the need to warm up the rigs on a 'maybe.' Now we do it on a 'probably.'"

What you need in your magazine or newsletter brief

A summary of the overall objective of the newsletter or magazine
For example: "to communicate our brand values to our customers, and by explaining about our business, to encourage them to call on our services more often"

A profile of the target readership, with insights wherever possible
For example: "predominantly male, aged 18 to 35, single, with a reasonable disposable income—they love our products, but they are not aware of the full line we offer"

Details of the strategic messages that must be communicated
For example: "our line of men's toiletries performs better than most premium brands, yet they don't have a premium price tag"

Contacts for sourcing raw material (copy and images)
For example: "our formulation experts have the scientific data, our toiletries buyer knows the key selling points, and the brand manager has a tone-of-voice guide that you can use"

A page count and information on frequency of publication
For example: "the budget will allow us to print 100,000 copies of a 32-page magazine six times a year"

A list of key clients involved in editorial and signing off
For example: "the toiletries buyer and head of beauty will need to sign it off, and the marketing director will have to give final approval before it goes to print"

The Internet and e-mail are very cost-efficient and effective methods of communication, and many newsletters and magazines are now published online. Digital media offer low-cost distribution and very rapid speed of delivery, but readers may only view the message a single time, and are often distracted by incoming mail or other sites that become available. Print offers messages a longer shelf life and the chance to be read in greater detail, and the opportunity to be displayed and discovered. It's all about the best way to reach the audience, and it is common for print publications also to appear online. As the writer, your goal is to communicate effectively with the readers and developing a clear, human voice is more important than worrying about the format being used.

Creating and writing a company newsletter

There are many types of newsletter—from a few sheets of paper photocopied at the office, or a round-robin e-mail, to a sophisticated, full-color publication— and because they can be produced cheaply it's not unusual to find "unofficial" ones thriving in larger organizations. These usually begin life as a series of memos, e-mails, or word-processed documents that someone collates and distributes to a group of people within their business. This is not such a bad way to begin because, if nothing else, it proves that there is enough content to support a regular communication (it can always be made more professional, but if there is no news there is no newsletter).

Many newsletters are digital, distributed through e-mail and the Internet rather than being printed. Blogs are simply personal newsletters. The process of creating the publication and its articles is the same, whether they are intended for print or online publication (except where the digital newsletter has to be written with the navigability of the text in mind—see chapter 8, page 201).

A basic editorial plan for a newsletter

FRONT COVER:
news items

INSIDE FRONT COVER:
a message
from the top

AT THE START:
shorter news items

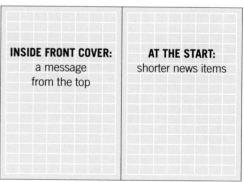

IN THE MIDDLE:
a few lead articles

AT THE END:
a focus on the future

BRITISH AIRWAYS
News

T5 Our amazing new home

104 days to go

THURSDAY, DECEMBER 13, 2007   FOR THE PEOPLE OF BRITISH AIRWAYS   No 1701

T5 MAKES DEBUT IN AD CAMPAIGN
Page 5

COME TOGETHER THIS CHRISTMAS
BRITISH AIRWAYS

RESULTS OF THE SPEAK UP! SURVEY
Page 2 and 3

WIN A STAY IN SALZBURG
Page 8 and 9

NOW YOU CAN APPLY FOR A SEASON TICKET LOAN ONLINE – PAGE 7

COMPLIMENTS A CLICK AWAY

Customers can praise service on new website

By Peter Krinks

A WEBSITE that offers customers the chance to compliment British Airways staff for the service they receive is launched today.

The initiative is part of the airline's renewed focus on customer service, including the Refreshing Service campaign.

> "It's important to recognise staff for great service"

Customers can log on to ba.com/welldone to thank or praise staff for good or brilliant service.

It has been designed as a quick and easy way of letting staff know that their efforts have been recognised.

Last year's Warm Up Winter campaign, which invited customers to feed back on great customer service, saw the number of compliments received nearly double.

Vicki O'Brien, manager airport solutions and performance, said: "Our business is about delivering brilliant customer service.

"It's important therefore that we recognise our staff when they deliver great service.

■ Turn to page 2

BEHIND YOU! ALADDIN'S THE STAR OF PANTO PRODUCTION

Gary Collins as the genie with Jane McGill as Aladdin and, inset, Ken Williams as Widow Twanky and Eddie Hinds as Abanazer

Pictures: Denis Wesson

Stage is set for genie-us

THE adventures of Aladdin are being brought to life by the Concorde Players.

The group will be staging its production at the Concorde Club next month.

Tickets are now on sale for the panto, which runs from Wednesday, January 23, to Saturday, January 26, at 7.30pm, with a Saturday matinee at 2pm.

The show promises singing, dancing, mirth, merriment, antics, cross-dressing, thigh-slapping and audience participation.

The cast and crew, which is made up of BA and other airport staff and their families and friends, have been working on the show since October.

Tickets for the Wednesday and Thursday performances are £8 for adults and £4 for children, and £10 for adults and £5 for children on Friday and Saturday.

Call 020 851 32000 or log onto www.concorde players.co.uk

● LETTERS: PAGE 6 ● JOBSCAN: PAGE 10 ● MONEYWATCH AND TIMEWATCH: PAGE 16

Using an energetic, motivational, and inspiring tone of voice, *British Airways News* is packed with information and news about new initiatives and projects, and ideas for the staff about how to make the best use of the discounted travel that they enjoy.

The precise boundaries between a newsletter and a magazine are blurred. Usually, a newsletter will be a regular publication with up to 16 pages (black and white or color), usually letter-sized or A4, that is distributed free of charge to a defined readership. Anything more substantial than this would fall into the category of a magazine, reflecting the amount of extra time, effort, and money required. A newsletter audience is characterized by their common interest, for example the company they work for or a club they've joined.

When planning the editorial content of a company newsletter, consider how many issues will be produced each year, and how this fits with the company's calendar. For example, when is the conference, when is their busiest period, are there seasonal trends? Avoid monthly editions, if possible—it's a relentless slog to hit these tight deadlines unless you are part of a highly motivated team—and if you do publish monthly stick to ten issues a year, doubling up issues for July/August and December/January to give you time to catch up (and have a break!). If the publication is biannual, your content has to be fresh for up to six months, so be careful to avoid too many references to dates or specific events.

From the earliest stage, try to work closely with the graphic designers to create a **page plan**. The designer should welcome your input, as you will be helping to shape the most successful approach to the brief. The main things to consider include whether there will be a full-bleed (to the edges of the page) photographic image or text-based news stories on the cover, whether you're including an editorial comment and, if so, from whom, how the content will be split between short news items and more in-depth articles, and what these will look like. It is always a good idea to start with some lighter material (news in brief, for example) and to include a detailed feature article in the center.

Your newsletter ought to have a strong title and properly designed **masthead** and an editorial **style sheet**. The best way to create the overall publication title is to brainstorm words associated with the client's business, avoiding anything that is a cliché or bad pun. It is better to play it safe than risk undermining the credibility of the publication by giving it a daft name. "Company News" is perfectly acceptable. Get the content right as a priority, and experiment with the style only if you are sure it suits the brand and your audience.

Next, create your schedule and the accompanying editorial calendar, based on the time available and the amount of copy required. You may want to leave some of your articles until the very end, adding them in just before the print deadline, so that your news is fresh and newsworthy. If necessary you can then quote for your time based on this schedule. It can take a surprising amount of time to gather information, conduct interviews, process and collate the raw material, and draft copy for your newsletter, so get off to a quick start and include some contingency time if you can. You'll need as much time as you can get—and don't leave the writing until the last minute, as this type of writing, unlike pure creative copywriting such as advertising or direct marketing, does not lend itself well to burning the midnight oil.

Creating and writing a company magazine

A carefully thought-through, well-written, and well-designed company magazine is a very powerful brand communications tool that can play a leading role in ensuring that a client's employees and customers think favorably about their organization. As the writer, it is essential that you take the time to understand the context of your story fully, research the background, and present your information credibly to an informed audience.

Company magazines are far less common than newsletters, and are far weightier projects in every sense. Some are designed for customers, to encourage their loyalty and raise their awareness of the client's full range of

A typical editorial plan for a company magazine
The cover and front sections should be designed
to win attention, while the middle to back sections
should present material for regular readers.

FRONT COVER:
Intriguing cover lines

INSIDE COVER:
Editorial and
contents list

EARLY SECTIONS:
News items
and reviews

Cover and front sections

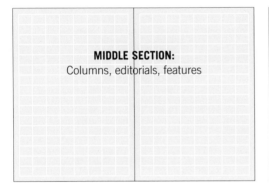
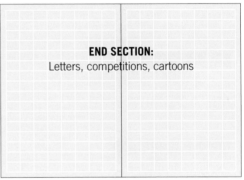

MIDDLE SECTION:
Columns, editorials, features

END SECTION:
Letters, competitions, cartoons

Middle to back sections

OTHER OPTIONS:
Lists of facts, people profiles,
humorous articles, questionnaires

Checklist: Editing

Whether you're editing material supplied by the
client or by other writers, or your own copy, you
will be aiming to:

achieve maximum clarity:
Can the message be misinterpreted? If so, change it.

hit the word count:
Remove all padding, and be prepared to add material.

remove repetition:
Don't waffle, be as succinct as possible.

get the facts right:
Is the material accurate?
Are you sure it is correct?

remove the jargon:
Explain things to everyone, and everyone will get it.

perfect the spelling:
Use the spell checker as backup.

check the punctuation:
Apostrophes really matter—just keep the rest simple.

maintain the right tone:
Express the brand, and relate to the audience.

products or services, while others are created to carry **internal communications** in a highly professional manner. In both cases, company magazines are printed on high-spec paper, and make good use of quality photography and graphic design. Too often they are let down by poor editorial content. Gone are the days when pictures of staff handing over charity checks, getting married, or showing off their hobbies can hold the audience's interest.

The process for creating a company magazine is similar to that for a newsletter, but there are significant differences. A magazine will have bigger budgets, larger circulation, and a higher profile than a newsletter. Because of this, every element of a magazine carries greater importance than the equivalent in a newsletter.

An article for the employees of a company that explains a new strategic initiative would be written differently depending on the type of publication for which it is intended. If it was for a newsletter it could have the following header: "Moving some manufacturing to China allows us to compete globally." This is fact-based, clear, and unambiguous. The same material could be shaped for a more in-depth magazine, perhaps aimed at shareholders or investors: "Tackling the competition head-on: our new initiative opens up lucrative new markets." This is more intriguing and thought-provoking, and draws in the reader to the body of the article.

As the writer you have to invest more time and energy in magazine articles and features than you would for a newsletter, and so does the designer. A newsletter is usually set to a fixed **house style**, but a magazine will include a lot more original design. When there's enough freedom to develop design concepts and enough budget for quality imagery (photography and illustration are not cheap) a magazine is one of the most exciting environments for a graphic designer, and it is up to you to help the designer to achieve his or her best work by working with the words as the design ideas are being developed.

The tone of voice of the magazine is a major part of its style and impact. This will be the voice of the client organization, but it must be relevant to the audience. Throughout a company magazine the copy has to speak in a consistent and appropriate tone of voice, which can be easier said than done. Work closely with the client or the magazine's editor to determine content, and with the designer to ensure that the words and imagery complement one another and that the designer understands the messages you've written and helps to highlight these.

Keep the magazine reader to the forefront of your mind. If it's a loyalty magazine mailed out three times a year to a bank's teenage savings account holders, it should be written with a teenage style, not a corporate bank style (taking care to avoid anything that might compromise the bank's brand). The audience must be able to identify with the messages and feel that they relate to their lifestyle, so be careful to select the content carefully and be sure to shape it with them in mind.

A good way to maintain consistency is to create a word bank and copy style sheet (see page 18) for reference. Create and share these with those leading the project and signing it off, as this consultation process will enable you to explain your approach and incorporate their direction and guidance from the start (which is far better than doing it at the end).

Plan the main editorial content for your magazine six to twelve months in advance. This will help if it is intended that advertising space (which suppliers are often keen to buy) is to be made available within the magazine, as the advertiser will want to appear alongside relevant articles. There will be a number of articles, including feature articles, which you can compile well before the issue deadline, leaving yourself free to focus on the last-minute hot news just as the publication is being put to bed.

"At a magazine, everything you do is edited by a bunch of people, by committee, and a lot of them are, were, or think of themselves as writers. Part of that is because magazines worry about their voice."

Chuck Klosterman

Fairmont Hotels' customer magazine uses relaxed and sophisticated copy to present details of the company's move into sustainable tourism. The importance of conserving local traditions and heritage is conveyed by maintaining an enthusiastic and inclusive tone of voice.

AN AFRICAN LEGACY

At four properties in Africa, Fairmont shows its guests the new way to travel: not just with a light footprint or a green conscience, but by joining local communities to make life better in some of the world's most unique and beautiful places.
BY STEPHEN JERMANOK

> At four properties in Africa, Fairmont shows its guests the new way to travel: not just with a light footprint or a green conscience, but by joining local communities to make life better

> *"Thanks to Fairmont bringing guests to our village, we have become part of the equation."*

Thanks to Fairmont bringing guests to our village, we have become part of the equation.

Interview: Conan Kisor, American Medical Association

Conan is the editor of a number of print and electronic publications for the American Medical Association (AMA), the largest organization for physicians in the United States.

I am 35, and the son of a newspaper editor and book critic for the *Chicago Sun-Times*. My mother was a children's book critic, so there were lots of opinions at home! I did a four-year BA in English at Kenyon College in Ohio, and my first job was working for a public relations firm. I called them 50 times and they eventually let me become an intern with them. In my last year at college I started writing spots for the college newspaper, even though my mother made me promise never to work in the newspaper business— the competitiveness, long hours, and hard living takes its toll.

I stayed in PR for a year and then I got a job as a news reporter for the City News Bureau of Chicago, a wire service that covered crime, government, and courts. I learnt the who, what, where, how, and why of journalism and developed my interviewing skills—it's very difficult to try to get the person on the other end of the phone to say something quotable.

My "client" isn't really a client, it's the entire American Medical Association, my employer, and I focus on what we put in the magazine to convince the readership to keep their membership in the AMA, come to our meetings, and collaborate with us.

My publications are intended to demonstrate the many ways the AMA is working on behalf of doctors. The goal is retaining and growing our membership of 250,000 physicians and students, which is a broad audience. Our readers include everyone from 23-year-old students to 65-year-old physicians.

The doctors in our audience could be working in accident and emergency in a hospital or be in private practice in an office on their own, each having very different experiences within the medical profession. We focus on the broad, national issues that affect every member of the profession. Our tone of voice aims to be one that doctors trust. We try to include subject matter for everyone, but recognize that not every article will appeal to every reader.

We produce a number of publications. *AMA Voice* is a bimonthly newsletter mailed to every member. It has eight pages and plenty of photographs. I am the editor and I have two writers on my staff; together we produce a handful of publications. The writers draft the content. I write one or two articles and edit the rest and I also write some of the issue-based advertising. We're part of a large, integrated in-house marketing agency of about 20 people— we handled over 13,000 creative projects last year from advertising and posters to magazines and newsletters.

We work with a design manager and five designers, and we share the process of working out the initial layouts. We follow a loose template and use consistent graphic elements in the publications, and we all use a booklet of house fonts and colors.

We plan the editorial and approve the content, which gives us a great deal of freedom. We highlight frontline medical doctors and students in a real-world approach—it's not "top-down" and we include lots of profiles of our members. The issues don't change much year to year, but the solutions and tactics we use do change. We are always asking ourselves "How can we demonstrate concisely that AMA is doing something to make the problem better?"

The big features, usually covering two pages, are planned a couple of months in advance. We are given the design input at the front end, and then plan a photographic style to suit the article's content and angle. For example, the government's payments to doctors under Medicare (for the over-65s) is a big problem. The government plans cuts in the payments to doctors by 10 percent each year, which makes it hard for older patients to find a doctor who can afford to take care of them. We will find those whose practices have to

AMA Voice
Helping doctors help patients — September 2007

Medicine's voice strong on care for kids, seniors

Aggressive and sustained advocacy by the AMA and its members advanced two priority issues when both the U.S. House and Senate passed separate legislation to reauthorize the successful State Children's Health Insurance Program (SCHIP), which covers millions of children in low-income families.

The House approved a bill that would both reauthorize SCHIP and replace two years of scheduled cuts in Medicare physician payments—totaling 15 percent—with two years of positive updates.

The increased spending would be paid for by a federal tobacco tax increase and the elimination of overpayments to insurance companies that offer private Medicare plans. The Senate passed a bill that reauthorizes SCHIP but does not address the Medicare physician payment cuts.

Payments are slated to fall 40 percent over the next nine years.

A joint TV campaign with AARP, as well as phone calls and notes to Congress from AMA members had an undeniable impact on the passage of these bills—but the battle is far from over. Both chambers of Congress must come to an agreement on provisions in the final legislation. That's why the AMA is aggressively lobbying lawmakers to and finalize a bill to both stop the Medicare payment cuts and reauthorize SCHIP. The campaign includes grassroots lobbying, e-mails, letters, phone calls, direct mail brochures, as well as TV, print and Internet ads to get medicine's message across. With current SCHIP funding set to expire Sept. 30, the clock is ticking.

Time is also running out to avert the reductions in Medicare physician payments slated to begin with a 10 percent cut in 2008.

AMA member Julia Anne Bowlin, MD, a family physician in Versailles, Ohio, a rural community about 90 miles north of Cincinnati, said a 10 percent cut would force her to stop seeing any new Medicare patients. "Loving the patients," she said, would be her sole motivation for continuing to care for her current Medicare enrollees if the cuts take effect. As with many medical practices, even the first year of cuts would strain Dr. Bowlin's practice's financial resources.

Meanwhile, AMA member Michael Deren, MD, described the prospect of seeing his Medicare payments slashed by 10 percent as devastating. A thoracic and general surgeon in New London, Conn., a rural community about 45 miles south of Hartford, Dr. Deren said such a steep cut could force him to close his practice. "People say, 'Just cut down on patients,' but that'll be pretty hard to do," Dr. Deren said. "If someone comes in with lung cancer, you have to take care of them."

Urgent matters

Complete our survey

All AMA members are strongly encouraged to complete a brief online **AMA Member Connect® Survey** about the issue of the uninsured and how their experience with uninsured patients affects their practice. The results will be used to strengthen the voice of AMA members in influencing national and local policy initiatives to enable more people to secure health coverage. Make your voice heard today.

>> www.ama-assn.org/go/survey

Surgeon Michael Deren, MD, said losing Medicare physician payment cuts threaten his practice.

> "Patients who show up to their doctor's office without a referral may need to be rescheduled."

Feature story

Focused on change

Ophthalmologist Ravi D. Goel, MD, sees that keeping cuts in Medicare payments will prevent him and many colleagues from investing in new equipment and technology.

Any way you frame it, the law governing the way Medicare pays doctors is unsustainable. Will Congress have the vision to fix it?

AMA member Ravi D. Goel, MD, is one of many physicians who believes Medicare needs to undergo some serious changes for the good of America's patients, such as replacing the flawed sustainable growth rate formula with a system that reflects the economic realities of practicing medicine.

An AMA-led campaign helped avert an across-the-board 5 percent cut in 2007 Medicare physician payments, and the AMA is again leading an effort to stop a deep 10 percent cut in payments for 2008, demonstrating to lawmakers the disastrous effect such a cut would have on seniors. Meantime, the privately administered Medicare Advantage plans are exacerbating matters by giving patients more hoops to jump through and costing the government more than the traditional Medicare plan.

"The biggest stumbling block is patients' access to care," Dr. Goel said. "Medicare patients are used to being seen without a referral, and many Medicare Advantage plans require referrals. So patients need to plan ahead, obtain referrals and verify that both their primary physician and specialist are participants in their Medicare Advantage plans. Patients who show up to their doctor's office without a referral may need to be rescheduled."

Results of a recent AMA Member Connect® Survey on Medicare Advantage plans, administered earlier this year, revealed similar views. The survey found that more than 80 percent of patients have had difficulty understanding how their Medicare Advantage managed care plan or Medicare private fee-for-service plan works. While inconveniencing and confusing patients, Medicare Advantage plans are paid on average 12 percent more than traditional fee-for-service providers—to the tune of $65 billion over five years and $160 billion over a decade. With physicians facing cuts in payments of about 40 percent by 2015, Dr. Goel wonders why Medicare uses such an unseen playing field to pay for seniors' care. "I'm not sure exactly what the government is getting for its money," Dr. Goel said.

He's not alone. As part of a separate AMA Member Connect Survey released in June, fully 80 percent of physicians said Medicare should stop subsidizing Medicare Advantage plans. That falls in line with a recommendation by the Medicare Payment Advisory Commission, which has called for Medicare to pay the same amount regardless of which Medicare option a patient chooses.

The survey also found that 60 percent of new Medicare patients they treat if payments are cut by 10 percent in 2008. Worse, if cuts totaling 40 percent are instituted over the next nine years, 77 percent of physician respondents would limit the number of new Medicare patients they treat. AMA member Nathan Laufer, MD, a Phoenix-based cardiologist, worries that such steep cuts will have a devastating effect on the physician population in states with a high number of medically underserved communities. A serious access-to-care problem for seniors wouldn't be far behind.

"When you start cutting reimbursement so practitioners have difficulty running offices, then you're driving the physicians that are here either to other parts of the country or to other lines of work," Dr. Laufer said.

The survey also found that 72 percent of physicians would defer the purchase of new medical equipment if the 10 percent cut takes effect. For Dr. Goel, those updates are essential to his practice and maintaining a high level of service for his patients.

"If these cuts go forward, and in the future we have more, it will be more difficult to invest in these new technologies," Dr. Goel said. "Ophthalmology is a very precise specialty, and we need to be able to make those investments."

And at a time when the government and others are asking physicians to measure, track and report data about the quality of the care they provide, 67 percent of doctors said next year's cut will force them to delay the purchase of information technology systems that are critical to participating in quality reporting initiatives.

Of course, technology investments aren't even a possibility for physicians struggling to keep their practices viable. "If Medicare keeps cutting, we'll reach a point where overhead is higher than income," Dr. Laufer, noting that some primary care physicians already have stopped seeing Medicare patients. "I can foresee a time with all these cuts when we not only will be forced not to see Medicare patients, but we will just shut our doors."

> "I can foresee a time with all these cuts when we not only will be forced not to see Medicare patients, but we will just shut our doors."
> —Nathan Laufer, MD

AMA members have spoken

Results of AMA Member Connect Surveys are frequently cited by policymakers in Congress, patient-advocates and the news media.

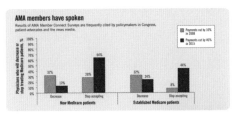

Legend: Payments cut by 10% in 2008 · Payments cut by 40% in 2015

	New Medicare patients		Established Medicare patients	
	Decrease	Stop accepting	Decrease	Stop accepting
Payments cut by 10% in 2008	32%	13%	32%	8%
Payments cut by 40% in 2015	64%	28%	24%	44%

AMA ads put a face on the issue

Making the case for change

This summer, the AMA is dialing up the pressure on federal lawmakers to stop the 10 percent cut in 2008 Medicare physician payments and even the playing field between the traditional Medicare program and Medicare Advantage plans. The AMA has provided testimony to several congressional committees on these issues.

Meanwhile, the AMA National House Call campaign is making stops across the country this summer to focus public attention on this issue, most recently in Arkansas and Utah. The AMA also has launched an ad campaign in key areas to highlight the urgency of stopping payment cuts to doctors.

The AMA encourages individual members to help by making their voices heard among their lawmakers. "The AMA is the strongest voice we have if it is used properly," said Nathan Laufer, MD. "Physicians have tremendous political clout if they choose to use it, and I'm in favor of a very strong united front and sending a message loud and clear to Congress."

The AMA Physician-Grassroots Network can help.

>> www.ama-assn.org/go/grassroots
>> (800) 833-6354

"The issues don't change much year to year, but the solutions and tactics we use do change."

limit the number of Medicare patients they can accept, and report on how the AMA is working with lawmakers to help them. We use graphic headlines and imagery. For example, we'll feature an ophthalmologist standing in front of an eye chart supported by a headline that uses "focus" as its theme.

We have a staff photographer who travels around for us, and we hire local photographers too. We art direct them remotely by giving them a creative brief and the article to read, so that they can bring the story to life. Sometimes we fly a designer out to art direct the shoot in person too. The doctors are usually helpful, finding 15 minutes in their diary for us. We do a lot of phone interviews with doctors,.but lots of the material hits the cutting room floor because we can't publish it or don't have room for it—800 words is our maximum for an article.

Our staff writers are highly informed. Two have been with us for three and four years, and we have a new writer on the team too. We have to be conversant in the subject matter and also in the correct tone of voice—getting the tone right is 80 percent of the battle. I aim to complete an interview in about 15 minutes, prepare a short article, and make sure that the headlines say a lot. We know our audience is intelligent but very busy, so the editorial has to be "idiot-proof" so that our readers will "get it" in a couple of seconds as they flick through the pages. We sacrifice cleverness for simplicity. We're translating for a general audience, so it can be strange to interview doctors who are leading experts in their field and then simplify their words.

After I hang up the phone I have to type up the interview straight away, as I can lose the essence of it, even with the stacks of notes I take. I bang it out as quickly as possible in order to keep it as fresh as possible. We use focus groups to learn the reactions to our work, and I am always astonished by the take some people have

on it. For example, if the words "choice" or "life" appear in a headline, they tend to conjure up images of the debate on abortion in the US.

My advice to other writers is to try to imagine that you're the audience—think about how much time you have to read these sort of articles, and what you will think about each article under these circumstances.

Interview: Sarah McCartney, *Lush Times*
*This quarterly newsletter is the way Lush Cosmetics
talks to customers worldwide. It features 40,000 words
of insights and inspiration into the unique products
the company creates. For over ten years Sarah has been
its editor, looking after the words, as well as many other
aspects of this significant newspaper-catalog.*

Writing is like football: everyone can do it but you wouldn't pay everyone to join your team. I've been working with Lush for 11 years, and as I've always had an interest in writing I jumped at the chance to write copy for them. My background is in science; after studying I was a media planner for an ad agency. I have a good memory, which helped me get good grades, but always had a range of interests: I studied classical clarinet but also played saxophone in a big band. I draw on my experiences when I write; it seems to me most people don't fully observe what's around them.

I write copy for products and promotions, but the bulk of my work is the newsletter. We produce *Lush Times* quarterly for a one million-strong audience in the UK, US, Canada, Australia, and beyond. We don't advertise, so *Lush Times* is our main piece of direct communication with customers. It's informative and interesting, and provides a memory-jog about our products that helps with retail sales.

I don't get a written brief; it is much more of an organic process. I speak to the directors about how we should tackle the content for each issue and my only rule is to include all current products within the pages. I include a lot of content written by customers, as we get so many great letters and contributions from all over the world. A lot of readers really enjoy the newsletter and reply to articles or suggest new products. It recently got so packed that we split it into two publications: *Lush Times* presents our viewpoint, and *Scent* features customers' viewpoints, reviews, photos, and ideas.

I keep a notebook with me at all times and am always scribbling ideas about our products that I can incorporate into the newsletter. Things said in meetings provide good quotes and lots of material I can develop and build on. We promote the concept of "long candlelit baths" but are also committed to innovation and creativity; I always enjoy finding new and stimulating ways to talk about new products. I pick up ideas all over the place and use them in my work. Nothing is cheating—except stealing other people's words.

There are days when you don't want to write, but have to. You can't just sit down and write good copy all day long. I surround myself with books, and make myself choose one of these, open it up, and find a word at random, which I then force myself to include in a sentence—it helps me to get into the flow of writing again. I like to go for a walk too; if the writing is proving really difficult I go to a park and sit on the swings. Swinging with my head back is really helpful!

We have a two-month lead time to create between 40–60,000 words, which doesn't give us much breathing space. I tend to work in chunks, doing all soap or deodorant products separately. With soap products I tend to say little—there are only so many ways to discuss their benefits—and with others, such as moisturizers, I include lots of detail, facts, figures, supporting information. It's all to do with the way customers use products.

I work with in-house and freelance designers; the whole creative team is busy all the time. We don't have a fixed house style as we like to create a fresh, unique version every time. There is always a bit of give-and-take between design and copy, but we're working to create the best effect on the page.

If we had to get all of the copy signed off we'd never get it to print, so I'm trusted to sign off my own copy. We share proofreading and give a collective sigh of relief when we get to the end, only to realize it's time to start the next one!

I enjoy these challenges a lot, but writing is a difficult business. I'm not a carrot or stick person, so don't try and bribe or push me into doing my best. I thrive when I'm given recognition for work I do, whether it's sheer volume and organization, or the creativity I put into the finished text. I'm compiling a collection of articles we've published to create an archive for the business, and I've discovered that over the last 11 years at Lush I've written something like 1.6 million words!

"I include a lot of content that has been written by our customers in the newsletter."

A Ballistic in your morning bath makes the day special. If you were in a hurry and only had time for a shower, then looking forward to your evening Ballistic is possibly even more of an occasion! (It depends on whether you prefer your gratification to be instant or planned.)

Youki-Hi—named after one of the world's most beautiful women; she bathed daily in jasmine scented water to keep her lovely skin smelling delicious and so will you when you try it. She also divorced her princely husband to marry his dad, the king. That we don't recommend.

GO GREEN

NEW

Greenwash
**Don't believe the greenwash.
Get clean with palm-free soap.**
Lush is gradually working towards replacing palm oil with different kinds of soap. Our first step is Greenwash, an environmentally helpful soap scented with woody oakmoss and seasonally suitable frankincense. One of its green credentials is that it's made with no palm oil at all. We make each big soap in the shape of a Christmas Tree; use it as a yuletide decoration, then cut it into bits on Twelfth Night, give it to all your friends and family and you'll have a packaging-free, waste-free, beautifully scented all-in-one decoration-plus-gift!
2731 100g £2.50
Ingredients: Water (Aqua), Propylene Glycol, Sodium Palmkernelate, Sodium Cocoate, Perfume, Sodium Stearate, Sodium Lauryl Sulfate, Stipa Paou (Stearine acid), Gommosa Absolute (Evernia furfuracea), Frankincense Oil (Boswellia carterii), *Cuminal, *Geraniol, *Sodium Chloride, EDTA, Tetrasodium Editronate, *Limonene, Gardenia Extract (Gardenia jasminoides), Chlorophyllin. Green Glitter (Polyethylene terephthalate).

Squeaky Green
**Our greenest shampoo bar ever!
Use it and save 3 green bottles.**
Squeaky Green is the first aromatherapy Shampoo Bar made with our new noodles, to get your hair squeaky clean in the greenest way possible. It smells of our gorgeous Go Green scent, with rose and vanilla balancing out all the scalp-purifying herbs: fresh rosemary, nettle and peppermint, powdered tea tree and chamomile essential oil. Peppermint stimulates your scalp; tea tree and rosemary help you to avoid dandruff (and help to get rid of it if you've got some). It's amazingly refreshing and reviving for your whole head, and not half bad for the environment.
2736 55g £3.95
Ingredients: Sodium Coco-Sulfate, Perfume, Rosemary (Rosmarinus officinalis), Nettle (Urtica dioica), Tea Tree Powder (Melaleuca alternifolia), Peppermint (Mentha piperita), Rose Absolute (Rosa centifolia), Chamomile Blue Oil (Matricaria chamomilla), Vanilla Absolute (Vanilla planifolia), *Coumarin, *Geraniol, *Benzyl Benzoate, *Limonene, Linalool. Hydroxycitronellal, Chlorophyllin.

The Greeench
Naturally effective herbs and absorbent powders to banish the gremlins from your armpits (and other smelly parts).
The Greench is the best deodorant Lush has ever made. This one is in powder form but not just any old powder: powdered rosemary, sage, clubmoss and tea tree leaves to deodorise, refresh and soothe your skin, mixed with absorbent bicarb and microfine magnesium trisilicate. It's got no preservatives, no aluminium salts and nothing else that could possibly cause offence. The herbs biff the pong-causing bacteria into submission to keep your armpits as fresh as a daisy in springtime.
2695 100g £4.95
Ingredients: Talc, Sodium Bicarbonate, Magnesium Trisilicate, Lycopodium Powder, Perfume, Thyme Oil (Thymus vulgaris), Tea Tree Oil (Melaleuca alternifolia), Bonzoin Resinoid (Styrax benzoin), Powdered Sage (Salvia icterina), Powdered Tea Tree (Melaleuca alternifolia), Powdered Rosemary (Rosmarinus officinalis), *Limonene, *Linalool, Chlorophyllin.

It's A Wrap!
Take your Lush naked products away with you in our reusable and washable, fair trade cotton wrap designed and made [...] them up [...] safe.

Go Green
Refreshingly green fragrance for eco-warriors, enviro-mentals and complete cycle paths.
Our Go Green fragrance is part of Lush's decision to make a bit of noise about our greenness. Greenness is the opposite of greediness. It's all about considering what's best for the rest of the planet, not just ourselves. But it doesn't have to be sackcloth, ashes and misery. Absolutely not! Sustainability is about appreciating the wonderful things we have and having a lot of fun while we're at it.
Go Green is inspired by environmental activist, Rebecca Lush (honest, that really is her name) who now works for Transport 2000, heading up Road Block. She cycles and takes the train, recycles with a passion and buys fair trade, organic food. (She also pied Jeremy Clarkson for his glorification of the car.)
Mark created Go Green in its two forms for Rebecca and other people who cycle and take public transport to work. Spray on the refillable* spritzer (just stick it under your t-shirt and squeeze) or dab on the solid perfume which comes in a 100% recycled, post consumer waste tin.
It's a refreshing blend of grapefruit, bergamot and neroli, with calming smoky vetivert. Herby scents of fennel, thyme and cedar wood make you smell like you just walked out of a forest, carrying a basket of citrus fruits, rather than you just got off a squashed train or a bicycle.
*Coming soon.

Fragrance Spritzer
2727 180g £9.95
Ingredients: DPF Alcohol, Perfume, Grapefruit Oil (Citrus grandis), Bergamot Oil (Citrus bergamia), Tarragon Oil (Artemisia dracunculus), Thyme Oil (Thymus vulgaris), Vetivert Leaf Absolute (Vetis riberia), *Galimosa Absolute (Evernia prunastri), Neroli Oil (Citrus amara), Sambacwood Oil (Santalum album), Cedar Leaf Oil (Thuja occidentalis), Fennel Oil (Foeniculum vulgare), *Benzyl Salicylate, *Citral, *Eugenol, *Geraniol, *Benzyl Benzoate, *Citronellol, *Farnesol, *Isoeugenol, *Linalool. Hydroxycitronellal.

Solid Perfume
2694 10g £4.95
Ingredients: Jojoba Wax, Perfume, Cocoa Butter, Grapefruit Oil (Citrus grandis), Camellia Otto (Camellia sinensis), Bergamot Oil (Citrus bergamia), Limonene, Grapefruit Oil (Citrus grandis), Vetivert Oil (Vetiveria zizanoides), Bergamot Oil (Citrus bergamia), Jojoba Oil (Simmondsia chinensis), Tarragon Oil (Artemisia dracunculus), Thyme Oil (Thymus vulgaris), Vetivert Leaf Absolute (Vetis riberia), *Galimosa Absolute (Evernia prunastri), Neroli Oil (Citrus amara), Sambacwood Oil (Santalum album), Cedar Leaf Oil (Thuja occidentalis), Fennel Oil (Foeniculum vulgare), *Benzyl Salicylate, *Citral, *Eugenol, *Geraniol, *Benzyl Benzoate, *Citronellol, *Farnesol, *Linalool.

Vegan

POST ORDERS: LUSH TIMES, UNIT 3, 10 WILLIS WAY, FLEETS INDUSTRIAL ESTATE, POOLE, DORSET, BH15 3SS.

2727 LUSH GO GREEN Perfume
Reviving scent for eco-warriors, enviro-mentals and complete cycle-paths. With organic butters and essential oils.
34 HIGH ST, POOLE, DORSET, BH15 1AB
MADE IN ENGLAND, WWW.LUSH.CO

[...] in a tub.
[...] one of the most amazing [...] to pack into a bath bomb. [...] in a tub, what with its red [...] refreshing, green Ballistic mix. [...] and harvested, it gets a coat [...] gives it an interestingly sweet [...] skin feel better too. With the [...] cypress, it's like bathing in the [...] the trees on the shoreline.
[...], Hawaiian Sea Salt (Sodium chloride), [...]press Oil (Cupressus sempervirens), [...]um album), Seaweed Absolute (Fucus [...]ardenia Extract (Gardenia jasminoides).

21

Our Go Green fragrance is part of Lush's decision to make a bit of a noise about our greenness. Greenness is the opposite of greediness. It's all about considering what's best for the rest of the planet, not just ourselves. But it doesn't have to be sackcloth, ashes, and misery. Absolutely not! Sustainability is about appreciating the wonderful things we have and having a lot of fun while we're at it.

Generating quality editorial content

The fundamental role of a regular publication is to build a relationship with an audience, establishing rapport, trust, dialogue, interaction, and, in extreme cases, friendship. Your editorial content has to relate to the audience, and a good way to achieve this is to find out what they are like by creating two-way communication: invite them to write in, take part in competitions, fill in questionnaires, or comment on your website.

The information you glean will give you a strong sense of how to pitch the messages, and the precise tone of voice to use, but you must also present the client's personality clearly and openly. Don't simply reflect your audience; be confident and let the client have a stance, an opinion, a viewpoint. This will promote mutual understanding, and let the relationship develop.

The fundamental difference between writing for magazines or newsletters and other forms of copywriting is the requirement that you source your raw material. With most copywriting projects the bulk of your raw material—facts, figures, detail—is supplied by the client company, either directly or through the immediate briefing process. It's up to you to decide how best to use it.

Journalists know all about researching the story, and in many ways writing for a magazine or newsletter is more of a journalistic than a copywriting challenge. A good journalist will focus on preparing the story so that it provides as much detail and background as possible, and will follow a format that presents the material objectively and unambiguously. Always lead with the most important, interesting, or relevant information, using sentences no longer than about 20 words and paragraphs with no more than three or four sentences.

"If you don't get noticed, you don't have anything. You just have to be noticed, but the art is in getting noticed naturally, without screaming or without tricks."
Leo Burnett

When you are writing copy for a company magazine or newsletter, whether for the people who work for the organization or for its external customers, you will be combining your copywriting skills (creative, targeted, commercial writing) and your journalistic ability (balanced, researched, informative writing). Each of your articles or news items has to be accurate, provide detail, and hold the reader's interest, but this is still copywriting and your finished copy has to reflect the organization's tone of voice and overall strategic objectives.

As with all copywriting, your key principles must apply: identify and understand your target audience, maintain a consistent tone of voice that is relevant to your audience, and work hard to make sure every item is at least interesting, and compelling wherever possible. Unlike other formats, with a magazine or newsletter you have a range of copy styles to play with, so make the most of these.

Play to the strength of each type of article. These can include an editorial introduction, short news items, commentaries from key figures, interviews, analytical articles, and competitions. You can also feature readers' letters or articles by readers, and don't forget that the audience may be very interested in the advertising you include.

Look at the big picture: will it achieve the client's objectives?

Before launching into writing your articles, stand back and consider the magazine or newsletter as a whole, as a series of regular publications that will provide a collection of information for the readership. Whether you're dealing with a four-page, single-color news sheet or a glossy 48-page corporate magazine you should be thinking "how do we link the publication to the company's overall strategic objectives?" and "how accessible will the key influencers in the company be, and are they supportive of the publication?"

Proving that good copy does not have to be highly creative, so long as it is clear, informative, and accurate, Pearson Education's employee magazines work hard to ensure the audience is always up to speed on all of the essentials in their industry.

Pearson's MasteringPhysics will be the platform of choice for a nationwide physics talent competition sponsored by Pearson Singapore, the Institute of Physics Singapore and National University of Singapore. Targeting top high school students, the competition aims to groom outstanding physics students to participate in the International Physics Olympiad.

What do our higher education student customers really want? How do we know what they are really thinking? And how can we reach them more effectively? The new Pearson Student Advisory Board, and students@ pearson newsletter, are helping answer these questions as we reach out to students to learn more about what matters to them—and their 15 million peers—when it comes to their college education experience.

We're giving customers the help and support they need to stop smoking, lead a healthier lifestyle, and get healthier-looking skin. But this year, the main focus is going to be on weight loss.

Your Local Boots Pharmacy

The new-look stores set to take 2008 by storm. Page 6

Our Forum is a fantastic place for people from all over the business to come together, resolving issues and coming up with the ideas that will help us take the business forward. Here are just a few of the really successful projects that have come about as a result.

The editorial of this company magazine is closely tied to the strategic plans of the business. The articles and features help explain what the initiatives mean to customers and to the business, giving insights to both the head office and retail operations teams.

Planning the editorial as a whole

This can become very complex and before you know it you can become bogged down in all of the variables; the number of editions per year, the correct page counts, the best angle for features, the value of competitions, and the approach to imagery and photography will all have an impact on your budget and will need to be considered both in isolation and as a whole. Ground yourself by remembering one thing: you are writing a publication for a defined audience for a client with a specific objective. Every decision you make has to improve significantly the impact of your messages on the target audience and deliver the client's objectives as effectively as possible. Focus on the written elements of the publication and let the others in the team work out the rest.

Drafting articles and interviewing for copy

News items are relatively straightforward to draft if you have a structure in mind—the real challenge is getting your hands on the raw material, especially if you want a good photograph to go with it. Contact key players within the organization and brief them about the sort of news you're looking for, and how and when you want to receive it. Many professional people are put off by the thought of having to write copy, so reassure them that all you need from them is the raw material, ideally in brief bullet point format. Give them your contact details and a deadline, and interview them in person wherever possible.

Longer articles require a different approach. The designer should have a style sheet of sorts, and a typeface and size defined, and from this you should be able to work out a target word count. Remember, you are not a columnist, you are a copywriter, and no one wants to read your personal views.

Interviewing is the best way to source fresh new material. In many cases an interview has to take place over the phone. After sourcing your contact, begin with an e-mail or introductory phone call to explain who you are, who you are working for, and what you require. You can then book some time for the interview as, even over the phone, it may take up to half an hour. If you do meet face to face, a good approach is to bring a photographer (or even just a camera and lights) so that you can illustrate your article with a good mugshot.

Prepare your questions in advance but be prepared to wing it, and develop the craft of being able to scribble down responses, formulate your next question, and look the interviewee intelligently in the eye, all at the same time. Write up your draft copy as soon as you can after the interview, as you will otherwise forget some of the finer detail.

Include more than one interview in an article to make it more stimulating. If you're talking to the director of part of the business, why not also talk to someone who works in the team? If you shape the article carefully it can provide great insight into the workings of an organization. Obviously, your role is to present the positive aspects and not to expose any weaknesses.

Structure for news articles

The basic approach is to spell out the story concisely
in the headline, **topping and tailing** the piece with
paragraphs showing some personality, and presenting
the facts clearly in the main body copy.

Headline:

Summarize the key message in as few words as possible
(this may be all that is read).

Opening paragraph:

Explain the main story and its key features, accurately
and clearly, and promise what's coming up in the article.

Following paragraphs:

Present the full details in order of priority, giving each
new point a new paragraph.

Last paragraph:

Draw a conclusion, and maybe include an editorial comment
(from the point of view of the client). Lead the reader to
additional sources, if relevant.

Structure for feature articles
Feature articles can often take a more complex
and adventurous approach, as below.

Conceptual headline:
Play with the themes in the article and be as bold as you like—
keep it short and punchy, and be as intriguing as possible.

Qualifying line:
Give meaning to your intriguing conceptual headline—
explain the content of the article in a sentence.

Opening paragaph:
Connect the concept of your headline to the content
you're about to present and promise what's to come.

Main body copy:
Present information from a variety of sources—it must, however, read
as a coherent train of thought.

Subtitles:
Break up your text with subheads and highlighted
quotes to entice skimmers to dive in.

Conclusion:
Highlight your client's message, and communicate the brand values clearly.

Extras:
Translate some of your
information into tables,
charts, or illustrations to
add life to your message.

Picture captions:
Give plenty of life and
personality to these,
as some people read
only the headers and
the captions.

Competitions, letters, and editorial

These peripheral items should be included only if they can be fully justified. Too many company publications have been cluttered with boring news about someone's fiftieth wedding anniversary or shots of a proud angler holding a giant fish caught one weekend. To generate quality material from your readers' letters you must give them a brief and some direction about what you're looking for. Ask them for specific comments about a core subject. Tempt them with a prize for the best letter and develop themes with them that can be carried through over different editions.

The editorial is a form of welcome, and is usually best placed on the opening pages. A familiar face is helpful, so a senior manager would be suitable. Keep it real, and don't create a false editor—it could catch you out. It's perfectly acceptable for you to appear as the editor yourself, if necessary, with your photograph and signature. In any event, it is more than likely you will draft the editorial column for the editor.

Competitions are also popular with readers, and these give them a reason to check out your next issue too. Whatever you do, keep the rules very simple, make it challenging, and always, without fail, include legal disclaimers explaining how the result is subject to availability of prizes and liable to change at your discretion. Estimate the response and the amount of handling this will take. A competition that is attractive to a reasonable-sized audience can create sacks and sacks of mail for someone to manage.

Internal communications are marketing communications

Internal communications have often been the poor relative of marketing communications, with "poor" being the operative word. However, with increasing global competition, new ways of working with suppliers and customers, new technologies, and changing marketplaces, companies are undergoing consistent change more than ever before. Keeping employees properly informed and briefed is becoming increasingly vital, and this can be achieved using the tools developed for marketing communications.

The audience for internal communications is very different to the external audience. To a certain extent it's a captive audience that has a vested interest in what you have to say, but you can't assume they are going to pay attention or buy into your message just because they work for the company. They may be more critical than customers (if they know the cold reality of life within the organization), but they are more likely to respond in a positive manner if the message is constructive and clear.

Traditionally the voice used for internal communications has been patronizing or overly formal. Messages from the top speak down to the staff on the ground, often use **jargon** or fail to explain the full context, and generally leave the reader cold.

You can overcome this by creating a fresh and upbeat tone of voice and using targeted copywriting to make the messages relevant, interesting, and compelling. Create a communications strategy and calendar to ensure all of the key points are covered and that each new piece builds on the previous one. There can be a lot of value in creating a word bank and company dictionary. Document whether a company's retail network consists of "branches," "stores," or "shops," and whether it referes to its people as "employees," "staff," "our people," or even "you." Define jargon that needs to be explained, such as "RDC" and "cascade communication session" (see page 20).

When you're writing communications to staff, remember that you're talking to a diverse audience, from senior directors to junior office workers, from people

Checklist: Editorial content for newsletters and magazines

☐ Have you created a formula for the page plan, showing where news, reviews, articles, features, and other regular items appear?

☐ Do you have a plan for generating the material you will need for your large pieces (booking interviews, allowing time for research, etc.)?

☐ Do you have a process for gathering the news and smaller items, such as product reviews or guides?

☐ Have you created, with the designer, style sheets for news, articles, and features, with word-count guidelines for you to follow?

☐ Do you have a grasp of the tone of voice for the publication, and the boundaries that your copy can't cross?

☐ Have you identified how the newsletter can give additional exposure to messages you are communicating in other media, such as online?

☐ Have you planned to get a response from readers? For example, are you offering a subscription or competition entry?

☐ Does your newsletter have an attention-grabbing name that will appeal to a wide section of readers?

☐ Do you know what advertising content will be featured?

☐ Will the newsletter be on display at a checkout, or customer service point?

☐ Have you started keeping a folder where you can collect ideas for future editions of the newsletter or magazine?

out in the field to those in head office. Finding a voice that suits everyone is your challenge. A key technique is to link your content to the overall company strategy. If the board have announced a new initiative then feature this in your communications and bring it to life by finding out what the implications might be for people in the business—as an overall group, as departments, and individually. Interview some store staff and some head office managers and pool the information to give everyone an insight into each other's situations.

Your content has to be open, honest, and accurate. There is simply no point telling a demotivated workforce that there is a new initiative to save money by cutting back on their perks and making them work in a different way. If you're talking to a tough crowd, make sure you show understanding and empathy. Find respected people in different areas of the organization who support the project, then communicate through them.

Stakeholder mapping can help you decide how to communicate effectively. Some of your stakeholders will be low interest, low influence—for example, the project delivery team. They're not decision makers, but they need to know what's going on. Think about the frequency of updates and how much detail you need to go into. In the initial "boardroom" stages they might just need monthly summary bulletins, but later on the updates might become detailed weekly or daily task lists.

In other cases you might be writing to someone who has high stakes in the project, such as an investor, who has a high level of interest and lots of influence. You need to turn these people into advocates for the company, gaining their support, and encouraging them to use their influence positively. If you need to sway their opinion your copywriting will need to work harder. You might want to create personal letters to be sent from the company directors, or perhaps provide content for face-to-face meetings.

Exercise: developing article-writing skills

Choose a magazine that you like, ideally one that is focused on a specialist subject in which you have an interest (football, music, travel).

Work out the audience profile by studying how the magazine is angled at the readership.

Prepare news
Make up a piece of news and draft it in three paragraphs, with a compelling headline and strong opening paragraph.

Draft an article
Take a topic that you know something about (or make one up) and draft a 400-word article for the magazine, making sure you relate to the audience.

Write a feature
Choose a topic relevant to the magazine and conduct some research into it on the Internet. Collate your notes, create a structure for them, and write the article as a 1000-word feature, exploring the pros and cons and drawing a clear conclusion.

Round-up

Newsletter and magazine articles have to be informative, stimulating, and interesting.

Researching the content for news items, reviews, interviews, and articles will be a key part of your role.

A magazine is a themed collection of interesting material, and a newsletter is an update on what's going on.

The Internet and e-mail are very cost-efficient and effective methods of communication.

The process of creating the publication and its articles is the same for print or website.

Try to work closely with the graphic designers to create a page plan.

Create your schedule and the accompanying editorial calendar, based on the time available and the amount of copy required.

It can take a surprising amount of time to gather information, conduct interviews, process and collate the raw material, and draft copy.

Every element of a magazine carries greater importance than the equivalent in a newsletter.

The audience must be able to identify with the messages and feel that they relate to their lifestyle.

Before launching into writing your articles, stand back and consider the magazine or newsletter as a whole.

Case Study: *Land Rover Onelife*

Few brands are as well traveled and adventurous as Land Rover, and Land Rover Onelife *is, in its own words, a truly global project with a worldly view, regularly heading to the ends of the earth in search of a good story. It uses beautiful imagery and combines high-profile contributors with stories "you won't find in any other automotive customer magazine." Deputy editor Christa Larwood found the time to tell us how they keep this thing on the road.*

The Objective:
communicating Land Rover's brand values

Land Rover Onelife is a biannual 68-page magazine that goes to owners of Land Rovers and Range Rovers bought in the last three years (they can opt out of receiving it); it's seen as a benefit of owning a Land Rover. The client's brief is that the magazine must reflect the adventurous, gutsy yet premium heart of the brand.

We translate the magazine into eight languages and distribute it to over 60 countries. It's a full-time job; we don't get any downtime. For each country we include a combination of global content and some pages with local news and information, which we source through local agencies. We also prepare pages here to appear in foreign-language editions.

The audience for *Onelife* is existing customers, so our remit is to build the brand, not sell directly. We create editorial using a lifestyle approach based on the brand values. Our tone is "the Freelander 2 enables us to go to an amazing place, exemplifying the Land Rover spirit," not "we drove the Freelander 2 from A to B." The characteristics of the brand are based on six "pillars" we all innately understand: authentic, adventurous, worldly, gutsy, premium, and sustainable. These are fantastic characteristics to editorialize, and all the values lend themselves to interesting content. As Land Rover is all about adventure and travel, it's easy to do a good job.

We have space for four advertisements and include products such as Bang & Olufsen, which reflect our magazine and associate well with the Land Rover brand.

The Approach:
taking the editorial to extremes

The editorial team challenges itself to produce the most adventurous, unique stories possible. *Onelife* has explored Northern Canada's Barren Lands on a road made of ice, journeyed to the blistering heat of the Libyan Sahara to catch a total solar eclipse, and dealt with Bolivian revolutionaries setting off pipe bombs in the middle of a shoot.

In the last few years, editor Zac Assemakis has pushed the magazine further than ever, particularly in its structure and content. A good example is the editorial treatment of the Freelander 2. Instead of communicating this new product in a conventional way, Zac decided to represent different features of the vehicle through a series of different stories, so the car's interior was highlighted with a travel story "on the inside" of a hotel converted from a prison in Oxfordshire; the car's styling was showcased with an exciting illustrated car chase created by a renowned US graphic artist.

We sometimes throw out all of the sections and dedicate the magazine to a theme: for example, we did a Paradise issue and a Carbon Neutral issue. As we publish just twice a year there isn't much time for the customer to build a relationship with the magazine and elements within it, so we can be flexible and do it slightly differently each time.

The majority of the team is in-house and we have a number of external contributors to each issue. This adds variety and allows us to feature specialists and authorities—for example, we wanted to send someone to the edge of space and used Andrew Smith, who'd written a book on people who have walked on the moon. For our Paradise issue we sent Kevin Rushby, who has written a book about paradise, on a search for Utopia in the US.

The client gives us a lot of freedom; we're very lucky. They appreciate good editorial and we tend to have only a few corrections. There's a more rigorous sign-off when we're involving Land Rover itself, but even this is usually mild. The client is sophisticated, not banging on about putting cars in everywhere!

The Result:
the magazine is helping to lead the brand communications

We want people to keep the magazine, and research shows we have a good retention, as readers keep it for a month or more and show it to others too. We measure our effectiveness with reader surveys; it is claimed that 6 percent of Land Rover customers bought or upgraded their Land Rover as a result of reading *Onelife*, a huge statistic for a customer magazine, showing what an effective medium it is.

The Association of Publishing Agencies has all sorts of statistics about customer magazines, and has awarded *Onelife* its "customer magazine of the year" title. Surveys show it's considered a compelling read, as indicated by 75 percent of respondents, and showcasing the Freelander 2 was very effective: 23 percent of respondents requested a test drive as a direct result of reading the magazine. Overall, 52 percent of respondents took some action, compared to a 38 percent automotive average.

Land Rover is a storytelling brand, and the *Onelife* team "gets" the brand, probably because we've spent such a long time working with it. Land Rover is moving away from traditional views, and *Onelife* is seen as representing this—the magazine is doing absolutely what it should be.

This is the surface of the world's coolest road. It's 350 miles long, hewn from ice that's 42 inches thick, and is a lifeline for Canada's Barren Lands. The truckers who drive it warn of savage blizzards, blinding white-outs, and temperatures of 55°C below. They tell us axles snap like twigs, and bare hands freeze to metal when they touch it. They also tell us not to go there…

25 WAYS TO MAKE GOOD THE ADVENTURE

Question: what do Scotland's very own Jurassic Park, a biodegradable golf ball and a heavily tranquillised elephant all have in common?

Answer: they each represent different ways to enjoy the adventure, while doing your bit for the environment, too. Who says it's not easy being green?

1 HANG OUT IN BORNEO'S RAINFOREST CANOPY
Rock yourself to sleep in a hammock hanging 300 feet up in the canopy of the forest's tropical rainforest – and help protect the forest's orangutans, birds and flora while you're at it. The Rainforest Canopy Study Tour in Danum Valley Conservation Area provides training in canopy climbing from expert guides. Once up there, what you experience is recorded to support the Global Canopy Programme – a network of research, education and conservation projects aimed at preserving those vital biospheres. www.canopyaccess.co.uk

2 STAY SUSTAINABLE IN THE SUN
A very easy step towards making your adventures impact-free is to use an ecologically sensitive suncream. Traditional suncreams can leave harmful chemicals in the sea and cause long-term damage to coral and marine ecosystems. Instead, try something like Green People's Intensive Sun Cream, which contains no petrochemicals or artificial perfumes – and it's made from organic plant extracts, so on top of its eco-benefits, it's also better for your skin. www.naturalcollection.com

3 HEAD DOWNTOWN FOR THE GOOD LIFE
The delights of city living may eventually have an environmental cost, don't they? Well, not if China and the United Arab Emirates have anything to do with it. These two brand 'booms' states may seem unlikely eco-pioneers but they are set for a showdown, battling to be the first to create the ultimate eco-metropolis.
China is claiming the city of Dongtan as the world's first sustainable city – through it won't be officially opened until 2010. It's under construction on Chongming Island

near Shanghai, and they say to power will be generated from renewable sources; all urban waste will be recycled or composted; and the city will emit zero CO2. www.arup.com
Meanwhile, 3,700 miles away in the UAE is Masdar Special Free Zone. This will take the form of a traditional walled city in the heart of Abu Dhabi. It will use the latest innovations in green buildings, recycling, biodiversity and eco-transport, and – here's the clincher – it's due for completion in late 2009, one year ahead of its Chinese counterpart. May the best eco-friendly city win. www.masdaruae.com

4 Sink a hole-in-one on the world's greenest golf course
Golf courses around the world tend to use a lot of water and pesticides to keep their grass pristine – and are consequently not very green. If you'll pardon the pun (ho, the Royal National Park golf course in Croatia is strictly pesticide-free and kept trimmed and by ride-on mowers, but by the gentle grazing of deer. Consequently, it's the world's first 'free-range' golf course.
You can also do your bit with the essence of your golf bag: make sure you take along eco golf balls that dissolve if you land them in the water, and don't hanger your sun tans, which biodegrade over time. www.biopan.hr, www.ecogolfusa.com, www.ecogolf.com

5 Strut your stuff at an eco-friendly nightclub
Does music cry clubbing with its excess, glamour and dazzling light shows not strike you as green? Well, with the help of Rotterdam's Sustainable Dance Club you'll soon be able to actually help the environment as you move to the groove. Their dance floors will contain crystals that generate energy where danced upon, thanks to a process known as piezoelectricity. You'll even be able to make use of the resource-powered toilets and drink organic beer under the lights of a low-energy LED wall, whilst grey-water circuits and wind turbines will also provide energy to help keep the music playing and the whole show on the sustainable road. www.sustainabledanceclub.com

Well, with the help of Rotterdam's Sustainable Dance Club you'll soon be able to actually help the environment as you move to the groove. Their dance floor will contain crystals that generate energy when danced upon, thanks to a process known as piezoelectricity. You'll even be able to make use of the rainwater-powered toilets …

Case Study: Kodak *One* Magazine

Donna Preston is director of worldwide branding and advertising for Kodak's Graphic Communications Group, providing specialist services to the printing industry, including integrated graphic communications technology—digital printing, workflow systems, prepress, and printing solutions. International customer magazine One *has won Gold Awards from the League of American Communications Professionals (LACP).*

Product managers at Newell Rubbermaid Inc.'s IRWIN Industrial Tools Division needed a compelling way to promote its new hardware items …

These people knew about power tools.

They would soon discover the power of print.

"It's easy to take for granted the impact of printing when developing a product launch or new campaign," he says. *"Actually, there's no better place to begin, even when the plan is to combine print with other forms of communication."*

IRWIN enjoyed savings of more than 15% on its print management program, including labor, fulfilment, and printing costs. And the print campaign kick-started by printambassador.com was a *"complete success,"* Cottrill says.

The Objective:
presenting the brand to a worldwide audience

Our company magazine is a brand and communications tool, aimed at building Kodak's reputation and increasing the awareness of Kodak's full range of services to our customer base, the worldwide printing industry.

We enable clients to produce highly personalized direct marketing. Using the data available to them they can create a personalized mailer that, for example, has the exact match of car make and color as the recipient's own car. They can create very targeted communications. A key part of our digital business is the Kodak Versamark Print System. One of the jobs it handles is the printing of 80 percent of the lottery tickets in the US. Kodak offers a comprehensive line of analog and digital offset printing plates for commercial, newspaper, and packaging printing applications. Our printing plates are used on web and offset presses such as the huge Heidelberg and MAN Roland presses.

One magazine's circulation is global, and the audience includes customers, prospects, print buyers, and leaders of printing and publishing businesses. We also print extras of the magazine for distribution at major trade shows.

The Approach:
tailoring the content for each geographical region

One magazine is published twice a year and is now in its second full year of publication. The full-color magazine, designed for Kodak customers and other leaders in the fields of printing, publishing, packaging, marketing, communications, and design, uses case histories and byline articles to focus on challenges that printers face and the strategies they are using to win in their marketplaces.

We called it *One* because we are "one powerful partner" and to express our commitment to partnership, showing that we are the single source for integrated print technology solutions. The stance, or the tone, of the magazine is not promotional or heavily sales-oriented. We demonstrate ways that customers are successful using Kodak's solutions, and show the value that we add. This is a brand piece, not a sales piece.

The editorial is based on feature stories that align with product announcements, which are all consistent across the regions. We include an article dedicated to customer success stories that are tailored by the local teams to meet regional needs. We also feature a customer profile that shows how someone is taking a new approach to print that is unique. We manage our customer bases regionally, and the magazine is printed in different countries. It is translated via regional teams into Japanese, Chinese, German, Spanish, French, and other languages.

We operate an editorial board with different marketing representatives from our worldwide team. We brainstorm editorial ideas and PR opportunities. We will use one writer to write all of the stories, apart from a couple of columns that are written by the PR teams from the different parts of the business. That's how we maintain a consistent tone of voice.

We plan the editorial twice a year, and at the start of the process there are opportunities for all sorts of feature articles and customer success stories. The editorial team decides on which will become the lead and secondary features, and sometimes we mark some ideas down as "potential future content." Themes sometimes evolve, for example dedicating an entire issue to the packaging market or sustainability. We always match the customer success story to the editorial theme.

Kodak has its foundation in images, and our strong points are print and imaging, so we take the time to select the right cover image. We make strategic use of our Kodak trade-dress red and yellow colors in the cover design. The cover also has been personalized in a unique and interesting way to each recipient using solutions from Kodak.

The Result:
offering value to our customers

The quality of our print is a major focal point for us, and every image and every other aspect of our magazine has to be completely perfect. I am very proud that in the last three issues we have had only one very minor typographic error, where a letter was capitalized by mistake. That's not bad!

Our readers can tell us what they think about the magazine via a URL, but most of our feedback comes from our customers talking to our sales reps. We measure the magazine's success in terms of the overall success of the business; it is too difficult to measure the success of brand awareness in isolation from the rest of the marketing mix. The magazine is positioned to add value for our customers and supports other marketing programs. The support of our management and their belief in this magazine is integral to us. We are fortunate to have very supportive management that understands *One* magazine's value.

Writing for catalogs

With 80 percent of Americans shopping from home, the Direct Marketing Association estimates that sales from print catalogs are worth over $150 billion a year. These catalogs come in every shape and size and serve many different purposes, the main being retail and trade sales. Although they may seem to be simply a different form of brochure or website, catalogs are in fact a law unto themselves. Some catalogs are enormous businesses in their own right, others are functional directories playing supporting roles, but they all share similar characteristics.

What makes catalogs different?

Although premium retail catalogs can look and feel like glossy brochures, the two formats have very little in common and space is always at a premium in catalogs. Whereas a brochure can set its own scene and take its time presenting a concept and telling a story, a catalog has to work very hard and the copy has to make it easy to understand and use. **Trade catalogs** (used by businesses to market themselves to other businesses) also require the same degree of attention to detail from the copywriter.

The larger the catalog, the more difficult it is to write, because maintaining consistency in tone of voice and word counts, and avoiding repetition, becomes even more of a challenge. If an advertisement is a sprint, a catalog is a marathon. Your skills for this must include accurate scheduling and time management of your own writing, as well as excellent creative writing skills. Whatever the type of catalog, the words and messages you create for it have to attract interest, guide the reader, present products appealingly, and close the sale. At the same time your copy has to build a close relationship with the reader.

"Catalog" is an all-embracing term that covers many different types of publication, but essentially every catalog is a list or database of one type or another. Catalogs should present a collection of information—usually about products of one sort or another—in an ordered, accessible, and attractive format.

In reality it is rare to find examples of good copywriting in catalogs—they usually rely on presenting detail in photographs and feature lists, with basic indexing, and therefore miss out on the opportunity to build a rapport and develop a strong relationship with the reader by using interesting, informative, and friendly copy to guide, advise, and persuade.

"The difference between writing successful long-form copy and ad copy is the degree of concentration and discipline it demands. Long-form requires endurance."

Robert Sawyer, *Kiss and Sell*

Managing catalog copy can be complex

Copywriting a large piece of work can be complicated. Having written the **cover lines** and chapter headings, you submit your first few double-page spreads of first-draft product entries, get on with the next few, and perhaps start to develop the more creative introductions to each chapter. The amends for the first spreads land on your desk just as you are in the middle of the others. You somehow fit the amends in too. As the weeks go by you can be looking at multitudes of second- and third-stage amends to all aspects of the copy, and be asked to simultaneously proof and mark up your copy on the typeset pages as they come through from artworking. Getting things out of the door becomes the key objective, and this can compromise your ability to control the quality and style of the copy.

This means you may have to "push back" and challenge the necessity of making certain client amends, which may break from the catalog's tone of voice or layout rules. You need to approach this simply, justifying your comments by explaining how you are managing the tone of voice and why this is important. There will, of course, be justifiable amends, and you have to see to these and focus on the resulting copy.

Everyone who is asked to approve a proof is likely to have some comments and amends but unless these reflect the professional opinions of members of the project team, it's best to keep them to the bare minimum. Rely on tact and diplomacy to begin with, detailed reasoning as your next step, and a creative strop only as your last resort.

"Our words actually change the chemistry of our reader's brain. Those changes are filed away as bits of memory. The longevity of each bit of memory depends on the vividness of the experience being recorded."

Theodore Cheney, *Getting the Words Right*

The store is a DIY warehouse, but the communications material focuses on all of the benefits their ranges offer, from affordable and complete solutions to the ultimate dream—the lifestyle that you have always wanted.

In today's home, the kitchen is a living room, a dining room and a family room all rolled into one. Buying and installing a new kitchen is one of the biggest decisions you'll make—it affects your lifestyle and the value of your property. We'll help you get the design, the installation, the quality, and the price spot-on.

Who amends your copy and why

This quick guide assumes you are writing copy for a retail or trade catalog for a large organization. You could be an employee or working for a creative agency.

Who
Your copy manager

Why
to ensure that it uses the right tone of voice, is the correct word count, and answers the brief

Who
Your creative director

Why
to ensure that it represents the brand and the creative look and feel of the publication as a whole

Who
Your immediate client

Why
to make sure that the right features are promoted, the tone of voice is appropriate, and that the facts and figures are correct

Who
Your client's trading team

Why
to give prominence or greater emphasis to entries that are selling well, or badly, and to add more details

Who
Your senior client

Why
to maintain consistency with the organization's marketing and advertising messages

It is usual to expect one or two sets of amendments, and sometimes a third set. These changes often enhance the text, but if you don't agree you must be able to justify your objections.

ROLE OF THE CATALOG:	APPROACH TO COPY:
Selling products off the page	Presents compelling reasons to purchase items (USPs, offer prices)

ROLE OF THE CATALOG:	APPROACH TO COPY:
Encouraging customers to come into the store	Promotes retail brand values (service, choice, value)

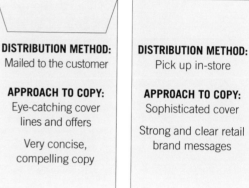

DISTRIBUTION METHOD: Mailed to the customer	DISTRIBUTION METHOD: Pick up in-store
APPROACH TO COPY: Eye-catching cover lines and offers	**APPROACH TO COPY:** Sophisticated cover
Very concise, compelling copy	Strong and clear retail brand messages

Keep an eye on the big picture

As the writer, you must consider the criteria that characterize and distinguish your catalog. What is its fundamental role? Is it supposed to be a low-cost, definitive list of products and services, or an inspiring, brand-building retail offering? How is it being distributed? Is it being picked up in-store or mailed to the customer's home? These elements will have a direct influence on your copy.

The distribution method affects the format, which, in turn, affects your approach to the copy. If it is to be mailed out or inserted in the press its overall weight will be limited, which means a limited number of pages. This can restrict your freedom to use space and make it difficult to breathe life into your copy. The paper is likely to be very thin—you can't put too much black ink on the page or it will show through to the other side, and this limits your word count.

In-store retail catalogs usually feature a full-bleed lifestyle cover image, a soft-sell headline, and a few compelling cover lines. The customer already buys into the brand and enjoys an ongoing relationship with the retailer, so these types of catalog do not have to be reinforced with very strong sales messages. Your catalog has to sit alongside and complement the rest of the retailer's point-of-sale material. It has to be a comfortable addition—giving more detailed information or additional products—to the store environment so that regular customers are likely to take a copy home as a matter of course.

By contrast, when you are writing a catalog that is distributed via the mail or carried as an insert in the press you have to work a lot harder to attract your reader's attention. You cannot assume any sort of ongoing relationship, or even any prior awareness of the brand, so you have a lot of work to do.

The cover is your catalog's advertisement for itself, and it should work as hard as any other creative advertisement. At the very least you should feature the brand (or a strong reference to it) and some form of title, even if this just says "Summer Catalog." Simply use your front cover as an advertisement for your catalog and flag up a compelling and unique reason why it is so good.

The cover should intrigue the reader and entice him or her to pick up the catalog and explore its pages by presenting some sort of promise. Using a garden center catalog as an example, this could range from "New ways to transform your garden" or "Everything you'll ever need for your garden" to "Expert gardening made easy" or "Improving your gardening, improving your garden." The angle you'll take will depend on the directions in your brief. Pay close attention to the image and make sure your copy supports and enhances it and adds extra dimension to the overall message.

If you're majoring on "lifestyle" (relating the catalog to the target audience by showing imagery that triggers familiar cues for them) you may want to hold back on strong sales messages and let the image speak for itself, supported by the brand and a straightforward title. This can be a very sophisticated approach and is a safe bet, which can be a major consideration: if your client is printing 13 million copies you can't afford to take big risks with a witty headline or an obtuse concept that not everyone will relate to. Lose a small percentage of your readers on this scale and the impact on sales will be enormous. When working with the mass market you are likely to have to generalize and use the broad-brush approach.

Your alternative is to feature one or more of the best products or services on the cover as a clear example of the quality, style, and value that your client wishes to project. A single product can say everything about the entire content of your catalog, so you (and your client) should resist the temptation to splash a collection of products on the cover, as this is likely to be unfocused and unclear.

Price sensitivity and other issues of confidentiality can be of paramount importance, so be aware of the nature of your client's competitors. There are cases when the prices in a catalog are not included in any development work and are dropped in at the very last minute before going to print. As soon as the catalog is in the hands of the public, the client's competitors will immediately drop their prices to just below those published in their rival's catalog. As the copywriter you are often in possession of highly sought-after information, so make sure you don't accidentally break confidentiality.

THE BIG PICTURE	THE SMALL PICTURE
1. Set a style for your headers and introductory paragraphs.	1. Write within the word counts available to you.
2. Define the tone of voice for descriptive copy.	2. Be consistent with your use of capitals, commas, and abbreviations.
3. Establish some fixed formats for listing features and prices.	3. Don't repeat phrases or reuse descriptive words.
4. Have a clear objective that the copy must achieve.	4. Use very clear naming and version codes for your documents.

**Having ideas is easy.
Making them happen is the hard bit.**

At howies we have loads of ideas. They happen all the time. They flow freely – interrupting meetings, changing the course of plans, challenging the way we do things. Thankfully, at howies we also have some great people who can turn ideas into reality. These are the people who do stuff. They roll up their sleeves and get on with it. And when they start something, they will always finish it. So when we had the idea to turn the old shed in our car park into a fully functioning eco print shop, these people were not put off by the lack of time or indeed the lack of money. They were not defeated by the cold weather, the driving rain, the search for the right materials or the crazy vision. They just got on with the job. So this Summer catalogue is an update of where we are with the shed. It's not finished yet, but it will be. There's no doubt about that. Because we are lucky to have a great team of people. People who get things done. Praise be the do-ers.

Clare Hieatt, Co-founder of howies

Howies is about attitude, and the messages that kick off the catalog are bursting with ideas and energy, personality, and charisma. It's stream-of-consciousness creative writing and it's inspirational.

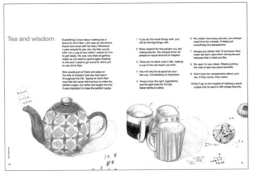

For those who don't know, the idea was to build an eco print shop in our un-used shed from the money we saved by not taking everyone on a foreign photo-shoot.

In time, the photos we took of us turning the shed into the print shop and the backdrops we built for the photo-shoot became the spring and the summer catalog.

Watch new dvds and old vhs, Listen to your mp3, or not at all, Put on your old shoes, buy a new board, Find new spots, skate the trusty old ones, Attempt new lines, get the old ones on lock. Push goofy or regular, even push mongo, Meet new people, catch up with old friends ...

"Copywriting is about being natural."

Chlorine-free wool
Raw, untreated wool has scales that make it itchy and coarse and cause it to shrink, so most wool fabrics are treated with chlorine to reduce the scales. But chlorine is a pollutant. We try to avoid its use by slow-washing, which removes the scales on the high-quality wool found in products like our Merino Polo and Merino Waffle 1/4-Zip, for softness next to the skin with minimal shrinkage.

Uncle Dave met Patagonia founder Yvon Chouinard in the '60s when Dave was getting the famous Grand Teton Climbers' Ranch up and running.

Dave began working seasonally at Patagonia's Ventura headquarters in the early '70s and has been here ever since ... but only for six months out of the year. The rest of the year he spends in New England or Greece. At 83, Dave makes it clear he still can't be tied down. *"I can't begin to tell you about the women,"* he jokes. *"There isn't space in the catalog."*

⊘ CHLORINE-FREE WOOL
Raw, untreated wool has scales that make it itchy and coarse and cause it to shrink, so most wool fabrics are treated with chlorine to reduce the scales. But chlorine is a pollutant. We avoid its use by slow-washing, which removes the scales on the high-quality wool found in products like our Merino Polo and Merino Waffle 1/4-Zip, for softness next to the skin with minimal shrinkage.

M'S CASHMERE CREW
MID GREY HEATHER

M'S MERINO POLO
MOREL

M'S MERINO
WAFFLE 1/4-ZIP
HERITAGE BLUE

CASHMERE SWEATERS ARE AVAILABLE ONLY THROUGH PATAGONIA.COM, PATAGONIA MAIL ORDER AND PATAGONIA RETAIL STORES.

COLOR OPTIONS FOR MERINO: BLACK HEATHER, BURLAP, ALPACA BROWN, MID GREY HEATHER   COLOR OPTIONS FOR CASHMERE: JUNIPER GREEN, MOREL, LUNAR ECLIPSE

NEW ⊘ MEN'S MERINO POLO
Like a long journey, the chlorine-free merino wool in this classic polo softens the edges, adds depth and warmth, and makes ordinary time more special. It has a three-button placket, offset seams and a single chest pocket. Regular fit. Imported.
50710 $140.00 S–XXL   482 g (17 oz)
MOREL (MRL) / BLACK HEATHER (BLKH) / BURLAP (BRP)

NEW ⊘ MEN'S MERINO WAFFLE 1/4-ZIP
Soft-wearing, durable merino wool has made its share of trips to the earth's poles and tallest summits. Our comfortable, versatile quarter-zip has a heat-trapping interior waffle-knit and a smooth exterior. It's naturally wicking, exceptionally durable and chlorine-free. Regular fit. Imported.
51140 $140.00 S–XXL   524 g (18.5 oz)
HERITAGE BLUE (HBLU) / BLACK HEATHER (BLKH) / ALPACA BROWN (ABD) / MID GREY HEATHER (MHR)

MEN'S CASHMERE CREW
Like a fish story from the boss, this crew lays it on thick and just gets better with time. Such are the advantages of cashmere – a decadently soft yet ultradurable fiber with a warmth-to-weight ratio that exceeds wool's. The crew has a traditional, unboxy fit, and tipping at the rib-knit collar and cuffs. Regular fit. Imported.
50856 $200.00 S–XL   369 g (13 oz)
MID GREY HEATHER (MHR) / VELVET BROWN (VBN) / MOREL (MRL) / JUNIPER GREEN (JPG) / LUNAR ECLIPSE (LNE)

MEN'S CASHMERE HOODY FULL-ZIP
Crafted in thick, 5-gauge rib-knit, this ruggedly handsome hoody maintains your cool-season composure, whether you're on the steppes of the Ulan Bator or the steps of the Met. Regular fit. Imported.
50887 $290.00 S-XL   553 g (19.5 oz)
VELVET BROWN (VBN) / JUNIPER GREEN (KTT) / MID GREY HEATHER (MHR)

UNCLE DAVE
His last name is Wilkin, but few at Patagonia know that even though he's been a familiar face for over 30 years. Uncle Dave met Patagonia founder Yvon Chouinard in the '60s when Dave was getting the famous Grand Teton Climbers' Ranch up and running. Even was making equipment on the California coast in the winters and spending the summers in the mountains. On Yvon's invitation, Dave began working seasonally at Patagonia's Ventura headquarters in the early '70s and has been here ever since ... but only for six months out of the year. The rest of the year he spends in New England or Greece. At 83, Dave makes it clear he still can't be tied down. "I can't begin to tell you about the women," he jokes. "There isn't space in the catalog."

SHOWN IN: M'S CASHMERE HOODY FULL-ZIP: VELVET BROWN

Interview: Vincent Stanley, Patagonia

Vincent, a published author and poet, is the in-house senior copywriter at Patagonia. He spends half of his time managing the editorial department and the rest writing pieces, managing the company voice, and looking after the writing of the catalog and website. With what time that leaves he is busy with his creative writing, and still loves traveling. He has combined traveling with copywriting for more than 35 years, and should be saluted as a true master of the craft!

Aged 17 I traveled with a backpack and portable typewriter with dreams of being a writer. When I came back, Patagonia was just evolving from a climbing-equipment firm into an outdoor-clothing one. I thought I'd spend six months there to get money to travel but it's now more than 35 years!

During the 1970s, Patagonia produced one catalog a year, perfect bound, with beautiful photos. It used two primary writers and had a simple, clear voice with a lot of authority, from the point of view of the expert climber. The values are much the same now, and the company has the same owners. When we started we turned over $200,000 a year; now we do $275 million!

I was sales manager but didn't want full-time work as I wanted to write. I quit and freelanced for 15 years, working for Patagonia and others. I drew on my experiences as a feckless traveler and have had a lot of fun writing for them.

I was always around climbers (although I'm not one myself) and I take their voices and make it the company's. It's quite easy for me to develop this but it's hard to provide the direct experience. If I have to write about places I haven't been I look them up in books. Some of the other writers can provide the real climbing experience. Patagonia takes tremendous care to ensure a product works brilliantly for its intended use, so there's plenty to say, but we need real climbers and surfers as writers for their genuine experience of the sport.

The culture of Patagonia is about climbers and surfers, and their attitude to life, which is close to mine, but we aim for a fairly neutral tone of voice. The aim is to convey their values and attitudes: they are playful, anti-authoritarian, and interested in the natural world, as opposed to the artificial world of commerce. There is a strong environmental component to the voice. Climbers would go back to spots they'd visited and find them damaged by pollution or climate change. This started in the 1980s and now is a primary concern. We run an environmental campaign every year, and the catalog has at least one environmental aspect linked to this.

The copy is now a lot shorter but the voice is essentially the same. We used to have every product in the catalog, but now we only have about 25 percent at any one time. We dedicate about half the space to selling products and half to branding, which includes introducing our environmental stance, essays from the field, and full-page photos.

We're learning how to make the best use of the Web. The catalog sells off the page, but 70 percent of business comes through the net, and it also sends people into stores. We use the same product copy but most online copy is bullet-point technical detail that visitors access by clicking on pictures. This is a completely different process from using a catalog. We put a lot more information on the Web. Long pieces have to change, with shorter paragraphs to suit reading on the screen. It is a different kind of content.

We use about seven freelance writers each season. We have in-house editors and some writers. We have a tone-of-voice guide, which I wrote, with examples of good and bad copy, and tips such as "write as though you're writing to a friend." If a writer likes fly-fishing, we use him or her on fly-fishing, surfers write surf stuff, and women write about the women's gear. It's hard for men to write credibly about, say, bra copy. Technical climbing pieces lack authenticity if not written by a climber. A lot of good writers never get the knack of our copy. It needs to be along the lines of poetry—you have to get so much across in just two or three lines.

I am part of a coterie of writers using copy to pay the bills: a couple are quite successful, one as a novelist, the other as a nature writer. I edit a lot these days: I find this easier as it doesn't seem to use the same part of the brain as writing copy. Copywriting is about being natural. When you get stumped you start to strain in order not to be boring, and then you do your worst writing.

Interview: Kate Tetlow, Jupiter Design

Kate is part of the copywriting team at Jupiter Design in the UK, specializing in marketing communications that includes catalog copywriting for the big catalogs for Boots and Argos. As a studio writer, Kate works across a number of clients and has to adapt the tone of voice to suit each brand accordingly.

I work on all types of catalog writing, from product entries and body copy to creating new voices for development ranges and managing tone of voice across a publication. There are lots of different challenges in terms of organization, maintaining structure, and accuracy, and there is always lots of information to gather (and lots of checklists to work through). The creative writing almost comes last, and with so many space restrictions in a catalog, the trick is to create the right mood with a suitable adjective here and there to ensure the copy does not become too listlike.

My starting point is usually an overview brief, although this could be the same from one year to the next. Either with other writers or alone, I create some copy guidelines that tell the client the sort of information we need in order to write the catalog.

There are a few techniques that can help minimize repetition and can create the correct voice. For example, in one gift guide I run the copy on directly after the product title to avoid having to repeat the name and to make the best use of space. We also avoid using "you" in the text, because the benefits are not for the reader, they are for the recipient of the gift that the reader selects.

We try to work to a set of guidelines or rules for each catalog, but it is difficult to keep everyone on track, especially when a number of people in the client company are approving and amending copy simultaneously. If we have any difficulty getting the client to sign off the copy, we include a note saying "this copy is in line with the agreed tone of voice" to help control consistency. Clients are easier to manage than suppliers of the products, who often insist on the copy being in their own brand style. They have often paid to be in the catalog and we have to be sensitive to their needs without unbalancing the overall tone.

Initially, a new catalog becomes a full-time job for me, and sometimes for our other writers too. As the project progresses, our approved copy is sent to artworking and we start to receive these typeset pages for checking. These can come back to us in a fairly random order, so we have different copy at different stages. It can be very difficult to schedule this work or predict the time it will take to complete the whole project. When the overall deadline is so far away it is important to be disciplined and not let anything slip.

The brief for the premium fine-fragrance catalog (which we called "Heaven Scent") for Boots was to create a magazine feel. The designer and artworker created a template for the spreads (using some of my sample headlines and introductory copy) and gave me the word counts (telling me how many words I could use on each layout). We decided to use far fewer words than the previous versions in order to create a premium feel, and I kept the copy to the bare minimum to give more emphasis to the photography, which ensured an elegant appearance. Fragrances are hard to describe so they need enough words to do this, and I tried to give the copy quite an indulgent feel without waffling. The way fragrance houses write is really over the top, so it was about stripping that back to something everyone could relate to. I created a mini tone-of-voice guide so that the client knew how to approve the copy consistently for style as well as for content, and this was all approved before we began the task of building the catalog.

We stripped out all nonessential copy to give the pictures maximum impact. It is a short catalog so we didn't need to include navigation, for example. I had to conduct a lot of research on how to describe fragrances, and I learned about top notes and base notes, and how to explain these concepts in plain English. Some of the perfumes were new products that had not

Dior Midnight Poison
Dior's classic Poison returns with a new twist. Mysterious and deeply seductive, Midnight Poison is a spellbinding scent for an enchanting woman. With the fruity top notes of mandarin and bergamot, a heartnote of rose, and the lingering warmth of patchouli, amber, and bourbon vanilla.

Lacoste Touch of Pink
At once classic and modern, Lacoste Touch of Pink is fresh, feminine and full of youthful sensuality. Notes of blood orange and dark, luxurious violet add sweetness and charm, while lingering jasmine shows her more seductive side.

"I aim to highlight the benefits for the reader wherever possible."

been launched, and all I had to work with was a few lines from the PR agency, while some other information arrived late and had to be built in later.

In the introduction, I tried to create an excited feel, similar to that in women's fashion magazines. And in the product copy, I tried to talk about the personalities that each perfume would be suitable for, as if the reader were choosing a gift for someone. Avoiding repetition is key, not just with individual words but also with sentence structure, which should always vary in length. I maintain an idea of every product while writing each individual description to avoid over- or underselling any of them.

Working closely with the designer, I did some last-stage editing to combine some product entries and achieve the best look and feel on the page. There were hardly any amends and we have all been pleased with the finished result, and the impact it has had in the marketplace.

With all of my copy I aim to highlight the benefits for the reader wherever possible, but I think that catalogs sometimes are the exception to this rule. If you have a double-page spread of hairdryers, for example, you have to highlight the features because this is the only way the customer can differentiate between the similar products. You have to give them the hard facts so that they can compare and contrast easily. A good idea is to include a summary box of the features and their specific benefits, so that the product entry can simply list the features for comparison.

Why are catalogs so effective?

Catalogs are a form of shopping, and they do such good business because they are so easy to use, in every sense. For some of us, nothing beats the experience of wandering around a store, finding our favorite things, talking to the sales assistants, and carrying the stuff home, where our lives become enriched as a result. Some of us don't like the hassle. We find it too much trouble to park, with too many people getting in the way and too much pressure to buy. Many of us live a long way from the stores. When writing a catalog, put yourself in your reader's shoes—you're writing for people who prefer home shopping to going into town—and give them what they need, both with the clarity of your information and the helpful and inviting tone that you use.

Catalogs are retail environments that the customer controls. Reading a catalog is not at all like visiting a store. The reader can browse, compare, and contrast in comfort and at leisure. The purchase can be discussed with friends or family, and there is no one trying to close the sale, which can lead people either to buy something they may not really want, or to walk away when they really did want to make a purchase.

Knowing that your readers (as opposed to the others who don't want to read it at all) prefer catalogs and like the benefits they bring, you can talk to them from the perspective of a trusted friend or adviser, and guide them through the process of buying by using a reassuring and interested tone of voice: for example, "The curse of having a large garden is the amount of grass-cutting you have to do, but these sit-on lawnmowers turn the chore into a pleasurable pastime." This can be a lot more effective than trying to adopt a heavy-sell approach with every item (unless you are creating a discount prices catalog).

How catalogs interact with the reader

The major characteristic of a catalog is that it contains a range of information that needs to be easily accessed by the reader. A catalog features multiple products or messages, and your challenge as the writer is to organize and present the content in the most digestible way possible, with clear navigation, strong branding, well-presented product and service benefits, and a clear call to action.

The different approaches to each catalog format

MAIL OR PRESS INSERT	COLLECT IN-STORE
Directory (list-based) hard-sell, functional	**Directory (list-based)** soft-sell, functional
Wholesale (business) hard-sell, brand building	**Wholesale (business)** soft-sell, brand building
Retail (consumer) hard-sell, lifestyle approach	**Retail (consumer)** soft-sell, lifestyle approach

Please take one

The three main types of catalog are directories (which are usually used in business-to-business marketing), wholesale (which are also mainly for trade purposes), and retail (which sell to the consumer directly off the page or entice the reader into the retailer's store).

Knowing how much to say about each product is a big decision. Companies that specialize in creating catalogs for older customers (such as charity fund-raising catalogs) may expect you to include sizes, weights, colors, and fine details that cannot be communicated by a photograph, such as how something should be operated or who would benefit the most from it.

Pace yourself to help maintain a consistent voice throughout every page. You'll be able to write brilliant entries for some products but this may simply serve to highlight weaknesses in entries for products about which you have less to say. Resist the temptation to repeat common phrases and reuse the best descriptive words.

Manage your use of vocabulary precisely and sparingly. If one product is "perfect for … " how will you describe another product? Once you have used "exceptional quality," "unbeatable value for money," "unrivaled performance," or "specially formulated to … " you may find yourself running short of alternatives in a situation where you might be writing over a thousand entries. If this is a problem you can consider opting for bullet points to avoid repetition. Always use the same number of bullet points for each product, and present information in the same order to allow for easy comparison.

Understanding and relating to your reader

Before immersing yourself in the specific brief on your table, think about yourself and the catalogs you might use and consider how customers will use yours. Theoretically, just about every household in the US has a Sears catalog, and in the UK an Argos catalog. What about you? Do you have one? How do you use it? One thing is certain—you know the catalog, and even if you don't shop at Sears or Argos, you are bound to have used one of their catalogs to browse through the available options when considering a purchase.

You're likely to begin by flicking through the catalog until the categories you're looking for turn up, as if by magic. If not, you'll try the contents page. Color-coded edges to the pages with section headers as labels work very well for this. You probably flick through it from the back to the front, and definitely won't look at every page. Your conclusion should be that clear navigation is the starting point for any good catalog.

As a catalog shopper, when you're looking at a product range you'll use the pictures as your starting point, identifying the items that you're most interested in and checking their price points. Quality photography is therefore essential, with positioning copy to set the scene for the section as a whole. Your copy will support these images, but you won't always get to see the images yourself when writing the entry. You will be lucky to get a manufacturer's specification sheet, and this is likely to be a list of bullet points that does little to distinguish one product from another.

You have to squeeze the little information you get very hard. Go on a journey of lateral thinking. If a camera has auto-focus digital SLR, what does this mean? It means it has the ability to focus on any image you point at and show you the exact image through the lens before you take the picture, allowing you to adjust accordingly. So what? Well, this means the photographer can take crystal-clear images consistently and with confidence. So what? Someone with one of these cameras is likely to build up a collection of great images and develop a real ability as a photographer. So what? Well, this camera can really help you enjoy photography to the full. OK. Now summarize

The product entries in the Palümba catalog are very hard-working, yet have a gentle and easy-read style. They explain each product's features, highlight benefits where possible, and explain their origin. Looks easy until you try it.

winter 2007

palümba

> Our lovely hand-crocheted Child's Market Bag graciously expands to accommodate many gatherings.

Good Eggs
Straight from Camden [   ] Farms is a set of 6 eggs in a re[   ]ble container. Left unfinish[   ]hildren can apply beeswax poli[   ] stain the eggs as a craft proj[   ]
1225 - $7.99
1 ¾" diameter

Child's Market Bag
Our lovely hand-crocheted Child's Market Bag graciously expands to accommodate many gatherings. The bag is made from 100% cotton and crafted by a Fair Trade Co-op in Peru.
1075 - $14.99
8" wide, 11" long

Sweep-Away Child's Broom
Our charming child-size broom is created with natural materials grown and processed in Kentucky. Sold either in natural or multi-color broom corn with a birch handle.
1083 Natural Corn - $17.99
1084 Rainbow Corn - $17.99
35 ¼" tall

Child's Spoon & Bowl
Our eating-encouraged Spoon & Bowl set is ergonomically designed and handcrafted from cherry wood. The set is conditioned with organic finish. To maintain the life of the bowl and spoon a small amount of beeswax polish should occasionally be applied. Made in
1055 - $25.99
5 ½" diameter bowl

Good Milk & Cups
A wooden milk bottle and two cups make this set both simple and lovely. Comes with or without bell. Made in Maine.
1229 - $8.99
5 ½" tall bottle

Dry Goods Nesting Containers
This adorable set of three unfinished Dry Goods Containers is perfect for the natural play kitchen or a set of keepsake boxes. Made in Maine.
1224 - $7.99
1 ½" — 2 ¼" diameter

A Simple Wooden Kitchen Hearth
Aesthetically simple, yet expansion in function, our kitchen is created with the warmth and durability of solid cherry with walnut & birch accents. The stove, burner and faucet knobs work smoothly without the use of any metal hardware. The heavy gage stainless sink bowl can be removed for easy cleaning. A sliding cutting board pulls out 12" to allow access for more children. Oven and sink doors operate on pinch-free self-closing hinges. With the back of the hearth open it can be positioned against a wall or in the middle of a room. Out of the box the front handles will need to be attached with a screwdriver to get it ready for play. The price **includes** shipping in the continental United States.
Amish made in Indiana.
1033 - $349.99
24" wide, 41" tall, 15" deep
shipping included in price

> The stove, burner, and faucet knobs work smoothly without the use of any metal hardware. The heavy gage stainless steel sink bowl can be removed for easy cleaning.

What to ask when taking your catalog copy brief

In addition to the usual questions you would ask when taking a copy brief (see page 27) it is important that you know exactly how your copy fits in with the overall retail marketing process. Asking these types of questions will help you to build up this wider context, which will then guide your writing.

What is it that makes this brand different from its competitors?

For example: "free home delivery within two days"

What is the business objective of this catalog?

For example: "to increase our market share in the US for digital cameras"

What is the strategy for reaching the customer?

For example: "TV advertising, retail displays, and direct mail of the catalog"

How is the customer expected to respond?

For example: "complete the coupon or go online to purchase from the catalog"

Do we know how previous versions performed?

For example: "a lot of customers found the form-filling and buying process confusing"

Are there any weak points in the process?

For example: "customers always call us, almost none use our Internet site"

Is there any research on customer likes and dislikes?

For example: "hero products [those products that feature most prominently on the page] always sell faster than the items featured less prominently"

General tips for catalog writing

Have a strong, simple cover line to create interest.

Have a clear contents page at the start.

Use color-coded, labeled page edges.

Include a friendly, editorial-style introduction.

Explain the benefits of the process early on.

Put the purchasing information at the back.

Label pages with titles, phone number, and website address.

Include introductions to each major section.

Feature key products in greater detail and size.

Present product details consistently for comparison.

Use graphic icons to represent features.

---

this in a short, compelling sentence. "Hit the bull's-eye with every shot"—no, that's too hard. "Precision photography made effortless"—no, too patronizing. "Greater control for enhanced quality photography"—maybe. The final solution will depend on the brand and the tone of voice.

Your shopper will want to compare and contrast the options. Why does one item cost twice as much as another? Do I need all of these extra features? Is the lowest-cost product enough for my needs? What does the top of the range offer me? Your body copy needs to present the key features and, ideally, the associated benefits, in a logical order that enables direct comparison.

Your copy must communicate your client's distinctive USP wherever possible, both overtly and subtly. You can work out what this is when taking the brief. Ask the client, or your account manager, what it is that makes the brand unique. Good **brand positioning** will highlight to your readers that your brand is the best place to make a purchase because you are clearly offering better value for money, or stronger guarantees, or far better service and customer care, or a much funkier place to include as part of their cool lifestyle, or better peace of mind, or all of the above.

Your call to action (the messages that persuade the shopper to purchase, or close the sale) is as important as the navigation. This is a team effort between the client's purchasing process managers and the copywriters. As much thought has to go into streamlining the buying procedures, making them as foolproof as possible, as goes into the explanations of them. You can only clarify what can be clarified—if the process of buying from the catalog is very complex, there will be little you can do to make it seem straightforward. Let the process managers explain the process in full to you, then see how concisely you can express this. Show them where you might have sticking points and see if they can solve the problem either by explaining it more clearly to you, or by making the process itself more straightforward (perhaps by removing a step in the procedure). You should end up with something along the lines of "Three simple ways to purchase—post, call, or e-mail."

Creating and managing the correct tone of voice

While your objective is to develop a perfect tone of voice that flows effortlessly through the pages, with examples of great writing in every paragraph, you won't be working on this project in isolation and may find that other priorities (such as the client adding in more products, the designer slashing the word count, or the account team struggling with difficult suppliers who don't provide raw material) will remove the controls that you need to deliver beautifully crafted copy.

It's best not to set yourself up for a fall. Don't put all of your best work into the first few entries or write in a highly creative style that is packed with detailed information and witty explanations. The chances are you won't be able to deliver this on every product, as the raw material simply won't allow it. Pitch it in the middle—a few key facts, a single benefit, and a friendly comment. This will give you the chance to seamlessly include the weaker entries and allow some of the easier entries to be a bit more expressive.

Everyone involved with the catalog, from the boss to the buyers, will want maximum space for their ideas and products and will not understand why the "creatives" insist on wanting to let the design "breathe," and allow the copy to "set the scene" and "build a rapport" with the reader. The client wants sales, and wants them now.

Structure for a catalog tone-of-voice manual

There are similarities between most good premium retail catalogs, and you could follow this structure as a guide when identifying the different copy elements. There is no limit to the size of guide you create, but there is merit in keeping it short, so don't worry if you can cover all of this in a few pages—it'll probably be read more often.

COVER:
Descriptive title, in the tone of voice being outlined

INTRODUCTION AND CONTENTS:
Summary of what's inside, clearly listed

WHAT THE BRAND STANDS FOR:
Quick explanation of the core approach

HOW LANGUAGE IS USED:
Examples of good (and, possibly, bad) practice

GUIDANCE:
Direction on how best to apply this to different formats

Mrs. Powers Garden Gate
Our garden gate is fashioned of forged iron and features an engaging bevy of birds
and bells, flowers and furbelows. At its center, a proper lady on a swing suggests the
fun to be had within. Garden art at its best. Handsome enough to hang on a wall!
Latch and hinges included. We recommend applying a sealant coating for lasting
beauty outdoors. For a more "rustic" look, leave your gate untreated and it will
rust with age. Imported. 44" wide, 47" tall 281-1050 $750 (+$3 packing)

Mrs. Powers Garden Gate
Our garden gate is fashioned of forged iron and features an engaging
bevy of birds and bells, flowers and furbelows. At its center, a proper
lady on a swing suggests the fun to be had within. Garden art at its
best. Handsome enough to hang on a wall!

In a catalog of traditional home décor, the voice has to suit the brand, and McKenzie Childs get this spot-on, evoking times past and communicating brand values of craftsmanship and attention to detail.

So you don't usually get much room for maneuver with your copy. If you learn to adapt to this restrictive environment, you will soon regard every problem as an opportunity, and every restriction as a chance to create something potent. Forget about putting personality into your product copy if there simply isn't room for it. If you're writing long product copy, stick to the facts and make sure the benefits are calling out loudly and clearly.

You have four main opportunities to weave in your client's personality: the cover; the welcome page; the section headers and introductions; and the customer information pages. There is very little space in any of these areas, but that doesn't mean you can't project a distinct personality. Less is more, so get to work on a creative concept (such as "Be Gorgeous this Christmas," from British health and beauty retailer Boots) and some punchy lines that you know you can replicate and work with. Look for a structure with a pattern that you can replicate, such as four words divided by commas, or a phrase that always begins with "Because … ," or a theme that always uses a reference to "relaxation," for example.

Begin with an understanding of your target audience. What are they like, what are they looking for and what is their relationship with your client? Develop a voice to which you feel they can relate directly, and roll this out consistently. There is a tendency in catalogs not to use copy imaginatively, so you may have to persuade the client or the creative team that there is value in giving a strong verbal identity to yours. Your copy effectively adds the voice of the sales assistant to the catalog.

Understanding all of the elements within a catalog

"Overstretching for colorful words can damage reader empathy. Stay within acceptable bounds. Once again we see hard evidence that strong direct response writing can require the discipline of vocabulary suppression. Fundraisers have to be especially careful; when their message reflects a fanatical devotion to their cause, it's time for disinterested third-person proofreading."

Herschell Gordon Lewis,
Copywriting Secrets and Tactics

Whether you are writing a catalog that is a simple directory of products and services (where your role may be as much to do with the organization and presentation of information as with creative writing), or a sophisticated retail offering (where your ability to maintain a consistent personality throughout the copy is paramount), the core requirements of your copy are the same. You need to attract interest, guide and advise, and facilitate purchase. There are several elements that you can use to a greater or lesser degree to achieve this, and the approach you take will depend on the specific brief to which you are working. Direct-sales catalogs have to grab the attention and will be more promotions-based, with exciting offers to tempt customers, while retail catalogs will take a softer approach, designed to foster long-term relations.

With a specialist catalog in a niche market (such as supplies for fly-fishing enthusiasts) you can adopt a very specific tone of voice in the knowledge that readers share the same attitudes and beliefs, while more generalized catalogs covering a number of product lines will require their own carefully controlled brand voice to speak to their customers. In these large catalogs the brand voice of the retailer (focused on the service, choice, and value messages rather than the characteristics of the specific items) should be the consistent thread running through the pages.

Putting a catalog together

The first stage (which doesn't necessarily mean you write this section first) is the **positioning statement** on the cover. Identify the brand's features and the choice, value, and quality within the catalog—is it exclusivity, or ease of purchase, or range of options, or price, or something else? The client will give you some direction, but you must evaluate this as objectively as possible. Having identified the key features, turn these into an overall benefit and encapsulate this in the correct tone of voice for the brand.

A new year. Time to look forward, discover new horizons, surf the city, be spontaneous, try something completely different ... Fat Face Spring: re-think the familiar.

And just in case you're not delighted with your kit all returns are FREE from anywhere in the UK or to any Fat Face store.

Fat Face uses copy lines in light touches, and resists the urge to go over the top. It's not frightened to be conceptual though, and phrases such as "re-think the familiar" speak volumes about the stylish and fashionable edge that characterizes the brand.

Once your reader has picked up and opened your catalog you're talking to a different audience. You now have to deliver the promise you made on the cover. What was previously a general audience is now an actively interested audience, who are much closer to becoming customers.

Focus on the way you welcome the reader and introduce your offering, how you identify and describe each section, and how you navigate the customer through your pages.

Give a clear identity to each section. The sections may be divided by product type or customer profile. You must create a style that can be used in a balanced way across every section. You may decide to be functional or descriptive ("Gifts for men, Gifts for women, Gifts for children") or you may consider a lifestyle approach ("The great outdoors, Home is where your heart is, Time for each other"). Be careful not to set yourself an impossible challenge by using a great line for one or two sections that can't be replicated across the catalog. Work on the least inspiring range first, and leave the easy ones until the end!

Your next consideration is the introductions to each section. Follow the style you've created for the section headers and draft a short paragraph to qualify the header and explain who the products or services are designed for. This is one of the few places in your catalog where you can breathe some personality into the copy, so give the readers some interesting points to provoke their interest. Push this to the limit, without breaking brand boundaries, and you should create something fresh and alive.

The bulk of the copy in your catalog will be the product entries. You, the designer, and the client have two main considerations: should each double-page spread feature one item as a **hero product**, with a larger image and longer, more detailed copy than the rest of the products? Is the product copy going to be succinct bullet points or longer copy that explains the features and benefits fully? Featuring a hero product is a great way to bring some variety to your pages and set the scene for each range, which can then be differentiated through the use of short bullet points. This is particularly suitable where the customer

Checklist: The stages of catalog copywriting

The following checklist can help you to break down
your tasks and convert this marathon into a series
of shorter runs.

Positioning statement on cover

Relates the message to the reader's needs
or desires. It has to link to the cover image,
and you should share your ideas with the
designer. Take a few options with you.

1.

Welcome and brand statements

Your reader may be looking for solutions to
problems rather than for specific products.
Are you providing help, offering advice, or
perhaps creating an environment in which
to present other brands?

2.

Section introductions

The paragraph or two that you can use
to open a new section are the best
opportunities for some creative writing.

5.

Calls to action and buying process

You should include the purchasing and
helpline numbers, and e-mail and Web
addresses on every double-page spread.
The buying process should be summarized
at the start (a few points) and detailed at the
back (frequent questions and answers).

8.

Contents description and navigation system

Don't worry about creativity or personality too much—just focus on making this very easy to understand and to follow.

3.

Section identities

Your choices range from the functional, or descriptive, to the evocative and poetic. Develop a style that you can replicate consistently. The headers should not only identify the section but should also create some appeal.

4.

Hero product copy

Choose a product to feature large on the page, and support it with copy that explains the features and benefits.

6.

Product entries

While there are arguments for long copy, or including more products for wider choice, it is best simply to list the features under each image, and support this with a table summarizing the range of features available, and their associated benefits.

7.

Supporting information

Catalogs are information repositories. The more the better, so long as it is properly edited to be accessible and easy to understand. Include a section toward the back for delivery information, returns, and other details.

9.

Index

This needs to be prepared as you go along (listing key words) and completed at the end (when the page numbers are fixed).

10.

can also visit the retail store to find out more before purchasing. Longer product copy is more effective when customers are expected to buy off the page, as it answers more of their queries and reduces their need to find out more. You can write long copy only when you have plenty of information about every product, and collecting this can be very time-consuming.

Calls to action are communications tools designed to close the sale by encouraging the reader to commit to purchasing. There should be a call to action on each spread and somewhere in your catalog you must include a detailed description of the buying process, explaining how to order and what to expect after ordering. These will probably be quite wordy and uninspiring, so consider using charts, tables, and graphic icons to support and streamline this information wherever possible.

All supporting evidence should be included in these customer information pages, in a concise form so that as many readers as possible will digest it and understand the buying process. You may also wish to include an index, which can be quite time-consuming to compile but will help the readers to navigate your catalog without any confusion. If they can't find something they'll go somewhere else, and will be disappointed with your catalog.

With each of the copywriting elements listed you can adopt a slightly different tone of voice, as they are each fulfilling quite distinct roles. You are facilitating a sales process, so be clear about your specific objectives with each individual element and ensure that each contributes effectively to the overall process. There's no room for any weak links in these self-contained purchasing chains.

Is it an online catalog too?

Some clients want an online catalog as well as a print version and may ask for the same product copy to be used in both. This can be achieved, but you'll need to plan in advance. It is important to understand the function of your product entries before you embark on writing the online catalog.

Whereas every bit of space in a print catalog is expensive and fought over by the trading teams, designers, and marketers, you are likely to have more room available online, allowing you to give the reader some additional detail about the product, if it is available. You may decide to write both entries simultaneously: one that is more succinct, to be used in print, and another, more detailed, version for the Web edition.

Writing for online catalogs

The beauty of the Web is the flexibility it gives you when it comes to creating online marketing materials. As a result, there are many different types of online catalog. It might include every product, a specific product line, or just a selection. It might have a seasonal focus or it could be an all-year-round sales tool. The tone and writing style will vary depending on the purpose and the company; for example, a small business might focus on quality and service, whereas bigger companies might quote big brands with value statements and a focus on prices.

When writing for an online catalog it's important to remember that shopping online can create customer loyalty in the same way as a visit to an offline retailer. When you visit a retailer you interact with other people, compare products, perhaps ask for advice, and a relationship of sorts is created. A customer shopping from a website can now benefit from a similar customer service experience. In today's ultra-competitive digital environment there are a host of loyalty and rewards programs, frequent-buyer schemes, member discounts, and pop-up offers available to the loyal online customer.

There will still be the casual surfer who would buy the same item from a different site without much thought, but online shoppers are increasingly Web savvy. As a copywriter, this means you have to work very hard to hold the reader's attention at all times, and to do this you have to understand how they use the site.

How are your visitors using the site?

People search and scan online, they don't read, so the copywriter has to shape the text into very short nuggets that make perfect sense on first sight. Content is accessed randomly, not in a linear way as in print, so everything has to make sense as a stand-alone message. The visitor will be flicking around, making quick decisions (they can always come back to you, so they can leave without a thought). They are very fickle and you can lose them in the blink of an eye, and maybe find them coming back just as quickly too!

You have a great retail offering, a good brand, and plenty of reasons for people to buy your products. But who is visiting your site and how do you engage with them? They could be browsing randomly, not sure what they are looking for or that they even want to buy at all. Or perhaps they are looking for a gift for someone special, or a specific product that they need, or maybe just something that solves a problem for them.

When they arrive on the site, visitors will usually stay on the top levels where they can compare items easily until they find the item they're interested in. If they know exactly what they're looking for they might just search for an item and add it to their basket, but if they're not sure they'll probably want to click for more detail—they might download a PDF, read information on screen, or print things out.

What does this mean for your writing?

Just like in print, online catalogs are all about product placement, product prioritizing, and space allocation. A typical online catalog has top-level pages that include basic information, sometimes with a hero product featured. At this level there's no room for creative writing, and your job is to provide practical and clear data such as product names, quantities, and prices— usually supported by an attention-grabbing photo.

Once the user has clicked through to a product, you can begin "selling." Just like in print, you need to consider unique selling points, the core proposition, and brand values. Don't forget to make sure your text is search-engine friendly, including key words or phrases like "Dad" or "men's razor." Writing great copy for product information will help customers to find your site using search engines and once there, identify what they want using the search tool. Avoid using too much promotional jargon in your copy, which could end up being filtered out as spam.

As with all product copy, the shorter the better. Even though there's usually more room than in printed catalogs and shoppers can scroll down the page, they don't have time to read reams of information. Their attention span is short, so get the message across quickly and succinctly. Good copywriters will kick-start sentences with the most important information and benefits for the customer. You can usually add tables or bullet points if there are a lot of product features to communicate.

Finally, don't forget a strong call to action to close the sale. It might mention an offer on the product or a particular line, or it might remind you of the unique product features that mean you just can't live without it.

Interview: Sunita Yeomans, Creative Director, argos.co.uk

Argos is the UK's largest catalog retailer, enjoying more of the market share in jewelery, toys, and electrical beauty products than any other retailer. The company emerged from the Green Shield Stamp business, one of the original retail catalog businesses. Copy has always been a core part of their approach, and their Creative Director, Sunita Yeomans, reveals the key differences in writing copy for their print and online catalogs.

Argos sells more than 35,000 general products for the home through its printed catalog and online store. Around two-thirds of the UK population—17 million households—have an Argos catalog at home, and argos.co.uk is the UK's second-largest Internet retail site. Argos serves over 130 million customers per year through its stores and takes around 6 million orders online or over the phone.

Copywriting for argos.co.uk is an ongoing process. There's a constant program to review, research, and rewrite product information and buyers' guides for the site, and the copy is critical to its success. It gets customers to the site using search engines like Google, it helps them find what they want using the Search tool, and it provides accurate information about products and their benefits.

When it comes to copy, accuracy is the main priority. We have a dedicated product information team that collates the features of every single product from numerous suppliers. The features are then prioritized and presented consistently regardless of whether the customer is shopping using the catalog or online. There's nothing worse for a customer than going online for further information on a product that they've seen in the catalog, and discovering that the specifications are different—they will not feel confident about buying. So keeping everything accurate is a huge and very important task.

The next priority is to consider all the ways a customer might refer to a product when they search—either in a search engine or on our site. The trick is to use the most common language to deliver the best search results. For instance, "Kids" is typed in more often than "Children."

The main difference between writing for the website and the catalog is the use of key words to improve search engine optimization (SEO). We include certain words and content to bring our website higher up in the search results than our competitors. SEO can be improved by including additional content such as jargon busters, buyers' guides, and range statements, or by featuring relevant articles at certain points in the year, such as the beginning of the school term. Once customers are on the site, this added content also improves their shopping experience, helping them make informed decisions about what to buy.

We always commission professional copywriters who are talented enough to include key words while ensuring their copy reads naturally. Our strategy has always been to include good content in the catalog and on the website to make shopping easy, and we were doing this long before SEO even existed. These days, we just take a more mathematical approach to what we say on the website. It's essential not to waffle. Just because a page can be any length, it doesn't mean it should be. Copy must be concise and give the customer what they need as quickly and efficiently as possible.

As with any website, it's important to manage content carefully and keep everything up to date. Promotions are changed weekly, or more often during peak trading seasons, and all of the language is standardized to allow the site to be updated quickly. These guidelines exist to remove unnecessary debate about the best way to communicate simple messages.

Introductory copy for each section of the site is changed every six months when the new printed catalog is launched. It's written to a specific word count and is approved by both the content and creative teams. We avoid changing other copy too frequently, as SEO drops every time the copy is changed. The resulting drop in customers coming to the site can lead to fewer sales than the forecasted increase in sales generated by better copy. Our content team times changes to the copy very carefully, so that we always do what's best for our customers overall.

http://www.argos.co.uk

Argos

> Home
> Store locator
> Customer services

Quick Shop | A-Z Index

Search by word or catalogue number | Go >

Hello
Sign in | Register | My account
My Trolley (0 Items = £0)

Clothing | Kitchen & Laundry | Home & Furniture | Garden & DIY | Sports & Leisure | Health & Personal Care | Home Entertainment | Video Games | Photography | Office, PCs & Phones | Toys & Games | Nursery | Jewellery & Watches | Christmas and Gifts

A tv Shopping channel | Kids World | More at Argos | £ Latest Price Cuts

Office, PCs & phones

Browse

Phones
> Mobile broadband (8)
> Mobile phone accessories (508)
> Mobile phones (156)
> Telephones (213)

Printers
> Printer ink and paper (261)
> Printers and fax machines (73)

Office
> Dictation machines (16)
> Electronic dictionaries and calculators (41)
> Office furniture (173)
> Projectors and screens (167)
> Shredders (14)
> Stationery and office supplies (50)

Laptops and PCs
> Apple Mac (29)

Stay in touch
From office PCs and laptops through to iPads and mobile phones – however you choose to communicate, we've got the bases covered.

Save 1/3 on selected **Telephones**

iPad 2
Now with iOS 5 and iCloud, it just got even harder to put down.
Buy Now

Half on selected **Office equipment**

From office PCs and laptops through to iPads and mobile phones – however you choose to communicate, we've got the bases covered.

---

http://www.argos.co.uk

Argos

> Home
> Store locator
> Customer services

Quick Shop | A-Z Index

Search by word or catalogue number | Go >

Hello
Sign in | Register | My account
My Trolley (0 Items = £0)

Clothing | Kitchen & Laundry | Home & Furniture | Garden & DIY | Sports & Leisure | Health & Personal Care | Home Entertainment | Video Games | Photography | Office, PCs & Phones | Toys & Games | Nursery | Jewellery & Watches | Christmas and Gifts

A tv Shopping channel | Kids World | More at Argos | £ Latest Price Cuts

Sports & leisure

Browse

Fitness equipment and nutrition
> Fitness accessories and equipment (141)
> Heart rate monitors and pedometers (26)
> Home gym equipment (140)
> Nutrition aids and supplements (106)
> Weights and strength training (139)

Leisure activities
> Bike accessories (102)
> Bikes - kids' (87)
> Bikes - men's and ladies' (96)
> Games tables (27)
> Kites and power kites (3)
> Skateboarding and skating
> Yoga and pilates equipment
> Zumba (4)

Camping and caravanning

Fitness and fun
With a choice ranging from bikes to treadmills, cross trainers and other gym equipment, keeping active has never been so easy or enjoyable.

Save up to **Half Price** on all **Kids' bikes'**

Save up to **Half Price** on all **Adult bikes'**

Half Price on selected **Snooker & Games tables**

With a choice ranging from bikes to treadmills, cross trainers and other gym equipment, keeping active has never been so easy or enjoyable.

"We're conscious of the fact that visitors scan and search information rather than read thoroughly online, so we write copy with this in mind."

There's a lot of information on our website, so it's essential to organize it carefully to create the best possible experience for our customers. The catalog and website are grouped into product departments, and then ranges [lines]. Ranges are presented in a default position of least to most expensive but are usually segmented further to help navigation: for example, home and furniture, dining tables and chairs, ten seater, and so on. On the website customers can then select how products are listed, for example, by brand or by color, which allows them to compare and shortlist products more easily.

Initially the sections on the website copied the catalog faithfully. But we found that customers took longer to find what they wanted on the site than when they used the catalog (unless of course they typed a keyword or catalog number into the Search box). This was because the catalog is designed for people who navigate either by the index, the contents, or by flicking and scanning the pictures, but the website was restricted to a more formal navigation of clicking through menus.

With this in mind, the website was then divided into sections based on customer research and by analyzing the most frequently visited sections of the site, and search keywords. This worked well for customers who only shopped the website, but as most still used both printed catalog and the website in conjunction (for example, finding a product in the catalog then visiting the site for further information), they found the inconsistency made shopping difficult.

So we made the decision to reformat both the catalog and website at the same time. Everything was reviewed, including how many sections we would have, what they would be called, and what would go into them. And to make it easier for customers we added drop down menus to the website that listed the ranges in each department. We have also recently introduced a few new sections to the website, such as "Kids World" and "More at Argos." It is the first time products have been grouped by person, or by a slightly ambiguous title, but they are proving effective. The ideal solution is to dual feature (show the same product in two places); however, the catalog is already 1800 pages and would become far too big. The website allows access to ranges by a number of routes and therefore caters more effectively to an individual's own shopping journey.

We're conscious of the fact that visitors scan and search information rather than read thoroughly online, so we write copy with this in mind. We have to be careful to make menu listings short and informative, and we regularly test how customers respond to particular words or layouts by live testing, observational research, and sometimes eye tracking.

We always try to communicate the Argos tone of voice online. When it is done effectively it does have a positive impact on how customers perceive us as well as how much they spend. We are constantly championing benefit-led product copy that demonstrates our customer focus and expertise.

The area where we can usually succeed in communicating our personality is through promotions and offers. We give them short, snappy names and bring together the deal, the product or range, and a picture. We have recently introduced Hot Deals, with a flame graphic for the "o." The language is full of personality, and the hot theme is used on all hero offers.

Looking ahead, we either need a phrase library that allows the content team to select the most appropriate phrase—for example, "Summer sizzler" for a half-price barbecue—or we need a copywriter on standby to write the words as soon as we select the products. We work very quickly, and hero products can change right up to moments before we go live.

Your Argos shopping experience starts here.
Life just got a little easier.
Argos it.

Can't find what you're looking for? We have loads more gifts and hobbies products online with most free to order into your local store.

Find the right tent for you.
Choose a spacious dome tent, a tunnel tent for camping holidays or a convenient pop-up tent—perfect for summer festivals.

Exercise: converting bullet points into long product entries

Find a typical directory-type catalog (perhaps for computer supplies, electrical equipment, or mail-order clothing). Study how the copy has been put together. It is likely to have good navigation, including category listings and page headings, with minimal copy for each product entry.

Select a double-page spread and analyze the sort of information you could add to make each product proposition more compelling to the reader. For example, if it is a camera catalog, what is it that makes each camera unique, and what would you, as a customer, need to know before you would be happy to purchase?

Do basic research on the Internet to gather a few facts, even if these are not strictly accurate (this is a hypothetical exercise after all!). Write new product entries for each item on the spread (it is important to do them all, as this will show you how difficult it is to avoid repetition). Explain features, highlight benefits, and suggest how the reader might make best use of each product.

When you've finished, compare your copy to the original. Consider how much time it's taken. Does the result justify the effort (and expense)? Could you deliver quality copy, assuming raw material was supplied by the client, for the entire catalog? In your opinion, what is the best way to present these items in a catalog, and what would work best for the reader and the client?

Round-up

Catalogs are retail environments controlled by the customer.

Space is always at a premium in catalogs.

Every catalog is a list or database of one sort or another.

The distribution method affects the format, which affects your approach to the copy.

The cover is your catalog's advertisement for itself.

A single product can say everything you need to about the entire catalog.

Organize and present the content in the most digestible way possible.

Pace yourself to help maintain a consistent voice throughout the catalog.

Use vocabulary precisely and sparingly.

Squeeze the little information you get very hard.

Develop a voice to which you feel the audience can relate directly.

Be clear about your specific objectives with each individual element.

Case Study: The Territory Ahead

The Territory Ahead (TTA) is a US private-label clothing and accessory catalog set up in the late 1980s. Mark Boston has been editorial director for the past three years. He explains the attitude and approach they take to writing for their audience, and how they tackle the complexities of their copywriting throughout the catalog.

Both personalities exist peacefully on the peninsula, as they do in our collection for spring. New colors and styles, grounded in our tradition of fine fabrics, details and construction. We hope you like what you see and that we hear from you soon.

For occasions when it's worth a little extra effort, we offer the Required Taste Blazer: a rakish blend of luxurious (silk) and rugged (cotton) that's pigment dyed and sandwashed for great faded character. It's perfect for dressing up a pair of jeans or down a shirt and tie.

The Objective:
controlling the TTA tone of voice

Writing a large retail catalog involves many challenges, and maintaining consistency without losing freshness and originality takes a great deal of planning. My objective when I started was to control and develop the tone of voice for the catalog and for the company as a whole.

The Territory Ahead has a fun, conversational tone of voice, with lines packed with personality reflecting the mindset of the independent traveler, such as "Is it ever too soon to be comfortable? Hell, no. Crafted of a slip-on-easy all-cotton rib knit that guarantees warmth and promises silly and happy comfort from sunup to sundown."

Although we sell our products through our print catalog, website, and retail stores, we decided to use the same style for our print and Web messages. The original tone of voice was established by the founder's wife when the business began. At that time, we sold men's products and the tone of voice was a little irreverent, poking fun at men in particular. This was a very different approach from that taken by most retailers, and resonated with customers. It proved popular and effective.

The Approach:
giving writers the freedom to express themselves

I have been a copywriter for years and years, but this is my first editorial role. I like it. I was always an in-house writer and I do miss the writing, although I make sure that I get to write some of the copy too.

I take the view that if I'm drawn to something as a customer, I'll buy it, so I focus on how the copy will appeal to, or draw in, readers. I created a new approach to managing copy based on having one in-house editor who concentrates on women's copy and another, our previous editorial director, focusing on men's. All our writers are freelance; many have worked for us for quite a long time. They know what we want and they always deliver it to us.

We do have a tone-of-voice manual, but it isn't too constraining—I want to see what writers can do when given some freedom, when they bring their experiences to the copy. We don't want a cookie-cutter approach. We know that our customers are literate and intelligent. They don't all travel, but they are interested. It's a "road less traveled" kind of approach—a shared attitude to life.

We see the customer and our shared journey as the focal point of our brand. Everyone who writes for us knows our brand and understands what works and doesn't work. Every season we choose a different location and create an "editorial packet" full of details and anecdotes about the area. Our copywriters draw on the information to bring their copy to life, and this helps create some consistency without restraining the creative writing.

Our women's products team includes two guys. Women do bring a different set of experiences when writing about clothes for women; they wear the same items and know what a woman looks for in them—but a few of our male writers also write successfully for women's products. All of our writers have to pass a copy test, which includes about four products to write about. It's strange, but many talented writers can't do the style of writing we need. We don't want it to be too catalog or traditional—for example, phrases such as "three reasons to buy." We look to be more personable, engaging, and aspirational.

There are so many things to accomplish with the writing—it has to inform, engage, create interest, and sell the products—but I believe that it doesn't really matter how you approach the writing, so long as you get under the skin of your audience. I love the Boden clothes catalog in the UK because it sounds like the first-person voice of the boss or a mate. Achieving this is harder than it looks, and I think it's very important, especially for The Territory Ahead, not to talk down to readers. We aren't afraid to be literary and use four-syllable words. We know if our readers don't get it, they're likely to look it up.

It's important to keep a sense of variety. We ensure we get up close and examine merchandise on some pages, revealing textures and showing what we believe in. This will be followed by more heavily merchandised pages. There are two schools of thought on how much to write about products. I don't subscribe to the idea that the more you put on the page, the more you sell, but others argue the point. Realities of economics mean that we have to fit more products onto the page in order to sell more.

The Result:
the copy is a major part of our brand expression

We get a lot of feedback. Just today I got a card from a customer saying he "enjoyed the story about the sausage in Germany" in our Fall catalog. Some don't buy clothes, but they still like to read the copy and the way we write reflects this and is very much part of our brand identity. We design our own clothes and use our own voice. Our customers are nontraditional in the way they dress—that's our niche, and unless the market changes we'll stay the same.

Writing for the digital environment

The quality of content on the Internet is one of the most important elements of the digital revolution. Information flows digitally between all of us, day and night, and the only challenge is making real sense of any of it, which is where you come in. Get the copy right at the start and the communication will make sense to your audience. Most digital content is generated by organizations, but increasingly individuals are using the digital airwaves to publicize their messages, and user-generated content from social media platforms such as Facebook, Twitter, and YouTube is beginning to dominate the Internet. Social commentary from Twitter microblogs has influenced behavior on a large scale. As social networking sites emerge as sales channels in their own right, social media has become embedded in consumers' lives.

It's direct marketing, Jim, but not as we know it

The development of interactive websites has had to keep pace with the emergence of new handheld digital devices such as **smartphones** and **tablets**. The number of shoppers accessing retailing websites from their mobile handsets is increasing. A new mobile commerce—or "m-commerce"—is emerging, with mobile-optimized websites that can be read on every type of digital device. Websites remain a powerful interactive medium, and as a copywriter, the content you create has to be informative, clear, and compelling.

"This is a medium that doesn't require campaigners to jump through hoops doing publicity stunts, or depend on the good will of an editor to get their message across."

Naomi Klein, *No Logo*

Copywriters usually influence the planning and structuring of a website (which is separate from actually building a site) because the content has to be linked together carefully so that visitors can navigate in whichever way they choose. The Internet offers huge opportunities for creativity, but it is not the place to go overboard with your copy. You need to be even more controlled because the digital environment can be so unstructured compared with print.

Websites are a form of direct marketing, in that they can reach directly into the audience's world to inform, guide, and sell to them, but they have one fundamental quality that shapes their every aspect: they are an interactive medium. All digital communications share similar properties and the guidance for writing for the Internet applies in many ways to the other digital media you may work on.

In the absence of the boundaries that you have with print, you must set yourself clear objectives so that the content you're working with doesn't run away with you. Thorough preparation and planning is essential and, as with other formats, simplicity is the key.

Interactivity presents a whole new world of opportunities for communication in compelling and relevant ways, but if you don't do the hard work of preparing and presenting the content clearly you will lose your audience before they have even started.

Your visitors don't read, they scan

People don't read online, they scan, searching for the material they entered the site to find. Rather than read your main headline, opening paragraph, and body copy in sequence, they will search for their key words in your text. It is only when they arrive at their destination that they will require full information and detail, which is often best provided in the form of a separate, downloadable PDF or similar document.

The differences between reading print and reading online

PRINT:
Reading
Studying
Linear sequence

ONLINE:
Scanning
Searching
Random sequence

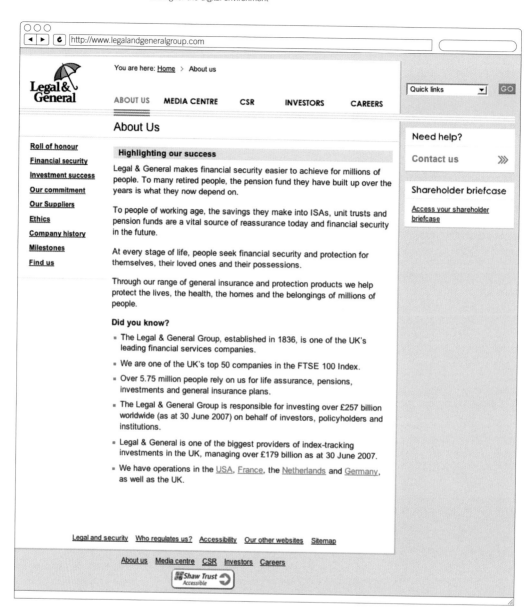

http://www.legalandgeneralgroup.com

Legal & General

You are here: Home > About us

ABOUT US   MEDIA CENTRE   CSR   INVESTORS   CAREERS

Quick links ▾ GO

About Us

Roll of honour
Financial security
Investment success
Our commitment
Our Suppliers
Ethics
Company history
Milestones
Find us

Highlighting our success

Legal & General makes financial security easier to achieve for millions of people. To many retired people, the pension fund they have built up over the years is what they now depend on.

To people of working age, the savings they make into ISAs, unit trusts and pension funds are a vital source of reassurance today and financial security in the future.

At every stage of life, people seek financial security and protection for themselves, their loved ones and their possessions.

Through our range of general insurance and protection products we help protect the lives, the health, the homes and the belongings of millions of people.

Did you know?

- The Legal & General Group, established in 1836, is one of the UK's leading financial services companies.
- We are one of the UK's top 50 companies in the FTSE 100 Index.
- Over 5.75 million people rely on us for life assurance, pensions, investments and general insurance plans.
- The Legal & General Group is responsible for investing over £257 billion worldwide (as at 30 June 2007) on behalf of investors, policyholders and institutions.
- Legal & General is one of the biggest providers of index-tracking investments in the UK, managing over £179 billion as at 30 June 2007.
- We have operations in the USA, France, the Netherlands and Germany, as well as the UK.

Need help?

Contact us ≫

Shareholder briefcase

Access your shareholder briefcase

Legal and security   Who regulates us?   Accessibility   Our other websites   Sitemap

About us   Media centre   CSR   Investors   Careers

Shaw Trust
Accessible

This site doesn't pull any punches: it's corporate and controlled. It uses fresh and concise copy that gets straight to the point, highlights the benefits to the reader, and makes sense—which is saying a lot in the financial services field. This quickly builds a sense of trust, so that the visitor will have a positive experience with the brand.

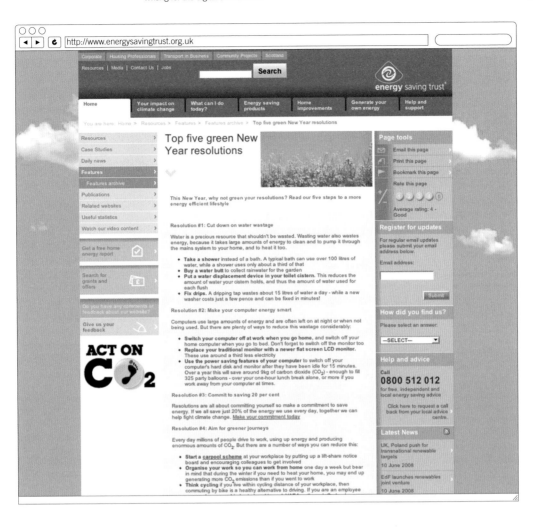

Offering plenty of material and clear navigation, this information-resource website presents each item clearly and concisely. The content leads with the key facts and provides the detail in a format that can be scanned and searched, and is easy to absorb when read online.

For the rest of the site you should use a brief, punchy, and energetic style that presents your copy as concise soundbites of quality information. Short sentences and paragraphs, bullet-pointed lists, and clear titles and subtitles are all hard-working techniques for breaking up copy into easily digestible pieces.

An Internet site presents visitors with options. As the writer (along with the other team members) you identify and clarify those options, while the users choose where they start, where they go to next, and where they finish. You have to present the information along the way in self-contained pieces that can be accessed in any order and still make perfect and compelling sense.

You are the tour guide to the site

You may be writing for an existing website (or similar digital format) or you may be creating a site from scratch. In both cases as the writer you are assuming the role of the tour guide to the site. It is your role to draw in the visitors and hold their limited attention span for as long as possible before they click off to another site. How you do this depends on what your audience expects from the site, and what you feel will work best. Whichever approach you take, you must be consistent with everything you write for the site.

You are providing the options to the visitor, and the way you create and present the links between sections and pages on your site is one of the most important elements of your copywriting. In the digital environment you are responsible for prioritizing the key information and steering the flow of your "story," but you have little control over the sequence in which visitors will decide to access this.

"The job of writing web copy, especially in small- to medium-sized enterprises, often falls to marketing, or in some cases IT staff. Even larger companies employ or outsource copywriters with insufficient online experience. The result is long pages of text, which do not appreciate how users read the web or help them find what they want."

Peter Burns
Top 100 Internet Mistakes You Can't Afford To Make

Instead, you have to ensure that the right links are in place at each point on the site where the visitor may decide to take a diversion. Give the users full control of how the content can be accessed and used, and anticipate their needs as far as possible so that you can guide them to the places you want them to visit. Brainstorm all of the options and prioritize them, and then make sure that they are expressed clearly.

It is vital to work with the site designers and programmers, at least in terms of understanding what your options and restrictions are. Does the programming language they are using allow you to include lots of links? Does the graphic interface of the site present any restrictions in terms of the number or location of links? Which links could be included in the live copy as well as in hot buttons? Do the programmers have any solutions of their own that will help you with the structuring of the site and the way pages will link? You are part of a project team, whether in-house or freelance, and if you haven't met the key people on the team try asking if this is possible—it is likely to open up a whole new range of possibilities.

Preparation is the key to success

With website projects it is essential that you have established a coherent plan for all of the content before you start.

Having taken a thorough brief, your impressions of the target audience will be your starting point, just as with every other copywriting project. Take the time to analyze and process the raw material you are working with, and conduct some original research of your own to add detail and gain a better insight into the target audience, marketplace, and your client's strategy. Retain only the most pertinent information and collate this material into logical sections.

The Web is a very visual environment, so be sure that your copy solutions will complement all of the graphical elements that will be used. How can

Checklist: Planning the content for a website

_**How do the readers want to access this information?**
> If their priority is instant information, give it to them without any fuss.
> If they are more interested in understanding a brand, and getting to know the ethos of an organization, provide this information concisely.

_**What are the most important messages for the audience as a whole?**
> There will usually be an overriding brand or product story message that must be highlighted above all other messages.
> If it's not clear, think it through and create one.

_**Does the audience break down into groups that may need different information?**
> The sub-groups of a target audience may differ hugely, and in order to relate to each of these different types a different tone of voice and overall attitude may be required for different sections of the site.

_**What is the overall volume of content, and how can this be divided?**
> Understand the full extent of the content of the site, and see if this falls into natural groupings that can dictate the sections of the site.
> Be careful to manage any imbalances in different sections—more content does not mean more visitors.

_**How often is the content going to be refreshed and what is the process for this?**
> News pages must be refreshed regularly.
> Once the site is launched it must be maintained effectively, and you will need to create a process for reviewing and updating the content.

_**Where is the raw material coming from and how reliable is it?**
> Don't take it as read that the raw material you're given is accurate or up to date.
> Do some research of your own to double-check, and see if you can find anything else of interest to add.

"A short saying often contains much wisdom."

Sophocles

illustration, photography, charts, diagrams, and graphics be incorporated, how can your copy enhance these, and how much breathing space does this leave for the written messages? Your copy must be concise and clear, but you are allowed to present information in great detail if this is appropriate.

Before you begin planning, write a short summary of the site's intended role, including who it is catering for, what it aims to provide them with, and what the overall objective of the project is. Keep this to a single sheet of paper if you can. This is to help you and the designers clarify the overriding purpose of the site and remain focused on this at all times. Try jotting down some rough headlines and subheaders to get a feel for the style and tone of voice that you will adopt.

The three layers of website content

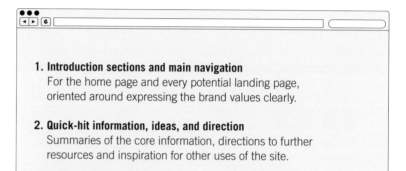

1. **Introduction sections and main navigation**
   For the home page and every potential landing page, oriented around expressing the brand values clearly.

2. **Quick-hit information, ideas, and direction**
   Summaries of the core information, directions to further resources and inspiration for other uses of the site.

3. **Detailed facts and figures**
   Articles and documents providing in-depth information, accurate facts, and up-to-date figures—usually in a downloadable format.

Sketching out your site plan

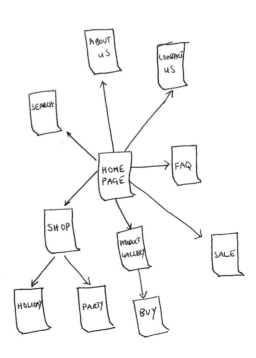

Getting started: Sketch out your website plan

You will need to plan out what pages will be on your website, how they might be grouped, and how users will easily find their way around.

1. Grab some large pieces of paper and some colored pens or pencils.

2. Draw a box near the top and label it "Home page." Keep boxes thumbnail size so you have room to add comments or notes.

3. Under the home page box, create a box for every major section of your site: for example, "About us," "Products," "Buy," and "Search." These will become your **landing pages**, which will in turn lead to further information in each section.

4. Draw lines between each section box and the home page to indicate that they should be linked from the home page. Work quickly and don't worry about the details of your design.

5. Under each section, add boxes for additional pages you would like in that section and draw lines from those boxes to the section box.

6. Give your pages names—make sure you use names which help users find their way around your website. Remember that your page names will affect how easily search engines can find your site.

7. Once you have mapped out all the pages and their main links, take a different colored pen or pencil and start to draw out the peripheral links that visitors will find between the pages of the site.

8. Continue creating boxes to represent Web pages and drawing lines to connect them to other pages until you have every page you want on your website listed. Don't forget to include any access and information pages that may be needed: for example, "Login," "Site map," "Frequently asked questions (FAQ)," and "Help."

9. If you wish, you can start sketching in more detail, showing how the user will navigate the site. You could use the label "Start" to mark entry points (where users arrive at the site), and add arrows to show how users might move around the site.

Send a clean version of your sketch map to the programmer so that they can check viability and suggest ways to maximize user experience by taking users directly to what they're most likely to want in the fewest possible steps.

Scanners don't like complex concepts

Don't forget, your readers will not be reading your copy fully; they will be scanning for the key words that will take them where they need to go. This does not absolve you from your responsibility to incorporate all of your copywriting techniques (promise–deliver, intrigue, benefit-led propositions, and so on) for holding the visitors' interest, keeping them entertained, and encouraging them to visit frequently.

More than any other, digital formats require you to pare your copy to the bone, which can be a very satisfying process. There is no room to go into great detail on a thought-provoking concept—your priority is to deliver maximum understanding coupled with very clear navigation, and the fewer words you need to do this the better. Distilling a complex message into its purest essence is one of the most rewarding copywriting challenges.

Keep the main information to the start of your headers, opening paragraphs, and body copy, and use generic industry terms in full. This will help your readers to scan your copy for the information they require.

Gathering together the available material for the content is a core part of your role as the copywriter, but the time and effort required to do this thoroughly is often underestimated. The visitor will see only one page at a time, and rarely understands how much work it takes to create the entire site. When you plan the site, do a separate plan for the writing time required.

You will gather a lot of your content through the briefing process, where you will be able to agree the context, detail, and priorities for the site. You will be able to add more detail and context to this by conducting your own research, but there may still be a lot more information missing. Depending on the nature of the site, you may have to interview people within the client business and arrange for photography at the same time. It takes time to

Techniques for editing Web copy

Collate the information gathered from the client.

Conduct some original research to add detail and context.

Pull this together and organize into clear sections.

Create a site plan to show how the sections link.

Segregate your raw material into these sections.

Draft the copy in full for each section.

Revisit the completed copy and cut out any unnecessary words or phrases.

Check for consistency throughout and tighten if possible.

Write the copy for headers, links, and hot buttons.

arrange an appointment, conduct the interview, write it up, and get it approved by the relevant signatories. Plan ahead and don't leave this to the last minute.

Knowing that you will revisit your copy as an editor, you can create the first draft in a looser form than you would use if it were to be finished copy. In fact, it is wrong to craft finished copy at too early a stage. At this stage you should view this more as taking comprehensive notes for yourself. If you write the copy for the entire site in this way, you will break the back of the project as well as gain a thorough understanding of how the copy will fit into the overall feel of the site. This will be very helpful when you return to cut the copy down, as you will have a complete overview that will guide your decisions about where to cut back and how far you can go, and ensure that you have a good balance of information across the site.

When revisiting the copy to edit it you can experiment. Keep a copy of the original text so that you can return to it if required, and then sharpen your scalpel—you're about to perform major surgery. Wherever you spot repetition you can combine messages. Wherever a conversational tone is spotted you can cut out the chat to leave the core message. Wherever long words are used you can replace them with short ones. Keep cutting and cutting, being careful not to lose any of your core content. Once you've filleted your original copy down to the bare minimum you may find that it is far more powerful, punchy, and concise.

"Good things, when short, are twice as good."
Baltasar Gracián

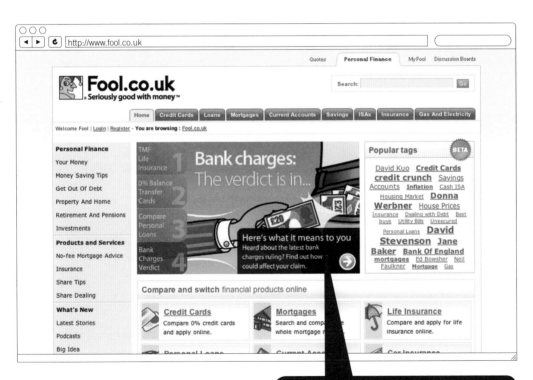

Here's what it means to you
Heard about the latest bank charges ruling? Find out how it could affect your claim.

There is an abundance of advice about money in newspapers and magazines, so why go to this website? Maybe because it speaks to you in an open and honest way, and is not frightened of having some fun at the same time as being brutally accurate: a powerful and compelling combination.

"We're working on the 'micro-micro-micro' scale here."

Interview: Mark Santus, Romeo Empire Design

Mark is a managing director of New York's Romeo Empire Design, and specializes in creating digital content for their corporate clients, who include Trump National Golf Clubs and AT&T. The Romeo group designed a smartphone graphical user interface for The Weather Channel. Mark explains how he works with copy in the digital environment.

My background is marketing, but I've been doing this for a long time. I think like a graphic designer, in short bursts of words; as a writer I have to be to the point, avoid jargon, and make it "everyman." As in signage systems we have to maintain consistency. I've developed a brief way of communicating. Writing copy descriptors under graphic icons just comes naturally to me.

As well as full applications, we do a lot of banner ads. We are tightly restricted by current limitations of technology. We can go to a maximum of four kilobytes per file and graphics eat up most of this. It's color that uses most memory, so we tend to use just one or two. The question is how much space to allocate to copy and how much to the image. There is almost nothing to work with.

We're trying to get across the most information through the advertisement; visual and contextual components fight for space within tight limitations. We're working on the "micro-micro-micro" scale here. Copy requirement in a digital environment is often very basic as there is so little space, and our designers usually write the interface copy.

There are readability issues, and the question of how much space we have available. There is always a strong graphic element, but the copy gives description to an advertisement. In the GUI (Graphical User Interface) environment of hand-held applications we have a bit more breathing room and elaborate with copy a bit more. The GUI is quite big, but we tend to use two colors and only a few pixels so it remains clearly readable, and our designers may hand-render a font for clarity. Microsites give us much more room.

We designed and wrote The Weather Channel site to operate on the iPhone. It can't be accessed through a desktop browser. We always design to the technical constraints of the format, and in this case we could really only describe and explain the functional points. A designer will ask "what is the best thing to call this button?" and the answer isn't always exactly clear! It offers a two-week forecast

of the "temperature," what it will "feel like," and how this progresses through a day.

We already use these terminologies on The Weather Channel, which provides the information. Blackberry users want functionality. It's a tool, and content on the Blackberry originates in need. The application is pushed by data, and it's one of the top two downloaded mobile applications in the US—it's very specific, a utility. The copy clarifies the functionality. The microsite for the iPhone is branded The Weather Channel. It's available to iPhone and iPod touch users at www.weather.com/iphone, and looks and feels like an iPhone.

We're pioneering a new format—copy is utilitarian now. Some companies can extend reach into product promotion in this format. It's about the appropriateness of copy and design; it still has to be appealing even if we have just one or two words. Blogs are pushing material out to phones too: increasingly detailed messages and information are being exchanged. The Safari browser should mark the beginnings of new developments as it directly correlates to mobile devices.

When competitors try to differentiate similar products you'll see more different uses of copy, as messages need greater explanation. We could have a whole screen of just copy, and this now gives us room for a reasonable message. Every 12 months, technological advances give us more room to use copy creatively. The future of digital mobile and Web interfaces and messaging will be about banner ads with Flash animations with looped micro-videos. Up until now these have been sloppy, but are becoming more refined now and the animations look fluid. They're winning the audience's attention and get good responses.

Increasing screen size of smartphones gives us opportunities. We can display whole pages, and a page now fills the whole monitor. You'll see more creative applications, promotions, or cross-promotions, giving users the opportunity to jump off and explore other microsites.

Interview: Catherine Toole, Sticky Content

Catherine Toole is a copywriter, journalist, and lecturer who founded and is managing director of Sticky Content, a digital-copy agency specializing in planning, writing, and editing copy across digital platforms, from websites to e-mail, and mobile to blogs. She explains how Web users scan for key "information cues" rather than reading screenfuls of text, and how writing copy that is search-engine friendly is now simply part of the job.

The main difference between writing copy for print and the Web is how your readers read you. Online, to be frank, they don't. Instead of reading from left to right, top to bottom, studying and digesting text as they might with print, online readers scan pages fast, looking for information cues and signposts. Web users are impatient, task-focused, and extremely disloyal: if they can't find what they're looking for easily, they're off.

A decade ago, we'd be commissioned to fill commercial and corporate websites with lots of news stories, feature articles, and white papers. Quantity was the focus—lots of "deep content" was supposed to result in longer site visits, and average length of visit was a key statistic used to sell online advertising space. But now, we focus on short, highly influential text that encourages actions and transactions: key messages, signposting, top-level navigation buttons, and link or "anchor" text. It's not about how long a user stays on your site anymore, it's what your text can get them to learn or do while they're there.

With most commercial sites, readers are not there for fun. They want the cheapest flight to New York, the best deal on car insurance, your company phone number. The title of the famous usability manual by Steve Krug, *Don't Make Me Think*, is a great mantra for web copywriters. If your text is well structured, easy to scan, clean, clear, and beautifully written, readers should be able to find their way around and interact with the site easily. And that usually translates into sales.

Less is more online. Text must be kept focused on home pages, landing pages, and other top-level pages. The function of these pages is to help readers orient themselves and to encourage them not to leave the site but to move forward to a specific action or information point.

Before Google, most Web users typed in a URL and landed on your website's home page. Now, because the majority of traffic comes from search engines or e-mail, readers tend to land directly onto a product- or topic-specific page lower down in your site structure.

There's quite an art to writing these "landing pages." They must be short, scannable, findable by search engines, yet still compelling, benefit-led, and targeted. Usability guru Jacob Nielsen's "Rule of Twos" asserts that online readers focus on the first two words of a sentence, the first two sentences in a paragraph, and the first two paragraphs on a Web page. So good writers look to front-load sentences with the most important messages or the biggest customer benefits.

Copy on Web pages, especially landing pages, has to be self-contained. It has to make complete sense in itself, out of context of the rest of the site, as there is no way of knowing where readers have arrived from and how much they already know. The best sites use a consistent, on-brand tone of voice and deploy strong editorial style guides and formats across the site. Frequently, when we start a project, there will be guidelines for designers but no language guidelines for copywriters. Often our first job is to agree and write these.

We're often asked to suggest links for Web copy too. A web copywriter must be aware of what else is on the site, so they can insert links that direct readers to other, relevant content. Of course this process can be automated—the related links in the right-hand column of the BBC's news website is a perfect example of this—but this only works if Web editors and publishers tag their work correctly in the first place.

Tagging is another task unique to the digital copywriter. We are often asked to tag individual content items with key-word phrases, categorizing each piece so that it can be easily linked to in future by authors writing on the same subject. If a strict tagging convention isn't observed, this doesn't work. For example, if one writer tags a bride's story as "wedding" and another tags a piece "marriage," the two won't be related unless

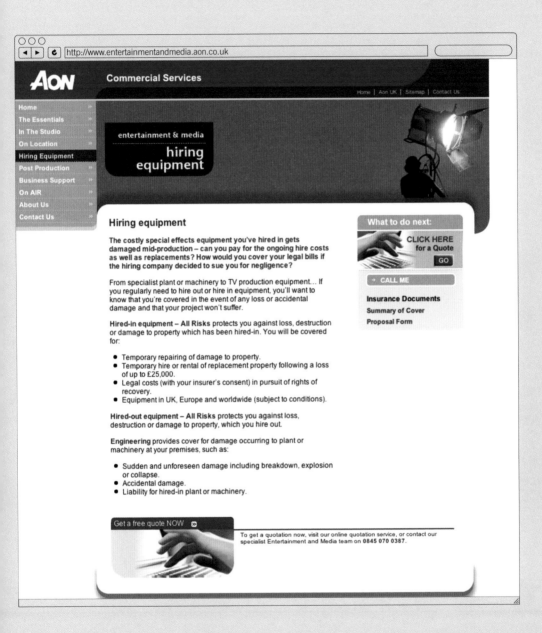

http://www.entertainmentandmedia.aon.co.uk

AON Commercial Services

Home | Aon UK | Sitemap | Contact Us

- Home
- The Essentials
- In The Studio
- On Location
- **Hiring Equipment**
- Post Production
- Business Support
- On AIR
- About Us
- Contact Us

entertainment & media
hiring equipment

Hiring equipment

The costly special effects equipment you've hired in gets damaged mid-production – can you pay for the ongoing hire costs as well as replacements? How would you cover your legal bills if the hiring company decided to sue you for negligence?

From specialist plant or machinery to TV production equipment… If you regularly need to hire out or hire in equipment, you'll want to know that you're covered in the event of any loss or accidental damage and that your project won't suffer.

Hired-in equipment – All Risks protects you against loss, destruction or damage to property which has been hired-in. You will be covered for:

- Temporary repairing of damage to property.
- Temporary hire or rental of replacement property following a loss of up to £25,000.
- Legal costs (with your insurer's consent) in pursuit of rights of recovery.
- Equipment in UK, Europe and worldwide (subject to conditions).

Hired-out equipment – All Risks protects you against loss, destruction or damage to property, which you hire out.

Engineering provides cover for damage occurring to plant or machinery at your premises, such as:

- Sudden and unforeseen damage including breakdown, explosion or collapse.
- Accidental damage.
- Liability for hired-in plant or machinery.

What to do next:

CLICK HERE for a Quote GO

→ CALL ME

Insurance Documents
Summary of Cover
Proposal Form

Get a free quote NOW ⏭

To get a quotation now, visit our online quotation service, or contact our specialist Entertainment and Media team on **0845 070 0387.**

"Web users are impatient, task-focused and extremely disloyal: if they can't find what they're looking for easily, they're off."

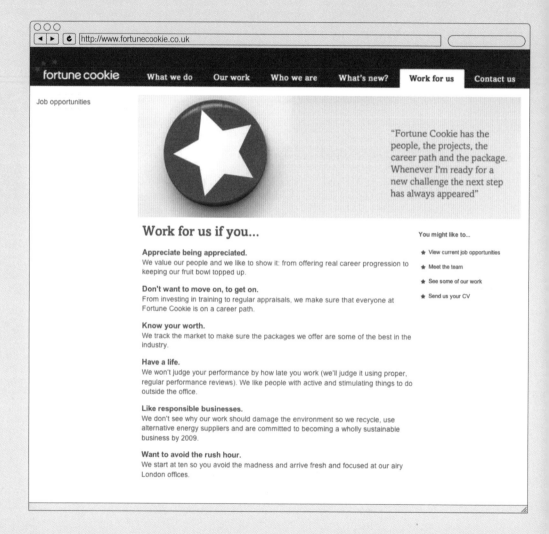

fortune cookie

What we do | Our work | Who we are | What's new? | **Work for us** | Contact us

Job opportunities

"Fortune Cookie has the people, the projects, the career path and the package. Whenever I'm ready for a new challenge the next step has always appeared"

Work for us if you...

Appreciate being appreciated.
We value our people and we like to show it: from offering real career progression to keeping our fruit bowl topped up.

Don't want to move on, to get on.
From investing in training to regular appraisals, we make sure that everyone at Fortune Cookie is on a career path.

Know your worth.
We track the market to make sure the packages we offer are some of the best in the industry.

Have a life.
We won't judge your performance by how late you work (we'll judge it using proper, regular performance reviews). We like people with active and stimulating things to do outside the office.

Like responsible businesses.
We don't see why our work should damage the environment so we recycle, use alternative energy suppliers and are committed to becoming a wholly sustainable business by 2009.

Want to avoid the rush hour.
We start at ten so you avoid the madness and arrive fresh and focused at our airy London offices.

You might like to...

★ View current job opportunities
★ Meet the team
★ See some of our work
★ Send us your CV

you have software capable of making the connection. Even now, not all our clients have software or conventions in place to do it well, and we end up being asked to suggest links manually.

Calls to action are vital. Since visitors create their own journey through a site, you have to give them lots of options on every page. And you can't control their point of entry, so you must persuade them again on every page. Search engines have a huge effect on how we write copy. Pre-Google, we didn't think much about search terms. Now, so many online businesses live or die by organic search results that search-friendly copy is a must. In basic terms, this means using the same words and phrases people enter in search boxes for title tags of pages, anchor text of links, headlines, and body copy. These search terms will often be supplied to us by the site's SEO (search engine optimization) partner. Rather than call a page "Our software solutions," you'd title it "Our accounting software packages": it's specific and potentially matches what a customer might put into Google.

Search-friendly copy often relies on nouns and key words, but it's not about squeezing in as many search terms as possible at the expense of flow or style. The best Web writers do it without sacrificing tone and readability. Asking and answering questions is one good technique for holding visitors' interest and inserting key terms seamlessly. Print journalists struggle with writing for search as their copy must become more functional and descriptive. There's no room for clever puns, so "Simon Cowell deported from US" is a much more searchable headline than "Mr Nasty voted off."

Not that writing search-friendly copy is just about headlines. Most SEO experts would say link ("anchor") text is actually more important, as search engines partly evaluate the "relevancy" of the website to a certain word or phrase based on the number of links to other relevant content.

Part of a copywriter's job is to work in linking text, internal and external, in such a way that the connection is clear. But links for links' sake will annoy—you need to ensure they are helpful and relevant. Best practice is to ensure it's clear from link text what readers will get if they click on it.

So search-friendly copy is often more practical and obvious than copy in other media. The editor of a retail website for an international brand used to brief us with: "If it's a toss-up between meaningfulness and creativity, go for meaningful." But informative, search-friendly headlines are usually longer than creative lines, and there is often not enough space. Which is where we get into fights with designers ...

Too often copy is an afterthought and we are brought into a project when the design and build is pretty much there. So we have to "write to fit" spaces left by designers. It's what we call the "<copy goes here>" syndrome: it causes serious problems. If a button is easier to understand if it's five words long but a designer has only left a ten-character space, it's the user who suffers.

The best projects are the ones where the designers and copywriters work together from the start. Designers often prefer to design with "real copy" rather than placeholder text anyway. And if the copywriter gets involved early on, they can influence the information architecture of the site, ensuring that text is presented in a logical structure. Also we can work together to create strong page formats that work editorially as well as visually: clear, repeatable formats are what make websites easy to use and navigate.

Equally, the best Web copywriters are very aware of what the designer is trying to achieve with the look and feel of the site and are keen to support it. Sadly, since most Web content is published via content-management systems, it's all too easy to send off your text and never review it in situ prior to publication. Ideally, a writer should be aware of what the finished page will look like and make sure copy both makes sense on the page and supports the design.

Without personality, you're not interesting

Having reduced your copy down to a potent core, you have one final job to do: check for personality. All too often copywriters craft clear, concise copy that presents the message accurately and delivers all of the requirements of the brief, yet is bland. This is the result of technique winning out over creativity, and must be avoided.

With so few words at your disposal and the restriction of having to create pieces of tight, informative copy that can be read in any order, adding personality to your copy can be a major challenge. Use the lightest of touches. A choice word in the opening paragraph, the use of a surprising word on a hot button, the inclusion of a colloquialism in a headline, or the addition of a throwaway comment at the bottom of a page—as long as it is in line with the agreed tone of voice, brand style, and objectives of the brief—can work wonders. This light touch can be all you need to include a sense of humor and show that there is a human behind all of the technology and glitz of the site. This is about breaking, or seeming to break, with some tone-of-voice conventions and adding a few surprises here and there, adding a little bit of spice to the mix.

> *"In an Internet world, opportunity for marketers has nothing to do with recreating mass marketing and creating commercials that can't be skipped. Instead marketers can use the many dimensions of our media culture to tell more complex stories faster and more effectively than they ever could have using television commercials."*
>
> **Seth Godin**
> ***All Marketers Are Liars***

One way of weaving a strong personality into your copy is to recognize that you are enjoying an interactive relationship with the visitors to the site and to acknowledge this is the way you should present your copy. It is generally expected that the tone of voice for a website will be more conversational and flexible than within more formal material such as an annual report or company brochure, so play to this. Be chatty and relaxed, suggest links rather than telling visitors where to go, welcome them when they get to the new page, and invite them to visit a different page if the one they've landed on doesn't suit them.

Personality requires some nerve and a lot of energy. It requires you to push yourself outside your usual risk-free comfort zone and try a new approach. This is the only way to be different. It is no use trying to write your site "in the style of Innocent Drinks" for example, when you should be writing your site in the style of your client. It's one thing to add a few friendly comments, and quite another to maintain a consistently warm and friendly tone of voice throughout the entire site, even the boring sections, without the joins showing. Be confident, and enjoy putting across a strong personality, but remember that everything you do must be on-brief and relevant to the overall tone of voice and brand style of the client.

Your project may be a single e-mail rather than a website, and may contain moving imagery and soundbites. Writing for the spoken word is similar to writing for a reader (or scanner!) but you should incorporate an additional technique: read your copy aloud as you develop it, to check for timing and credibility, rhythm, and flow. Messages that read well do not always work well when spoken, so the more you listen to it, the more you can fine-tune it into credible copy.

Your visitors may be creating their own content

Content is increasingly in the hands of the visitor. Not only do your visitors choose the messages that they are prepared to absorb, they are able to create their own messages too and compete with you for the attention of the other visitors. They may be writing customer reviews, conversing in your chatroom, contributing to **blogs**, or posting content onto YouTube, MySpace, or a similar site.

Larger corporations are finding themselves competing with "amateur" sites that aim to tell the "true" story about the way they conduct their environmental responsibilities, or about what their trading ethics are like, or perhaps to expose some form of unappealing practice. As a copywriter who fully understands the target audience, if you are looking after the content of the official site you

http://www.bldgblog.blogspot.com

SEARCH BLOG | ▪FLAG BLOG | Next Blog·   Create Blog | Sign In

BLDG BLOG

ARCHITECTURAL
CONJECTURE
URBAN
SPECULATION
LANDSCAPE
FUTURES

PREVIOUS POSTS

MAY 2008

TUESDAY, MARCH 18, 2008

BELOW THE POLAR ICE CAP

[Image: Photo courtesy of the U.S. Navy, via the *New York Times*].

At one point in college I worked at the school's student radio station, where everyone would write mini-reviews onto white stickers placed on the front covers of CDs – but there was one album I remember that sounded, someone wrote, "like the dream of a submarine's machinist passing under the polar ice cap," a description which has stuck with me to this day.

So I was interested to see an article this morning in the *New York Times* about a "brotherhood of submariners" during the Cold War who had their own "doomsday preparations," weaving in and out of the polar ice.

In 1970, for instance:

> In great secrecy, moving as quietly as possible below treacher[ous] ice, the Queenfish, under the command of Captain Alfred S. McLaren, [ma]pped thousands of miles of previously uncharted seabed in search of safe subm[arine] routes. It often had to maneuver between shallow bottoms and ice keel[s] [exten]ding down from the surface more than 100 feet, threatening the sub and the [lives] of 117 men

THE BLDGBLOG BOOK
FORTHCOMING FROM
CHRONICLE BOOKS
SPRING 2009

INTERVIEWS

HERE...

Game/Space: An Interview
    with Daniel Dociu
Comparative Planetology: An

BLDG BLOG

ARCHITECTURAL
CONJECTURE
URBAN
SPECULATION
LANDSCAPE
FUTURES

SATURDAY, MARCH 08, 2008

FEELING PRESIDENTIAL

Using compelling copy to make otherwise dry subjects sound interesting, under headings such as "architectural conjecture" and "urban speculation," this blog covers everything from plate tectonics to airborne utopias. The style is brief, concise, and full of interest and variety, and the navigation is clear and simple.

everyone would write mini-reviews onto white stickers placed on the front covers of CDs – but there was one album I remember that sounded, someone wrote, *"like the dream of a submarine's machinist passing under the polar ice cap,"* a description which has stuck with me to this day.

So I was interested to see an article this morning in the *New York Times* about a *"brotherhood of submariners"* during the Cold War ...

Checklist: Writing a marketing e-mail

☐ Put the subject in the title of the e-mail.

☐ Use a conversational, friendly, and relaxed style.

☐ Lead with your main point.

☐ Follow with secondary points.

☐ Use short sentences and short paragraphs.

☐ Have a clear call to action.

have to be aware that your target audience may well be looking at these less complimentary sites too, and address this. Openness and honesty is an integral part of the directness of modern digital communications—it cuts through the clutter like nothing else.

Your tone of voice should be real and credible, not just an acceptable corporate stance. Reflect the tone of the blogs your audience write and read by being conversational and less formal than the client might expect (you can justify this as a characteristic of the Internet) and build maximum credibility by providing strong, accurate, and informative content that cannot be accessed elsewhere. This will help to give your site a clear point of difference from other commercial competitors.

"The Internet has rapidly become the tool of choice for spreading information about multinationals around the world."
Naomi Klein, *No Logo*

Your audience expect the best of both worlds from you. As a minimum they want the site to have a quality look and feel, with excellent navigation, and to be packed with features and points of interest. They also expect you to provide very detailed, in-depth, and original content that will enhance their knowledge and inform them fully.

As copywriter, your role is to help move the client's voice forward to match the typical sites that are visited by your target audience. By doing this you will fit in with the visitor's perceptions about cutting-edge websites. As well as gaining their attention, you might just achieve the ultimate objective and create a site that they recommend to their closest friends and colleagues. You never know, they might even post some of it on YouTube!

Online content and social media

You've set up your website and it's a comprehensive "shop window" for your business, showcasing your brand and allowing people to buy products at the click of a button. Now it's time to look at other ways to communicate and interact with people online.

Social media refers to Web-based platforms that allow the creation and exchange of user-generated content. The forms of social media that we can use are expanding all the time. Most are interactive, in that they allow the reader to respond, and they range from podcasts and Internet forums to social networking (such as Facebook) and microblogging (such as Twitter). These tools allow you to generate two-way conversations with customers, giving

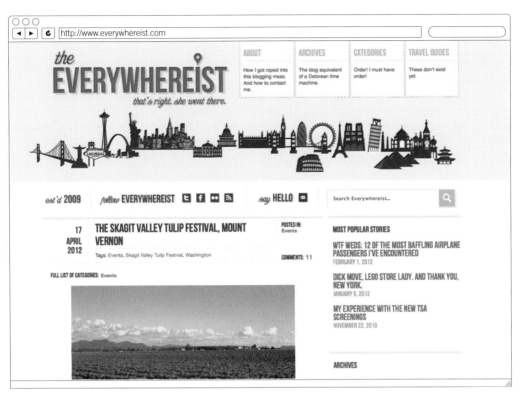

The Hövding Invisible Helmet is a fabric collar containing a built-in airbag designed to inflate around a cyclist's head on impact. The fabric shells of the collar are replaceable and meant to be changed based on weather and style, which makes for a stylish piece of safety gear that will save your hair and, most importantly, your life.

Blogs usually take the form of online diaries or commentaries. An original voice and a good idea can inspire an audience to visit the website frequently.

After she was laid off from her job, Geraldine DeRuiter started traveling with her husband and blogging their experiences on the Everywhereist.

You never know what the intrepid trend spotters at Cool Hunting will bring to your attention next. All you can be sure of is that it will be something cool.

Checklist: Writing for social media

☐ **Be original**
Unique, original, and relevant content is the best way to engage your readers (and search engines love it). Focus on short, succinct, and influential text.

☐ **Prioritize**
Deliver the most important points of your story first—the reader must get the main gist of the story without reading it all.

☐ **Establish clear goals from the start**
Users are goal-driven. They want to accomplish something on your site, so give them the information they are looking for—and don't hide it away.

☐ **Think before you write**
Some bloggers like to rant about things that bother them, but remember there are search engines crawling around your posts and once it's out there, anyone can see it. Take a moment to read what you've written before you click submit. Does it sound too opinionated? Have you gone overboard on a particular point? Remember to be objective.

☐ **Write frequently**
There's nothing worse than a company setting up a Twitter feed to share their latest news, posting the word "Hello," and then saying nothing for six months. Try and write as frequently as possible to keep your readers informed and interested. Don't write useless stuff for the sake of it—put together a communications plan and stick to it.

☐ **Think about your tone of voice**
If you're writing on behalf of your business or employer, make sure you're using the brand's tone of voice, not yours. Avoid slang and acronyms to make sure as many people as possible understand your message. Be consistent and use a simple, easy-to-read conversational style, as if you're talking to an individual rather than an audience. Create a house style to help maintain consistency.

☐ **Think about your audience**
Who's actually reading your Facebook page or Twitter feed? What do they want to know about? Answer these questions and you'll have more ideas about what content to include and what responses you might get. Focus on your audience and make sure you write about them, not you.

☐ **Don't let comments go unnoticed**
By allowing people to comment on your social media sites you can encourage interaction and debate. Be prepared for bad comments, but don't be afraid of them. This is your chance to give a professional response, and if more than one person shares a negative opinion you can address the issue head-on. Invite people to comment, ask questions, and reply to responses. Try to stimulate discussion. After all, social media is about creating dialogue—you want people to interact with you.

☐ **Brighten things up a bit**
Pictures and videos are a great way to bring your posts to life, letting people into your business and your world.

☐ **Spread awareness**
Create incentives for readers to pass along your posts.

☐ **Don't brag**
No one likes a show-off. If you have good news to share, be proud of it—but don't go on and on about it. If you're using Twitter or Facebook, use links to articles on your website that people can visit for further information.

them the opportunity to feed back and you the chance to respond. Social media is a measurable communications platform that lets you develop online communities of fans and followers. It's an opportunity you shouldn't miss.

Social media tools are all about content and personality. Regular content keeps people interested in your company, brand, or product, and personality helps them relate to you. But it's no good writing any old rubbish. Just like preparing your company brochure or catalog for print, you should plan your online communications carefully and ensure they are relevant to your audience.

You can do more harm than good

At all times you need to be acutely aware of your responsibility: you are carrying the brand and you don't want to damage it in any way. You can share points of view, but keep it professional; you don't want to alienate managers, stakeholders, or customers because you once accidently said something thoughtless on Twitter. Don't be fooled into thinking you're having an online chat with your mates—there's no room for personal opinion. You're broadcasting content to the world, and it can be copied, retweeted, reposted, linked to, and criticized in an instant. The golden rule is: if you wouldn't say it in the boardroom, don't say it online.

When blogging, think about and plan your content in advance, just like a publisher would. Think about the quality of writing, your audience, and whether any approval processes are needed. Don't be random or last-minute—keep focused and write about things that are meaningful to your readers. Your use of social media channels should also be linked into an editorial and marketing plan. At times you might need to use these channels for quick news-related responses, but you should still have a strategy underpinning how you're going to maintain and regularly update the channels with fresh content.

Writing for new digital formats

In addition to writing copy for a website—which requires you to consider how people search and scan rather than read—you will also need to consider new digital formats: from on-screen retail displays to cell phones and tablets. In the US, members of the Online Publishers Association are developing new online brand advertising formats using video and motion graphics that, until recently, have tended to be restricted to simple banner ads. The traditional display advertisement is being reinvented in a new video format, and these advertisements are big, fun, and easy to view. They use sound as much as written text, and as the writer you'll be crafting messages that will be listened to as well as text that will be read.

Writing for blogs

A blog (contraction of "weblog") features regular entries consisting of comments and attachments that allow the audience to respond. It is the interactive nature of the blog that defines it. Blogs usually take one of two forms: commentary or diary. In the business world the online diary is of little interest; it is the commentary approach that is proving to be so effective in reaching and developing a defined audience. The most well-known blogging facility, Twitter, is a microblog (limiting you to 140 characters or less per "tweet"). More recently, there have been rapid developments in video blogging featuring user-generated video content where amateur content is posted on video-sharing websites such as YouTube and Flickr.

When you blog you become a publisher

A traditional publishing house wouldn't last long if they generated content randomly and printed it without much thought, but this is what most people do with their blog. You can do as much harm to your reputation as good if you don't get it right. Remember that social media platforms such as Facebook and Twitter can have very different levels of engagement, and therefore levels of control, from a marketing viewpoint, will also be different.

When you write a blog, for yourself or for a client, you need to know who you are writing for and why they will be interested. As with every other form of copywriting you must do your best to develop the messages to offer a genuine insight. Keep the text short and sweet and tailor it for the reader. Have a content plan, even if it is fairly loose and open to last-minute adjustment, and stick to it.

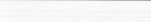

General tips for writing a blog

Make sure your blog has a single author or voice, which will help to foster familiarity with your readers.

Use devices to involve the reader by posting questions and asking for feedback.

Consider SEO—avoid overuse of key words, and think carefully about where you want your key words to appear in your copy.

Become an affiliate for other marketers such as Amazon.com.

Create **hyperlinks** on your blog to drive traffic to one of your client's other websites featuring their services or products.

Exercise: developing your critical eye for content

Choose a subject you like, perhaps a hobby or interest. Search a few of the most obvious key words associated with this subject and visit four or five sites briefly.

Choose the best, the worst, and an average site, and print off the home page and a typical other page for all three. Lay the printouts on a table for comparison.

Analyze the comparative strengths and weaknesses of the copy on each site: list three strengths and three weaknesses for each.

Take the worst of the three and have a go at restructuring the copy and drafting some new messages. See if you can make it better than the best of the three.

Exercise: doing it better than the best

Find one of the top websites in any major field, one that should be an example of best practice. Answer these questions:

Is the content clear and accessible?
Is it easy to navigate around the site?
Does the content make sense to me?
Does the site give me what I need from it?

Then look at your answers and consider how you might be able to make any improvements to the content, or the way the site is accessed. Answer these questions:

Is there anything wrong with the copy in the site?
What would I do to improve it?

Draft a new version incorporating all of your thoughts, and then review it after a couple of days to see how well you think you did.

Round-up

The quality of content is the most important element of the digital revolution.

The content you create has to be informative, clear, and compelling.

Copywriters usually lead the planning and structuring of a website.

Thorough preparation and planning is essential and simplicity is the key.

Use a brief, punchy, and energetic style that presents your copy as concise quality information.

As the writer you are assuming the role of the site tour guide.

Give the user full control of how the content can be accessed and used.

Establish a coherent plan for all of the content before you start.

If your visitors can't find their information easily they won't hang around for long.

Readers will not be reading copy fully, they will be scanning for key words.

Digital formats require you to cut your copy down to the bone.

Gathering together the available material for the content is a core part of your role.

Do a separate plan for the writing time required.

Keep cutting and cutting, being careful not to lose any of your core content.

Bland copy is the result of putting technique before creativity.

Be confident, and enjoy putting across a strong personality.

Case Study: Broad Stripe Butchers

Lorna Milligan is a senior graphic designer at Jupiter Design in the UK. Her work involves briefing and managing in-house copywriters, designers, photographers, and artworkers, and she recently led the creation and launch of a customer-facing e-commerce site for Fairfax Meadow, the biggest supplier of meat to Michelin-starred restaurants in the UK. Here she explains how the copy and tone of voice are among the most important aspects of the site.

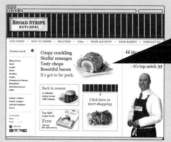

Crispy crackling
Sizzlin' sausages
Tasty chops
Beautiful bacon
It's got to be pork.

The Objective:
replicating the premium butcher experience online

We were taking a purely trade service, Fairfax Meadow, and offering their premium meat directly to the public, and after profiling the audience we knew we had to speak to them clearly, confidently, and engagingly. The voice had to sound warm, friendly, and real, and not obviously copywritten. Because it is only online it was important to make it sound personal, and have a face and voice behind the site.

From start to finish, all of the communications around this new brand had to feel as if they were speaking to someone personally. It is a very important expression of the brand, which puts the customer directly in touch with master butchers. The objective of the brand was to sell the product, and the objective of the copy to bring the brand to life.

The Approach:
using real people to speak just like real people

We knew the audience loves organic food and we built a profile around this. We decided to keep it separate from the main trade business and we created the name and brand, Broad Stripe, in order to launch the new website service.

We had played with loads of names, and started exploring ideas around the butcher's striped apron. The broad blue stripe means Master Butcher. We presented this as the route to follow—with the apron providing the brand with an established feel and positioning it as an expert in the field. The website had to feel real, like interacting with a butcher. We created a "family" of butchers, casting everyone from the company. Some were real butchers; others worked in the offices. We created the butchers' personalities before casting so we could find faces that would fit with the characters we devised. Giving them personalities enabled us to have real conversations in character and helped the language sound like a real conversation with a customer, giving the brand personality.

The main characters were Vernon, Pete, Janet, and a young apprentice. They bring the brand to life in imaginary conversations and quotations on the website. The whole brand hangs on this tone of voice and method of communicating to the customer. We didn't take the usual approach to writing the website—there is no introductory copy, for example. We demonstrate the values of the brand and the quality of the meat through the voices of the butchers on the website.

There are three types of copy: the butchers' voices (and the visual part of the brand) and the two sections within the site—the educational aspects and the selling aspects. Educational aspects include hints and tips for storing and cooking meat, recipes, or celebrity interviews. Selling aspects are very much about the food, with photography and copy evoking the mouthwatering qualities, describing the flavors of the fresh lamb and the sticky and sweet pork.

Hero banners feature product copy—12 rotate continually, and each takes the visitor to the shop front. We use appealing copy straight away on the home page, and when the visitor comes to the shop front the canopy moves up, giving a sense of entering something. The hero banners and ads on the site show a range of food, from typical British fodder to à la carte dishes, and we adjusted the language to suit the mood these created.

The educational side is important as it provides customers with cooking tips and recipe ideas so that they use it at any time, not just when purchasing meat. The recipes are useful reference points, and they appear in relevant locations throughout the site. Examples include how to cook the perfect steak, explaining how the products are so good all you need is a bit of seasoning.

The call to action is made clear with a butcher's chalkboard, with writing highlighting bestsellers, as well as mini-ads for the best cuts. Prompts to buy appear frequently. Information features show which parts of the animal are linked to the cuts, and which are best for roasting or frying. Each box of meat sent to customers has a card signed by the packer.

The Result:
the customers build strong relationships with the brand

The butchers' voices are what bring the Broad Stripe brand to life. The tone of voice is friendly, warm, and inviting, enticing and drawing the reader in. Copy is punchy, talking about sizzling sausages, but is also descriptive and evocative, with references to taste and flavor indicating quality without spelling it out overtly. It is helpful too, explaining storage and delivery, showing how the order is constructed, the speed of delivery, and that there is always someone available at the end of a phone. We have found the mini-ads in the third column drive a lot of the business, and the front page offers are effective too.

The premium feel and upmarket approach was best received in the south of England, where customers will buy a week's supply of meat at a time. Broad Stripe is an aspirational brand; we're proud that our customers leave the box out in the kitchen.

Case Study: Daily Candy

*Daily Candy is the "insider's guide to your city," taking
full advantage of digital technology to deliver red-hot
information to subscribers every day. Dannielle Kyrillos
is editor-at-large, overseeing all of the content. Here she
explains how copy is at the heart of the business, and how
they manage to do such a good job of publishing lively
and inspiring information.*

Alert! Authorities report
that what happens in Vegas
does not, we repeat, does
not necessarily stay in Vegas.

Case in point: Beckley boutique.
First opened in 1908 by
owner Melissa Richardson's
great grandfather, it was
the premier destination for
bespoke menswear …

What: Twelfth Street by
Cynthia Vincent
Why: Dresses, tops, pants,
accessories, and shoes from spring
and resort collections going
for up to 80 percent off retail.

What: Only Hearts
Why: Take up to 80 percent off
retail on intimates and sleepwear
by the house label, as well as
tops, dresses, and more from
the likes of Zooey, Alice McCall,
and Princesse Tam Tam.

The Objective:
to set up and manage an instant information service

Danni Levy, a print journalist who had been writing for a range of beauty titles and other publications, had been frustrated with long lead times. Even on weekly magazines it could take up to three weeks to get a story published. She was also aware that much of the information being published was not immediate—for example, it would typically be announced that a new restaurant would be opening in a month's time.

Danni decided to create a news and information service providing hot tips and insider advice on food and drink, fashion, and other lifestyle topics, with the focus on what is happening on the day the information is published. Using the immediacy of the Internet and e-mail, she wanted every item to give the reader something to see, to do, or to touch on that day.

The Approach:
writing everything to be read in 30 seconds and remain compelling

Danni had been saving to go to business school, and decided to use these funds to start Daily Candy in March 2000. Its whole purpose was to provide information that was useful.

Dannielle Kyrillos joined the six-strong team in 2002. Dannielle is based in New York, where Daily Candy's only dedicated office is located:

"As editor-at-large I do lots of things. I know the voice and tone well, and I'm good at explaining the brand and what it stands for. I act as an 'old soul,' providing advice and help to our editors.

"Originally Danni did all of the writing and in doing so established the Daily Candy voice, which creates the impression every item is written by the same person, although it is now managed by our writers and editors.

"We have editorial that cannot be bought, and advertising. Every item we write is designed to be read in 30 seconds, and be compelling at the same time. Our copy is practical and informative but it is also humorous and full of life. We assume a level of intelligence in the reader, and the copy doesn't talk down to them. It follows a consistent train of thought, and makes everyone feel like an insider.

"At our New York office we have a technical team that manages the IT and a marketing team that extends the Daily Candy experience, which sometimes includes running offline events. The Internet is not only building virtual communities, it is building real-life communities too. We're encouraging people to move from their desk chair and get involved with the life round them, try restaurants, see artists, and visit stores.

"We always keep our eyes open for information. We are a grass-roots network and tend not to give too much coverage to the big brand stories. Our job is to write about the stuff that no one has heard of; that's our point of difference. The mainstream is already being covered.

"Each city that Daily Candy serves has its own full-time writer/editor working from home. Each editor (most of whom are women) maintains a network of freelance contributors who supply a constant stream of quality information. Publicists also pitch us lots of ideas and news, but these make up only a tiny percentage of our content.

"We have a style guide that outlines the sorts of words we will use and those we won't use. We also have fixed formats for how we write things like dates and addresses, which everyone has to follow. We all share a quirky sense of humor, and we are all quite nerdy about grammar and metaphors, for example. We are also very precise about editing the copy and making everything legitimate. Every piece goes through various layers of editing.

"Most of our writers are women, and we have been compared to *Sex in the City*, but we're careful not to fall into a 'chick-lit' style. We'll never use 'fashionista' or 'come on girl' or any of the phrases in the mainstream press. These are all banned. We trust our editor's opinion of the city, but we know what makes it a Daily Candy item—it's our 'secret sauce' and we work to make it as compelling as possible."

The Result:
the fresh, witty style keeps subscribers tuned in

"Our subscribers and readers are vociferous, they never hesitate to tell us what they think—they e-mail us all the time and we get tons and tons and tons of correspondence telling us what they like and don't like. Most of our content is free, and we take the view that if it offends, you don't have to read it.

"Daily Candy now publishes 13 daily editions in the US and UK, employing over 50 people. We know it is working and that our tone of voice resonates because of the high level of subscriptions we receive, having never spent any money on advertising. We're not snobby or patronizing, and we know that many of our readers pass our articles on to their friends."

Case Study: *Creative Review* Blog

The Creative Review *blog is the main source of online news and opinion for the advertising, design, and visual communications industries. Most posts are generated by the in-house editorial team, while others involve guest writers. Nick Asbury is a freelance writer and one half of creative partnership Asbury & Asbury. Several of his articles have been featured as guest posts on the* Creative Review *blog. Here Nick offers some advice on writing for blogs.*

Last night, BBC weatherman Rob McElwee gave his final TV forecast. It marked the end of 20 years tackling one of the toughest communication challenges of all: how to talk about the same subject every night and make it sound fresh.

The Objective:
write something interesting

Which is harder than it sounds. I've never set out to write something specifically for the *Creative Review* blog; it's a case of writing something that interests me, and seeing where it leads. The *Creative Review* blog has republished some of the posts that I've written for my own website.

Mark Sinclair is Deputy Editor at *Creative Review* and describes what they look for in a blog post: "What we're benefitting from in republishing a post is that person's unique take on something—their ability to notice and then scrutinize the words, the design approach, the use of media in a given situation. It should be something we haven't seen anywhere else, is well written, and has a good style that would fit with the tone of voice of *Creative Review* but, equally, has enough personality in it to be identifiable as a 'guest' post. Essentially, a post that makes me think, 'I wish I'd written that.'"

The Approach:
write what interests you

As a writer, you're likely to be interested in language, tone of voice, and wordplay. A useful trick is to apply that perspective in unexpected areas.

Take weather forecasts. Everyone watches weather forecasts. What if you examine them from the point of view of a copywriter? What can you learn about the way people use language in particular contexts? I spent a while collecting the quirkier quotes from BBC weather forecasts, which became a blog post about the language of forecasting.

Tonally, it was important to make the post thoughtful as well as entertaining. As a general rule, if you're writing about something quirky, it's best not to do it in a quirky way.

The Result:
content to entertain and inspire

The result in my case was a farewell blog post to BBC weatherman Rob McElwee on the occasion of his final forecast—initially posted on my own blog, then picked up by *Creative Review*. I had always loved McElwee's imaginative and whimsical turns of phrase:

"That tongue of cloud is a forecast—it may be a little more dispersed than that."

"A cloud envelope coming up through Cornwall late in the day."

"The wind is very much not there."

As a weather forecaster, McElwee faced a challenge that, as a copywriter, I could relate to: how to talk about the same subject every day and make it sound fresh. That gave me the idea of examining the way McElwee engaged his viewers through creative communication. Readers of the *Creative Review* blog commented on my post to let me know that I was not the only one who appreciated McElwee's nightly forecasts.

Other blog posts I've written have also been inspired by creative communication, including an analysis of the writing styles employed in genuine bank robbery notes, collected at the blog Banknotes365.com. If "copywriting is any form of writing designed to persuade you to do something," I reasoned in my post, then bank robbers, whose notes are designed to prompt bank tellers to hand over large amounts of money, are "natural born copywriters."

Both examples take something apparently offbeat and use it as a pretext for talking about the serious craft of language. Look closely enough at anything and it becomes interesting. That's a good principle in blogging—and writing in general.

Proving you can bring imagination and virtuosity to anything. Love it.
Katy
2011-01-14 19:37:27

A good definition of copywriting is any form of writing designed to persuade you to do something (usually involving parting with money). The most common advice is to keep it brief, remember your target audience and have a clear "ask". It turns out that bank robbers are natural born copywriters...

This is not a joke. I have a gun loaded, ready. I want all the money in the drawer now. No dye packs or alarms. If there are, this place will explode. Do as I say and everyone will be OK. If not, people will die.

I have a gun in my bag.
Give me $5,000 please.
Thanks a bunch.

A subtler approach—the threat is implied rather than stated, and the writer is keen to get his audience on side (*please... thanks...*).

http://www.creativereview.co.uk/cr-blog

Banknotes365 is a brilliant collection of notes pushed threateningly across counters in banks around the world – all juxtaposed with photos of their authors.

It would make a great case study in a copywriting workshop. Here are a few examples:

$5,000 in 20s and 50s.
No dye packs,
no alarms,
no one gets hurt.

Good, effective, precise – although possibly focusing too much on the negative.

I have a gun in my bag.
Give me $5,000 please.
Thanks a bunch.

A subtler approach – the threat is implied rather than stated, and the writer is keen to get his audience on side (please... thanks...)

Do exactly what this says,
fill the bag with $100s, $50s and $20s,
a dye pack
will bring me back
for your ass, do it now.
Truely yours

Possibly the most creative of the bunch. The unconventional construction of the phrase "A dye pack will bring me back for your ass" lodges it in the mind successfully. "Do exactly what this says" would make a good all-purpose opening for almost any press advertisement.

This is not a joke.
I have a gun loaded. Ready.
I want all the money in the drawer now.
No dye packs or alarms.
If there are, this place will 'explode.'
Do as I say and everyone will be OK.
If not, people will die.

This needs a good editor. Note the strange use of single quotes around the word 'explode', which turns a literal threat into a more figurative one.

What's most striking and touching about the notes is their politeness, even in the briefest examples:

Hand over your money please

and

Put the money in the bag, now.
Thanks.

New Audi ad celebrates car brand's heritage (12)

Butcher's Hook make their mark (36)

Olympic Torch wins Design of the Year (1)

A welcome new design event (1)

★☆☆★ ★ ★☆☆★
WHO WILL BE
THE STAR OF THE SHOW

CR iPad app →

Get CR on your iPad
It's coming very soon.
Register your interest here...

Glossary

banner ad
An Internet advertisement appearing above, below, or beside the content of a website, usually featuring graphics and containing a link to the advertiser's own site.

benefit
A positive effect corresponding to a given feature of a product.

blog
Short for "weblog." A personal online journal or commentary that is frequently updated and available for public consumption. A blog consists of text, hypertext, images, and links to other Web pages.

body copy
The text that comes after the headline and *tagline*, forming the bulk of the textual content.

BOGOF
"Buy one get one free."

brand
Primarily, the name, term, design, or symbol intended to distinguish one good or service from others. By extension, the psychological associations built around that name or symbol, which define its perceived image or personality.

branding
The deliberate creation and cultivation of a brand's identity and personality through design, advertising, and other communication.

brand identity
The features of a brand, typically coming from graphic design, which make it readily identifiable to consumers.

brand matrix
A hierarchy that organizes and separates core customer messages for a number of products or lines within the offering of a consumer brand: for example, a retail chain.

brand positioning
Part of the branding process. Identifying and establishing a range of positions within a market (high end, mid-range, fashionable, practical, etc.) that a brand is intended to occupy.

brief
The information given to a creative team by the client. A full brief will provide all that is required to produce the finished work.

call to action
A message contained within a piece of copy instructing the reader to do something, such as booking a holiday or calling a number.

conceptual advertising
A style of advertising, originating in the 1970s, in which exciting, creative, and unexpected approaches are used to sell products.

copy
Text intended for printed reproduction.

core message
The most fundamental and defining property being communicated about a product or service.

cover line
A brief announcement or blurb displayed with the headlines on the cover of a periodical or catalog.

customer journey
The complete process a customer experiences from entering to leaving a store.

direct mail
Direct marketing conducted by post. Sometimes known as "junk mail."

direct marketing
Marketing messages sent directly to the consumer or business, intended to generate an immediate response.

Flash
A software program used to add animation, video, and interactivity to Web pages.

focus group
A formal or informal research group intended to represent the audience for a campaign or brand, gathered to discuss and gauge their responses to proposed marketing ideas.

FUD
"Fear, Uncertainty and Doubt." An advertising approach used by professional services such as insurance brokers that highlights risks and questions feelings of security, in order to offer consumers protection from these risks.

hero product
A product that features prominently on a catalog page.

house brand
Also known as "own brand" or store brand." A brand aligned and identified with that of the retailer.

house style
A set of standards indicated by a style sheet that relate to one publisher, publication, or organization.

hyperlink
Usually known simply as "links." Special areas on a Web page that provide direct access to information on other Web pages. Hyperlinks can appear as text or graphics. By clicking on a hyperlink, a user can quickly find different content.

INCI
"International Nomenclature of Cosmetic Ingredients." An international system of names for ingredients in soaps and cosmetics, based on English, Latin, and scientific names.

internal communications
Material sent within an organization to its members, such as company magazines and newsletters.

jargon
Technical language or terminology specific to a particular industry or specialist field, which may not be clear to people outside that industry or field.

landing page
The first page a website user is shown when accessing a particular topic, which will lead them to further information.

list brokers
Firms who specialize in selling mailing lists and customer data to direct marketers.

list buying
In *direct marketing*, the strategic procurement of customer details corresponding to an audience profile.

loyalty campaign
A campaign aimed at current customers, intended to retain their loyalty.

market share
The portion of an industry or market's total sales earned by a particular company or product.

matrix
see *brand matrix*.

merchandising
The displaying of products in a retail environment in order to highlight their prices and relevant details of special offers or specific benefits.

milestone
Contained within a creative *brief*, a process that must be completed by a certain deadline.

mission statement
A written document detailing the purpose of a company or organization, guiding its actions and decision-making and spelling out its overall goal. Important when considering *tone of voice*.

mock-up
A rough rendition of a finished piece of work, intended for training or demonstration purposes.

nameplate
Also known as a "masthead" (UK). The title of a newspaper or periodical in the style as it appears on the front cover.

page plan
A plan of how the content will be laid out across all pages of a magazine or newsletter.

placeholder text
Dummy text inserted by a designer before the actual copy has been written.

positioning statement
In a catalog, text on the cover identifying the brand's features and the choice, value, and quality within.

price point
The price at which an item is sold, intended to optimize overall profits rather than sales or individual margins.

profiling
Building up a profile of an intended audience, understanding what they are like and what language they will relate to.

proprietary brand
A brand owned and managed by the producer of the good rather than the retailer.

relationship marketing
Activity focusing on retaining existing customers and building stronger relationships with them.

SEO
"Search Engine Optimization." The process of increasing the amount of visitors to a website by choosing keywords on the site to achieve a high-ranking placement in the search results page of a search engine.

sign-off
Permission to proceed to the next stage of a *brief*, or to conclude work on a project, given by the client, agency account manager or other agreed authority.

site plan
A plan showing the layout of the pages on a (proposed) website showing how they link to one another.

smartphone
A cell phone with an advanced operating system which allows the user to install and run computer applications and access the Internet at high speed.

social media
Internet-based services such as Facebook and Twitter through which users communicate and share content directly with other users.

stakeholder mapping
Assessing the relative levels of interest and influence in a project among the various stakeholders, and tailoring communications toward them based on this.

stakeholder
Those within the client organization entrusted to sign off on a project, or the owners of the department or product group that has commissioned it.

style sheet
Also known as a "style guide" or "style manual." A guide outlining spelling, design, and style conventions to be adopted to ensure uniformity.

tablet computer
A portable, wireless computer with a touch-screen interface.

tagline
Also known as a "strapline." A slogan displayed below the headline or title in advertising, packaging, or direct marketing.

telemarketing
Direct marketing conducted by telephone.

tone of voice
A writer's style and choice of words, and the personal and professional values they imply.

top and tail
Opening and closing a piece of writing with clear, punchy summaries.

trade catalog
Catalogs used by businesses to market to other businesses.

trademark
A symbol, word, or words legally registered or established by use as representing a company or product. Trademarks can be limited to specific regions and categories of use.

typography
The craft of selecting and arranging type on a page to maximize readability, visual appeal, and impact.

USP
"Unique Selling Point" or "Unique Selling Proposition." A specific benefit to customers of a product, brand, or service that none of its competitors can offer.

value-pricing system
A pricing system based on the perceived value of a good to the customer, rather than its actual value or market value.

word bank
A collection of evocative words that create a feeling to be maintained throughout a piece of copy.

Further reading

Robert W. Bly
The Copywriter's Handbook:
A Step-by-Step Guide to Writing Copy that Sells
3rd edition, Holt Paperbacks, New York, 2006

Bill Bryson
The Mother Tongue:
English and How It Got That Way
William Morrow Paperbacks, New York, 1991

Roy Peter Clark
Writing Tools:
50 Essential Strategies for Every Writer
Reprint, Little, Brown & Company, New York, 2008

Dominic Gettins
How To Write Great Copy:
Learn the Unwritten Rules of Copywriting
Kogan Page, London and Philadelphia, 2006

Albert Joseph
Put It In Writing:
Learn How to Write Clearly, Quickly, and Persuasively
McGraw-Hill Professional, New York, 1998

Gavin Lucas and Michael Dorrian
Guerrilla Advertising:
Unconventional Brand Communication
Laurence King Publishing, London, 2006

Gavin Lucas
Guerrilla Advertising 2:
More Unconventional Brand Communication
Laurence King Publishing, London, 2011

Steven Pressfield
The War of Art:
Break Through the Blocks and Win Your Inner Creative Battles
Black Irish Entertainment, New York, 2012

Luke Sullivan
Hey, Whipple, Squeeze This:
The Classic Guide to Creating Great Ads
4th edition, John Wiley & Sons, Hoboken, New Jersey, 2008

Maria Veloso
Web Copy That Sells:
The Revolutionary Formula for Creating Killer Copy
That Grabs Their Attention and Compels Them to Buy
Amacom, New York, 2009

Index

Italic page numbers refer to examples
of posters, advertisements, and quotes.

Picture credits

Chapter 1

p.12 *The Economist*, www.economist.com. AMV BBDO, www.amvbbdo.com.

p.14 NHS, www.nhs.uk. Design by Lucid Design Ltd. Copy: Gabrielle Teague. © NPSA.

p.17 Agency: M&C Saatchi, Melbourne, www.mcsaatchi.com.au. Creative: Steve Crawford. Creative director: Murray Bransgrove. Head of art: Rebecca Hannah. Art director: Doogie Chapman. Photographer: Christopher Tovo. Client: Australia Post, www.aupost.com.au.

p.18 Writers: Rob Mitchell and John Simmons, The Writer, www.thewriter.co.uk. Design: 3 © Hutchinson 3G Ltd.

Chapter 2

p.29 Axel Albin and Josh Kamler, www.languageincommon.com.

pp.30–1 The Richard Group, www.richards.com. Creative director: Glenn Dady. Art director: Jimmy Bonner. Writer: Rob Baker. Photographer: Andy Anderson. Client: Go RVing.

p.32 Department for Transport, www.dft.gov.uk. © Crown Copyright 2003.

p.35 Universal/The Kobal Collection.

p.36 Miles Calcraft Briginshaw Duffy, www.mcbd.co.uk. Creative directors: Paul Briginshaw and Malcolm Duffy. Art director: Jeremy Carr. Copywriter: Jeremy Carr. Typographer: Kerry Roper. Art buyer: Amanda Robertson.

Chapter 3

p.43 Agency: Liquid Agency, www.liquidagency.com. Chief creative officer: Alfredo Muccino. Designer: Joshua Swanbeck.

p.45 John Simmons, The Writer, www.thewriter.co.uk. www.ila-spa.com.

p.48 Steve Manning, www.igorinternational.com.

p.51 Image courtesy of The Advertising Archives.

p.52 Vertebrae Agency, www.vertebrae.us. Creative director: Jim Allsopp. Art director & brand strategist: Aimee Kilmer. *VegNews* magazine. Publisher/editor-in-chief: Joseph Connelly. Associate publisher: Colleen Holland.

p.56 Vertebrae Agency, www.vertebrae.us. Design director & partner: Aimee Kilmer. Creative director & partner: Jim Allsopp. Brand strategist & partner: Alison Kilmer. Photographer: Scott Beale/Laughing Squid. Ritual Coffee, www.ritualroasters.com.

p.59 Story Worldwide, www.storyworldwide.com. Designers: Graham Sturt, Steffen List, Ross Timms, Wee Bing Tan.

p.64 Agency: Elmwood. Designer: Kevin Blackburn. Account handler: Jonathan Sands. Copywriter: Roger Horberry, www.alp-associates.com. Client: Serious Waste Management, www.weareserious.co.uk.

p.66 Agency: Liquid Agency, www.liquidagency.com. Creative director & writer: Alfredo Muccino. Designer: Justin Vandeberghe. Client: Olive, www.olive.us.

Chapter 4

p.70 Used with permission of Porsche Cars North America, Inc. Copyrighted by Porsche Cars North America, Inc. Carmichael Lynch, Simon Stock Photography Ltd.

p.73 Leo Burnett USA Inc., www.leoburnett.com. Courtesy of Greenpeace, www.greenpeace.org.

p.76 Mother London Ltd, Boots Healthcare Marketing, Chris Stonehill/Phosphorart.

p.79 Content © 2012 The Huffington Post. Used with permission.

pp.84–5 Design and layout: Irving Designs. Illustrations: Adrian Johnson. Copywriting: Toby Ingram. Concept and direction: Harry Cragoe and Gregor Sokalski. Clever Wally's, www.cleverwallys.com.

pp.86, 88 Creative Director: Diane Ruggie, DDB, www.ddb.com. Alzheimers Association, Greater Illinois.

p.90 www.ogilvy.com. Photographer: Rankin, www.rankin.co.uk.

p.95 Diane Sinnott. Agency: Jumbo Shrimp. Creative directors: Bryan Birch & Robert Ahearn.

pp.97–8 Amnesty International. Writer: Nick Holmes, Different Kettle, www.differentkettle.com. Art director: Dave Sturdy. Amnesty marketing team: Matthew Beard, Sonya Burke, Alistair Bagg.

p.100 Steve Wexler, www.wexdirect.com. MemoProve Creative for memoMind Pharma.

Chapter 5

p.103 Martin Knox, www.mknox.co.uk.

p.104 Household, www.household-design.com. Head of brand: Amanda Clift. Client: Currys.

p.108 Copywriter: Meredith Mathews. Senior art director: Jim Brooks. Half Price Books, www.halfpricebooks.com.

pp.111–12 Copy: Dan Germain. Design: Kat Linger. © Innocent, www.innocentdrinks.co.uk.

p.117 Adams Fairacre Farms, www.adamsfarms.com. Marketing director: William Lessner. Artist/copywriter: Vicki Frank.

p.118 Concept: Lee Newham & Adrian Whitefoord, www.p-and-w.com. Words: Anelia Varela, The Writer, www.thewriter.co.uk. Client: Loseley Ice Cream.

p.122 SpaRitual.

p.124 Method, www.methodhome.com. Industrial designer: Josh Handy. Graphic designer: Stefanie Hermsdorf.

pp.126, 128–9 Pret A Manger, www.pret.com. Co-founder: Julian Metcalfe. Commercial director: Simon Hargraves. Head of communications: Jay Chapman. Marketing communications agency: Fox Murphy, www.foxmurphy.com.

Chapter 6

p.132 Met Office, www.metoffice.gov.uk. Senior editor: Sarah Tempest, Met Office. Copywriter: Simon Jones, Ink Copywriters. Joint managing & design director: Ian Robson. Project manager: Robson Dowry. Senior design associate: Tony Grady. Images and design: Robson Dowry.

p.135 Courtesy British Airways, www.britishairways.com. Photography: Warren Potter.

pp.140–1 Fairmont Hotels and Resorts. Publishers: Spafax.

p.143 © American Medical Association, www.ama-assn.org. AMA copywriter: Randy Liss. Editor: Conan Kisor. Photographer: William Thomas Cain. Art director: Dan Fox. American Medical Association. Used with permission.

pp.146–7 Lush writer: Sarah McCartney, www.littlemax.co.uk. Designers: Reena Matharu and Michelle Leahy. © Lush, www.lush.co.uk.

p.149 *The Crescent,* Pearson Education, www.pearsoned.com.

p.150 Boots company magazine, www.boots.co.uk.

pp.158, 160–1 www.landrover.co.uk. Redwood Publishing, www.redwoodgroup.net.

p.162 Kodak, www.kodak.com.

Chapter 7

p.166 Wickes, www.wickes.co.uk.

pp.170–1 Howies, www.howies.co.uk.

p.172 Patagonia, www.patagonia.com. Copy: Vincent Stanley. Photos: Glenn Denny.

p.175 Design: Jupiter Design, www.jupitercreative.co.uk. Client: Boots.

p.179 Photos courtesy of Palumba.com, a Camden Rose Company.

p.183 MacKenzie Childs, www.mackenzie-childs.com. Copywriters: Jennifer Ellsworthy and Pleasant Rowland. Designer: Myland McGevey. Graphics coordinator: Beth Colvin. Photographer: Rudy Hellman.

p.185 FatFace, www.fatface.com. Photographer: Zed Nelson.

p.196 © 2012 The Territory Ahead, Inc.

pp.191, 193–4 Argos, www.argos.co.uk. Creative direction: Sunita Yeomans, Argos Head of Design.

Chapter 8

p.200 Legal and General, www.legalandgeneralgroup.com.

p.201 Catherine Toole, www.stickycontent.com. Energy Saving Trust, www.energysavingtrust.org.uk.

p.204 Sue George.

p.207 The Motley Fool, www.fool.com.

p.208 Creative director: Vincent Romeo, Romeo+co. Product manager, mobile downloads: Heather L. Wright. The Weather Channel, www.weather.com.

p.211 Catherine Toole, www.stickycontent.com. Aon, www.aon.com. Site designed by Sonaa, www.sonaa.co.uk.

p.212 Catherine Toole, www.stickycontent.com. Fortune Cookie, www.fortunecookie.co.uk.

p.215 www.bldgblog.blogspot.com.

p.217 Courtesy of The Everywhereist, www.everywhereist.com.

p.217 Courtesy of Cool Hunting, www.coolhunting.com.

p.222 Broad Stripe Butchers, www.fairfaxmeadow.co.uk. Created by Jupiter Design, www.jupitercreative.co.uk.

p.224 Daily Candy, www.dailycandy.com. Editor-at-large: Dannielle Kyrillos.

pp.226–9 *Creative Review* – CR Blog, www.creativereview.co.uk/cr-blog.

Acknowledgments

Writing this book was a labor of pure love (with the accompanying labor pains), and it was a relief to eventually get all of this proven thinking out of my head and into print once and for all. Finally I could rest, knowing that I had preserved all of the invaluable knowledge I'd built up over years of sweating and toiling, sifting and writing, squeezing my brain like a sponge to drip out juicy messages in the middle of noisy creative studios. I had fulfilled one of my lifetime's ambitions: I had created something that might actually last into posterity.

But it's only a book, and what can a book do? Well, this book traveled around the world and started to capture imaginations in many different and wonderful ways. I had little idea about the journey this book would take me on and the people it would lead me to. Soon after it was published I sold Jupiter, the design agency I founded and which had grown to £6 million turnover. This textbook then played a key role in my being recruited as a Design Associate at the UK Government's Design Council, where my fellow colleagues would mercilessly deride me whenever I dared to mention "my book" in meetings (I can only assume it must have been jealousy). Then all sorts of other unforeseen opportunities sprang forth, and I jumped at all of them: I've now been writing a weekly column ("Mark Shaw's Creative Nottingham"!) in the *Nottingham Post* for over three years now, and I was recently appointed a Visiting Fellow at the School of Art and Design at Nottingham Trent University. Most importantly, I got to know Alfredo Muccino from Liquid Agency, after interviewing him about his work, and this changed my life forever.

Alfredo was one of the best interviewees in the first edition, with such an interesting personality and so much fun too: a mixture of New York/Italian art scene punk rocker and Silicon Valley creative thinker. Open minded and approachable, opinionated and obstinate—everything I like in a friend. I was an instant fan, and when he suggested the possibility of collaborating I didn't have to think twice. In time I was to open the European office of Liquid, their highly successful branding agency, and I hope to be part of Liquid for the rest of my career.

I have the modest title of President of Liquid Agency Europe (but there's no need for formalities, you can call me "Mr President," or "Pres," I don't mind), and I have been lucky enough to develop a thriving brand design agency, based on some of Liquid's brand models and excellent reputation. So the biggest thanks for this new edition has to go to my current inspiration: Alfredo Muccino; his stalwart and equally inspiring business partner Scott Gardner; and our guru and thought-leader at Liquid, Marty Neumeier (thank God he didn't stay as the fifth Monkee!).

On a more practical level, this new edition is the result of a great team effort. I need to give full credit to Susan George, my editor at Laurence King, and to my brother Tim, who has been an invaluable collaborator. Lila Randall at Liquid Agency Europe has also played an essential role. Lastly I must thank my slightly bemused kids, Leilah, Sam, and Fin, who still haven't read a single page of this book (to my knowledge) and yet somehow seem to instinctively think and act like creative copywriters. I'm still working out how this osmosis effect works.

I am over the moon that this book has been translated into Chinese, and equally I can't wait to see this new edition in print—I'm curious to see where the next chapters in this journey will lead. Maybe there will be a third edition, in which I'll update you once more!

Remember, effective communication is the secret to great business, and to leading a happy and fulfilling life!